A TREATISE ON

THE CONFLICT OF LAWS

OR

PRIVATE INTERNATIONAL LAW

BY

JOSEPH HENRY BEALE

ROYALL PROFESSOR OF LAW IN HARVARD UNIVERSITY

VOL. I.—PART I.

CAMBRIDGE

HARVARD UNIVERSITY PRESS

1916

TO MY WIFE

PREFACE

In publishing this small portion of the treatise on the Conflict of Laws which he hopes eventually to finish, the author is not offering it as a complete piece of work, either in quantity or in quality. To finish the work as planned will be a labor of many years; to master, to think through, and to express one's thought on the topics herein discussed is not to be accomplished at the first essay. By publishing these few pages now the author hopes to benefit by helpful criticism, by further study and by more matured thought, and especially by that ocular demonstration of faulty thought and inept expression which seeing one's thought in print alone can give. Other parts are intended to follow from time to time; and when at last the work is complete, it will, it is hoped, include this part in a much improved form.

Joseph Henry Beale

CONTENTS

PAGE

PREFACE v

GENERAL BIBLIOGRAPHY

§ 1. The plan of this bibliography xi
2. The early Italian school xii
3. The early French school xiii
4. The early school of the Netherlands xv
5. Early German authors xvi
6. English and Anglo-American authors xvii
7. French authors, including French-speaking Swiss and Belgian authors xxv
8. German authors xxxviii
9. Dutch authors xlix
10. Italian authors li
11. Spanish and Portuguese authors, including Ibero-Americans lix
12. Authors of other nations and languages lxviii
13. Articles on the law of particular countries lxx
14. Periodicals lxxvi
15. Collections of cases lxxvii
16. Suggested collection for public law library lxxviii
17. Suggestions for private library lxxx

CHAPTER I

SCOPE AND NAME OF THE SUBJECT

§ 1. Definition of the subject 1
2. Other definitions 3
3. Practical necessity for this branch of law 5
4. Preliminary topics for investigation 5
4*a*. The nature of law as a necessary preliminary study 6
4*b*. The limits of jurisdiction as a necessary preliminary study 6
4*c*. Rights, acts and remedies as necessary subjects for preliminary study. 7
4*d*. Nationality and domicil 7
5. Whether criminal law is included in the subject 7
6. Public international law, how far included 8
7. Comparative law, how far included 9
8. Sources of private international law 10
9. The use to be made of authorities of various kinds 11
10. The method of treatment outlined 13
11. Names proposed for the subject 13
12. Criticism of names indicating conflict 14
13. Criticism of names suggesting international character 15
14. Difficulty of finding appropriate name 16
15. Reasons for adopting the name "Conflict of Laws" 16

CHAPTER II

HISTORY OF THE CONFLICT OF LAWS

§ 21. Identity of law in the Roman world: the *ius gentium* ... 18
22. Roman law following the edict of Caracalla ... 19
23. The rules of the Corpus Juris ... 20
24. The barbarian incursions: personal tribal law ... 23
25. The early middle ages: the law and the statutes ... 24
26. Bartolus ... 25
27. Baldus and the successors of Bartolus ... 29
28. The contribution to doctrine of the early Italian school ... 29
29. The later middle ages: the coutumes ... 30
30. The French statutists of the 16th century: Dumoulin ... 32
31. Argentré ... 33
32. Guy Coquille and other writers of the early French school ... 36
33. The Dutch statutists of the 17th century ... 38
34. Huber ... 40
35. The later French statutists of the 18th century ... 43
36. Boullenois and Bouhier ... 44
37. Summary of the doctrines of the statutists ... 47
38. The beginning of modern law: Livermore ... 49
39. Story ... 50
40. The influence of Story on European thought ... 51
41. Summary of this history ... 52
42. Efforts to unify the law: international conferences ... 54
43. Efforts to unify the law: comparative study ... 60

CHAPTER III

CURRENT DOCTRINE ON THE CONFLICT OF LAWS

51. The three modern systems of thought ... 62
52. The statutory system ... 66
53. The statute real and the statute personal ... 66
54. Modern statement of the statutory theory ... 67
55. Domicil or nationality as the basis of personal rights ... 69
56. Considerations in favor of the doctrines of nationality ... 71
57. Objections to the doctrine ... 72
58. The doctrine of the *renvoi* ... 74
59. The exception of public order ... 77
60. The principle of autonomy of the will ... 79
61. Pillet's theory of the continuity and the generality of law ... 80
62. Pillet's later theories ... 86
63. The international system ... 86
64. The early German school: Wächter, Schäffner, Savigny ... 88
65. The doctrine of von Bar ... 89
66. The doctrine of Zitelmann ... 91
67. The world-law of Jitta ... 95
68. Criticism of the international theories ... 98
69. International legal systems ... 99
70. The territorial system ... 100
71. The theory of comity ... 102

72. The doctrine of Story 103
73. The doctrine of vested rights 105
74. Dicey 107
75. The doctrine of vested rights in France: Vareilles-Sommières 108
76. Bustamante 109
77. Criticisms of the territorial theories 110
78. Answer to the criticisms 112

CHAPTER IV

LAW AND JURISDICTION

Topic 1. Sovereignty and Jurisdiction

§ 100. Nature of the discussion 115
101. Law as a function of sovereignty 115
102. The extent of sovereign power 116
103. Jurisdiction under international law 117
104. Territorial jurisdiction 118
105. Extent of territorial power 118
106. Extra-territorial rights 119
107. Legislative jurisdiction 122
108. Adoption of foreign law 122
109. Divided sovereignty 123
110. Legal units 124
111. What determines the legal unit 125
112. Legal units in the United States 126
112*a*. Is there a Federal common law? 127

Topic 2. The Nature of Law

113. Necessity for determining the nature of law 132
114. Definition of law 132
115. Statute law 133
116. Judicial law 134
117. Principle or doctrine 135
118. The difference between law and fact 136
119. Foreign law as a fact 137
120. How far knowledge of law extends 137

Topic 3. The Source and Growth of Modern Law

121. Legal systems 138
122. The principal modern legal systems 139
123. Other legal systems 142
124. Acceptance of a legal system 144
125. The part played by judicial decisions 146
126. The causes of change in the unwritten law 149
127. The part played by equity 150

Topic 4. The Characteristics and Function of Law

128. The social character of law 152
129. The generality of law 153

130. The universality of law 154
131. The continuity of law 154
132. The purpose and method of law 155
133. Social interests 156
134. Private interests of person 157
135. Interests of property 157
136. Interests of will and act 158
137. Vested rights 159
138. The legal protection of interests 160

CHAPTER V

RIGHTS

§ 139. The nature of rights 163
140. The analysis of rights 164

Topic I. PRIMARY RIGHTS

Sub-topic 1. Static Rights

141. The nature of static rights 165
142. Distinction between a static right and the rights which protect it . . 166
143. The nature of personal status 169
144. Personality 170
145. Artificial personality 170
146. Other examples of personal status 171
147. Relative status 172
148. What law governs status 173
149. The nature of property 174
150. The sort of interest protected 175
151. The sort of things which may be subject of interests 176
152. Transfer and extinguishment of rights of property 178
153. What law governs rights of property 179

Sub-topic 2. Dynamic Rights

154. The nature of dynamic rights 180
155. Interest-protecting rights 181
156. Interest-enjoying rights 182
157. What law governs absolute rights 183
158. Contracts and debts 183
159. Quasi-contracts 184
160. What law governs relative rights 184

Topic 2. SECONDARY RIGHTS

161. The nature of secondary rights 185
162. Rights of redress or restoration 185

Topic 3. REMEDIAL RIGHTS

163. Nature of remedial rights 186
164. Right to sue and to be satisfied 188

GENERAL BIBLIOGRAPHY

§ 1. The plan of this bibliography.
2. The early Italian school.
3. The early French school.
4. The early school of the Netherlands.
5. Early German authors.
6. English and Anglo-American authors.
7. French authors, including French-speaking Swiss and Belgian authors.
8. German authors.
9. Dutch authors.
10. Italian authors.
11. Spanish and Portuguese authors, including Ibero-Americans.
12. Authors of other nations and languages.
13. Articles on the law of particular countries.
14. Periodicals.
15. Collections of Cases.
16. Suggested collection for public law library.
17. Suggestions for private library.

§ 1. The Plan of this Bibliography. — In this bibliography are to be included such books and articles only as are of general scope, covering the whole or a substantial portion of the Conflict of Laws. Books and articles upon separate topics will be collected in a section of each chapter in which the topics are considered.

The books will be classified in two parts: first, books written before 1800; second, books written since 1800. Each part will be further classified according to the country in which, or, in the case of modern books, the language in which each book was written. In the case of almost every book a short note will state the nature and scope of the book, or something which will give a student unfamiliar with the book some idea of its helpfulness. When a book has formed the subject of another book or magazine article, the latter will be referred to. Special periodicals devoted to the subject and collections of cases follow.

With the books the names of articles which consider the subject in a general way will be given, classified according to the language of the periodical in which they appear. This form of classification has been adopted merely for convenience; since the possibility of consulting an article must depend, for each inquirer, upon the sets of periodicals to which he has access.

After the lists of books and articles, a list of books and special periodicals will be suggested as desirable for a public law library in America or England, and a smaller list as necessary for the working library of a lawyer who desires an office library on the subject. In suggesting these books, the author disclaims any desire to give dogmatic advice; but he wishes to indicate, as a result of his experience, books which in his opinion would for special reasons serve the needs of English-speaking lawyers.

PART I. AUTHORS BEFORE THE NINETEENTH CENTURY

§ 2. **The early Italian School.**—No work was written by any author of the early Italian school which dealt as its main subject with the Conflict of Laws. But two authors are so important for the development of the subject that their works should be included in a bibliography of the Conflict of Laws.

BARTOLUS OF SASSOFERRATO (1314–1347).

In primam Codicis partem commentaria. Various editions, 1571–1615. Also in *Savigny's Conflict of Laws* by Guthrie, App.

English tr., *Bartolus on the Conflict of Laws*, by J. H. Beale, Cambridge, 1914; pp. 84.

Bernabei, C. *Bartolo da Sassoferrato e la Scienza della Leggi.* Rome, 1881.

Meili, F. *Bartolus als Haupt der ersten Schule des internationalen Strafrecht.* Zürich, 1908; pp. 54.

Montijn, A. M. M. *Aanteekening op de leer van het internationaal Privaatrecht bij Bartolus.* Utrecht, 1887; pp. 80.

Woolf, Cecil N. Sidney. *Bartolus of Sassoferrato:* his position in the history of medieval political thought. Cambridge, 1913; pp. xxiv, 414.

For a life of Bartolus see Savigny, *Geschichte des römischen Rechts*, vi, 137–184; summary of this life in English, Beale, *op. cit.* For a statement of the doctrines of Bartolus and his influence on the law, see § 26.

See also Sir William Rattigan in the *Journal of the Society of Comparative Legislation*, v (N.S.), 230.

V. E. Hrabar, *L'époque de Bartole (1314–1358) dans l'histoire du droit international* (Rev. gen. dr. intern. public, 1900, p. 732.)

Meili, *Die theoretischen Abhandlungen von Bartolus und Baldus über das internationales Privat- und Strafrecht.* Zeitschrift für internationales Privat- und Strafrecht, iv (1894), 258, 340; v (1895), 363, 446.

BALDUS DE UBALDIS (1324–1400).

Commentaria in primum, secundum et tertium codicis librum. Various editions, 1526–1616; also a fifth centenary edition, by the University, Perugia.

Bonolis, G. *Questioni di Diritto internazionale in alcuni Consigli inediti di Baldo degli Ubaldi:* testo e commento. Pisa, 1908; pp. 194.

Solmi, A. *Di un' Opera attribuita a Baldo.* Modena, 1902; pp. 36.

Baldus was the pupil and greatest successor of Bartolus in the Italian school. His work is considered below, § 27.

Bonolis publishes, from a hitherto unpublished manuscript, nine *Consilia* of Baldus on questions of the Conflict of Laws, preceded by an excellent commentary.

See also Wilson, J. Dove: *Baldus de Ubaldis.* Yale Law Journal, xii (1902), 8–20.

ALBERICUS A ROSATE. *Commentaria de Statutis.* In Tractatus de statutis diversorum autorum, Frankfort, 1606; pp. 1–333.

Albericus (died 1354), an advocate at Bergamo, was a contemporary of Bartolus, who however did not see and use his work. His tract on statutes is in four books, and covers: Wills, Successions, Contracts, and Crimes. "Alberic de Rosate was an independent thinker, and his long experience in practice must have suggested to him individual views on the conflict of laws." Lainé, i, 125.

§ 3. The early French School. — Among a multitude of early French authors, a few only have written important works on the Conflict of Laws. Although these are not usually confined to that subject, they are included in this bibliography because of their historical importance in the development of the subject.

DUMOULIN, CHARLES. *In codicem Justiniani, I. 1., Conclusiones de statutis aut consuetudinibus localibus.* In his *Works*, Paris, 1681, vol. iii, p. 554. Also in Guthrie's Savigny's Conflict of Laws, Appendix II.

Dumoulin (Latin, Molinaeus), 1500–1560. "An advocate of the Parlement of Paris. Being exiled from France for his religion, he taught law at Basle, Geneva, and Strasburg. His principal work was Commentaries on the Custom of Paris." Guthrie's Savigny, 2d ed., p. 452. His writings on the subject also include his 53d Consilium, and a few scattered notes.

For Dumoulin and D'Argentré see also: Meili, *Argentraeus und Molinaeus und ihre Bedeutung im internationalen Privat- und Strafrecht* (Zeitschrift für internationales Privat- und Strafrecht, v (1895), 363, 452, 554.

D'ARGENTRÉ, BERTRAND. *Commentarii in Patrias Britonum Leges, seu Consuetudines generales antiquissimi Ducatus Britanniae.* 2 vols., Paris, 1640. (Paris, 1621, 1660.)

De la Lande de Calan. *Bertrand d'Argentré, ses doctrines juridiques et leur influence.* St. Amand, 1892.

D'Argentré (Latin, Argentraeus), 1519–1590, was President of the Presidial of Rennes. His work on our subject is contained in Gloss 6 to Article ccxviii, des donations; edition of 1640, vol. i, p. 646.

BARILIS, BERNARDUS. *De potestate legis municipalis in advenas et indigenas.* Lyons, 1641; pp. 124.

A rather elaborate doctor's dissertation.

BOUHIER, J. *Observations sur la Coutume du Duché de Bourgogne.* 2 vols., Dijon, 1746 [1742]; in his Works, Dijon, 1787.

Bouhier, 1673–1746, was President of the Parlement of Dijon. The passages bearing particularly on the Conflict of Laws begin with Chapter 21 of his Observations.

BOULLENOIS, LOUIS. *Traité de la Personnalité et de la Réalité des loix, coutumes, ou statuts,* par forme d' observations; auquel on a ajouté l'ouvrage Latin de Rodenburgh, intitulé, de Jure quod oritur e Statutorum diversitate. 2 vols., Paris, 1766.

Dissertations sur des Questions qui naissent de la contrariété des loix et des coutumes. Paris, 1732.

Boullenois (1680–1762) was an advocate in the Parlement of Paris. For a description of his works see § 36.

COQUILLE, GUI. *Les Coustumes du pays et comté de Nivernois;* in his *Oeuvres*, Bordeaux, 1625, 1646, 1703.

Coquille was an advocate of the Parlement of Paris, born at Decize in the Nivernois, and died there in 1603. This tract is found in the second volume of his works.

FROLAND, LOUIS. *Memoire concernans la nature et la qualité des statuts;* diverses questions mixtes de droit et de coutume; et la pluspart des arrests qui les ont décidées. 2 vols., Paris, 1729; pp. 1611.

Froland (died, 1764) was advocate of the Parlement of Rouen.

LEMEE. *Traité des statuts.* Paris, 1688.

§ 4. The early School of the Netherlands.

RODENBURG, CHRISTIAN. *Tractatus de Jure Conjugum: cum tractatione praeliminari de Jure, quod oritur ex statutorum vel consuetudinum discrepantium conflictu.* Utrecht, 1553. Also found in Boullenois, Traité des Statuts, vol. ii.

Rodenburg was a judge of the Supreme Court of Utrecht, and flourished about the middle of the sixteenth century.

BOURGOIGNE, NICHOLAS. *Tractatus Controversiarum ad Consuetudines Flandriae.* Antwerp, 1621, pp. 248; 1646, pp. 317; also in his *Opera Omnia*, Brussels, 1674.

Bourgoigne (usually known by the Latin form of his name, Burgundus) was born in Hainault, 1586. See also *Nicolas Bourgoigne et le droit international privé* (Pasicrisie belge, 1906, parts 9 and 10).

VOET, PAUL. *De statutis eorumque concursu.* Brussels, 1715; pp. 335 [also Utrecht, 1655; Amsterdam, 1661; the Hague, 1699].

The elder Voet was born at Heusden, in Brabant, in 1619, and died in 1677.

HUBER, ULRICH. *Praelectionum juris civilis tomi tres.* Leipsic, 1707 [also 1699]. The portion which treats of the

Conflict of Laws is printed in Guthrie's Savigny's Conflict of Laws, 2d ed., p. 508.

An English translation may be found in Dallas' Reports, vol. iii, pp. 370–377 *in notis;* reprinted in Carolina Law Journal, vol. i, p. 449.

Huber (Latin, Huberus) was born at Dockum in 1635. He was a professor in the University of Franaker, and died 1694. His writings on the Conflict of Laws are to be found under the title "De Conflictu legum diversarum in diversis imperiis," in vol. iii, Book 1, title 3. See also Meili, *Ein Specimen aus der hollandischen Schule des internationalen Privatrechts* (Ulricus Huber, 1636–1694). Zeitschrift für internationales Privat- und Strafrecht, viii (1898), 189.

VOET, JOHN. *Commentarionum ad Pandectas libri Quinquaginta.* Venice, 1827. 7 vols., The Hague, 1778.

John Voet, son of Paul, was born at Utrecht, 1647, and died in 1714. The chapter "De statutis" is found in Book 1, title 4, part 2, of his Commentaries.

§ 5. **Early German Authors.** — The early German works on the subject were, generally speaking, dissertations or other minor writings, difficult now to collect. The following are important essays which form part of well-known works or collections.

STRYKIUS, SAMUEL (1640–1710) professor at Frankfort.
De jure principis extra territorium. In Opera, 15 vols., Florence, 1837: vol. ii, p. 1.

MEVIUS, DAVID. *Commentaria in Jus Lubecense libri quinque.* 3d ed., Frankfort, 1679.

HERT, JOHANN NICOLAS (1651–1710).
Commentationum atque opusculorum volumen primum: De collisione legum. Frankfort, 1716; vol. i, p. 129 [also 1688, vol. i, p. 118]; also 1737.

HOMMEL, CARL FERDINAND. *Rhapsodia questionum in foro quotidie obvenientium nec tamen legibus decisarum:* Observatio ccccix. Baireuth, 1782; vol. i, p. 327.

The following are dissertations, separately published, which most obviously discuss the Conflict of Laws.

LYNCKER. *De statutis civitatum provincialium.* Jena, 1699.

DE WITZENDORF. *De statutis civitatum provincialium eorumque inter se concursu vario.* Jena, 1704; pp. 152.

MEIER. *De statutorum conflictu eorumque in exteros valore.* Giess, 1715.

ERNST. *De statutis eorumque conflictu.* Maintz, 1732.

REINHARTH. *De juris non scripti extra territorium efficientia.* Göttingen, 1734.

BOEHMER, J. S. F. *De efficacia statuti personalis extra territorium.* Frankfort, 1756.

BOSCHEN. *De vi legum civilium in subditos temporarios.* Leipzig, 1772.

WOLFF, C. G. *De vi legum et decretorum in territorio alieno.* Leipzig, 1777; pp. 29.

HAMM. *De statutorum collisione et praeferentia in causis successionis ab intestato.* Erlangen, 1792.

PART II. MODERN AUTHORS

§ 6. **English and Anglo-American Authors.** — This section includes Canadian books written in French.

ANONYMOUS. *Writers on the Conflict of Laws or Private International Law.* The Law Review, vol. 4 (1846), 318–335; vol. 6 (1847), 56–73; vol. 7 (1847), 30–55.

A short treatise on the general principles of the subject.

ANONYMOUS. *Private International Law.* Law Times, xcix, 210.

BALDWIN, SIMEON E., professor in Yale University.

Recent progress towards agreement on rules to prevent a conflict of laws. Harvard Law Rev., xvii (1903), 400.

BATE, JOHN PAWLEY, reader for the Inns of Court.

International Law, Private and Public. Lecture iii, in Century of Law Reform; London, 1901; pp. 67–80.

BATY, T. *Polarized Law,* with an English translation of the Hague Conventions on Private International Law; three lectures on Conflicts of Law delivered at the University of London. London, 1914; pp. xv, 210.

"The principle upon which these lectures were constructed was to pass briefly over the greater part of the subject, and to treat with thoroughness a few topics of special interest to the lecturer. Topics so treated are: nationality, marriage, divorce and marital property, and foreign theories of private international law. The discussion of these subjects is illuminated throughout by Dr. Baty's shrewdness, acuteness, and felicity of statement." Harvard Law Review, xxviii, 117.

"These lectures are vigorous and original work, and succeed in making a rather alarming special branch of jurisprudence appear in a much more interesting aspect than usual. Only students of mathematical physics will understand the title, but that is immaterial; the text is as clear as the subject admits. We agree with Dr. Baty that the rules for choice of the law governing a case are rules of municipal, that is, in an English court of justice, of English law. We do not understand him to deny that in the discovery of these rules the Courts ought to be guided by desire for general uniformity as an ideal, even if the ideal be sometimes remote." F. P[ollock] in Law Quarterly, Rev. xxxi, 106.

BERNARD, MATTHEW. *Manuel de droit international public et privé.* Montreal, 1901.

BURGE, WILLIAM. *Commentaries on Colonial and Foreign Laws generally, and in their Conflict with each other, and with the Law of England.* 4 vols., London, 1838; pp. lxxix, xii, 771; xix, 871; xx, 1080; xviii, 123. 2d ed. (unfinished; 3 vols. published), by Alexander Wood Renton and George Grenville Phillimore, London, 1907; pp. xxxviii, 420, xliv, 629, xlix, 987.

A valuable collection of the laws of the various British colonies, and an able though disconnected treatise on the Conflict of Laws.

CLARK, GEORGE L., professor in the University of Missouri. *Conflict of Laws:* in Modern American Law, vol. xii, Chicago [1915]; pp. 112.

A student's summary of merit.

DE BEER, REGINALD E. *Notes on Private International Law:* South African Law Journal, vol. 27, pp. 390, 551; vol. 28, pp. 36, 188, 336.

A serious work on the subject, published in this form only, and unfortunately incomplete. The author deals with the English law, basing his work on the theory of vested rights. Valuable for the collection of South African authorities.

DICEY, ARTHUR VENN, professor in the University of Oxford. *A Digest of the Law of England with reference to the Conflict of Laws.* London, 1896; pp. xliv, 853. 2d ed., London, 1908; pp. xcii, 883.

"Professor Dicey's book is highly satisfactory. He has succeeded in a few lines in stating the fundamental principles of his subject better than they have ever been stated before. . . . Professor Dicey has written the best book on the subject. His analysis and arrangement are strikingly novel, and commend themselves entirely. . . . The book has, in great degree, the merits of completeness, clearness of arrangement, of thought, and of statement, and enlightened dealing with the authorities." Harvard Law Review, x, 168.

Private international law as a branch of the law of England. Law Quarterly Review, vi (1890), 1–21, vii (1891), 113–127.

FARELLY, M. J. *The basis of private international law.* Law Quarterly Review, ix (1893), 242–260.

The New Italian school of private international law. Juridical Review, v (1893), 105, 121, 197.

FOOTE, JOHN ALDERSON. *A concise Treatise on Private International Jurisprudence,* based on the decisions of the English courts. London, 1878; pp. xxxi, 532. 2d ed., London, 1890; 3d ed., London, 1904; pp. xxxiv, 635; 4th ed. (by Coleman Phillipson), London, 1914; pp. xliv, 595.

"A collection for lawyers of the decisions bearing upon private international law, so-called. . . . The analysis is good, and the collection of cases is fairly exhaustive. In a few cases the discussion perhaps lacks something in perspicuity. . . . The greater part of the book is excellently done, the cases intelligently discussed, and the result of them fairly and clearly stated." Harvard Law Review, xxvii, 774.

GARDNER, DANIEL. *Institutes of International Law, public and private,* as settled by the Supreme Court of the United States, and by our Republic. New York, 1860; pp. v, 719.

A work of very broad scope, but of no great value today.

HARRISON, FREDERICK. *The historical side of the conflict of laws.* Fortnightly Review, xxxii (1879), 559, 716.

Translated into French under the title, Le droit international privé ou le conflit des lois au point de vue historique, particulièrement en Angleterre. Clunet, vii (1880), 418, 533.

HASSARD, A. R. *Private international law* (Westlake digested). Toronto, 1899; pp. 64.

A mere outline summary of Westlake's work, intended as a cram-book for students.

HOLLAND, THOMAS ERSKINE, professor in the University of Oxford.

De l'application de la loi. Translation by Ernest Nys of the last chapter of his Jurisprudence. Rev. dr. intern. vol. 12 (1880), p. 565.

HOSACK, JOHN. *A Treatise on the Conflict of Laws of England and Scotland.* London and Edinburgh, 1847; pp. ix, xvi, 317.

An unfinished work, of which only the first volume was published. After an introductory chapter the author treats of domicil, civil status, marriage and divorce. The law of England and Scotland only are considered.

KUHN, ARTHUR K. *Doctrines of private international law* in England and America contrasted with those of continental Europe. Columbia Law Rev., xii, 44.

LAFLEUR, E., professor in McGill University, Montreal.

The Conflict of Laws in the Province of Quebec. Montreal, 1898; pp. xvi, 259.

A student's book, but of scientific value because of the author's citation of the Canadian cases. It is a course of lectures delivered by the author as Professor in McGill University, Montreal. "The author cites few authorities except [Quebec] decisions and the commentaries of French jurists, — a proper course since Conflict of Laws is a branch of the municipal law, and decisions of a State where a different system of law prevails can be no safe guide to the law of Quebec. . . . The author's materials are well arranged, his exposition is clear, and his infrequent original suggestions are just and sound." Harvard Law Review, xii, 286.

LAWRENCE, WILLIAM BEACH, *Commentaire sur les elements du droit international,* vol. iii.

Volume III discusses private international law.

"All is business-like and colloquial. But in this simple and unrhetorical way are put together treasures of information, much of which would otherwise have perished, and all of which is needed to constitute a just system of private international law." Francis Wharton in vi So. Law Rev. N. S. 683.

LIVERMORE, SAMUEL. *Dissertations on the Questions which arise from the Contrariety of the Positive Laws of Different States and Nations.* New Orleans, 1828; pp. 172.

Livermore (–1833) was a distinguished advocate in New Orleans. His monograph is a defence of the theories of the French and Dutch statutists.

MERRILL, GEORGE. *Studies in Comparative Jurisprudence and the Conflict of Laws.* Boston, 1886; pp. xii, 247.

The law of various countries, with a discussion of the doctrines of the conflict of laws, on the topics of Nationality, Domicil, Alienage, Contracts (civil and commercial), and Bankruptcy.

MINOR, RALEIGH C., professor in the University of Virginia. *Conflict of Laws; or, Private International Law.* Boston, 1901; pp. lii, 575.

A concise but thoughtful and scholarly treatise, based on English and American authorities. The author's guiding principle is that "the great foundation and basic principle of private international law is Situs." "As an exposition of the law the treatise is very satisfactory. . . . The arrangement presents the law in clear-cut outlines, and the idea of *situs* has served admirably as a mode of classification." Harvard Law Review, xiv, 627.

PHILLIMORE, SIR ROBERT, judge of the High Court of England, Admiralty Division.
Commentaries upon International Law. Vol. iv: *Private International Law or Comity.* London, 1861; pp. liv, 772. 2d ed., London, 1871; pp. xlvii, 837. 3d ed. by Walter G. F. Phillimore and Reginald James Mure, London, 1889; pp. xlviii, 869.

The fourth volume of Judge Phillimore's work deals with private international law. His work throughout is influenced by that of the Continental writers.

RATTIGAN, SIR WILLIAM HENRY, professor in the University of the Punjab (India).
Private International Law. London, 1895; pp. xv, 267.

A student's text-book, with references to treatises (especially Gillespie's translation of Bar) and to English cases.

"The elaborations and wealth of reference of this little manual will render it no less useful to the practitioner than its lucidity of exposition will render it attractive to the student." Review from The Law Times, reprinted Alb. L. J. lii, 78.

REDDIE. *Inquiries in international law, public and private.* 2d ed., Edinburgh, 1851.

The first edition contains no discussion of the Conflict of Laws.

ROBBINS, ALEXANDER H. *Conflict of Laws.* St. Louis, 1915; pp. 25.

Brief lecture notes of no independent value.

RORER, DAVID. *American Interstate Law.* 2d ed. by Charles E. Estabrook, Chicago, 1893; pp. lxv, 508.

A summary statement of the doctrines of the Conflict of Laws merely as they apply between the states, together with a considerable body of constitutional law. The book has no independent authority, but is of value because of the large number of cases cited.

STOCQUART, ÉMILE. *Studies in private international law.* Brussels, 1900.

STORY, JOSEPH, professor in Harvard University.

Commentaries on the Conflict of Laws, foreign and domestic, in regard to Contracts, Rights, and Remedies, and especially in regard to Marriages, Divorces, Wills, Successions, and Judgments. Boston, 1834; pp. xxv, 557. Edinburgh, 1835; pp. xxiv, 559. 2d ed., Boston, 1841; pp. xxxi, 559. 3d ed., Boston and London, 1846; pp. xxxv, 1068. 4th ed. (by E. H. Bennett), Boston, 1852; pp. xxxviii, 1072. 5th ed. 1857; pp. xxxviii, 1047. 6th ed. (by Isaac F. Redfield), Boston, 1865; pp. xxxvi, 868. 7th ed. (by E. H. Bennett), 1872; pp. lvi, 823. 8th ed. (by Melville M. Bigelow), Boston, 1883; pp. xxxix, 901.

"Almost every page contains learned and valuable notes and a rich mine of authorities in support of the positions in the text collected from the civil and common law, and the writings of eminent lawyers and jurists." "Both the student and the practicing lawyer may resort to this work with entire confidence that they will obtain from it not only the best instruction and information which can be anywhere had upon the subject of the conflict of laws, but all the useful and important matter which can be found in any other treatise extant. The learned author has most judiciously rejected all the idle, theoretical distinctions and metaphysical subtleties which encumber the writings of the civilians, and at the same time has, with the most exhausting diligence, gleaned and collected from the numerous volumes of the common, civil, and foreign law and jurisprudence everything touching the subject which can be of any value in practice." From a review of the work in the American Jurist, i, 365.

"Marked by a deficiency of arrangement, and a too general absence of decision by the learned author between the discrepant authorities whom he cites." Law Magazine and Law Review, vi, 235.

"Story was essentially a man of powerful common sense and extensive legal learning, and though his language might lack precision, it was always intelligible to any one who wished to understand it. . . . His work deserves the respect and gratitude of all English lawyers." A. V. Dicey in Law Quarterly Review, xxviii, 342, 347.

TOWERS, WALTER K. *Conflict of Laws.* Law Student's Helper, xx (1912), 296–299, 329–331, 358–360, xxi (1913), Jan. 5–7, Feb. 5–7, March 13–16, April 6–8.

An elementary essay on the subject, of no independent value.

VINEYARD, B. R. *Interstate Law.* Missouri Bar Association Reports, v (1884), p. 167.

WESTLAKE, JOHN, professor in the University of Cambridge.

On the relation between public and private international law. Jurid. Soc. Pap. vol. 1, 173.

A Treatise on Private International Law, or The Conflict of Laws, with principal reference to its Practice in the English and other cognate Systems of Jurisprudence. London, 1858; pp. xix, 407. Philadelphia, 1859; pp. xvi, 251. 2d ed., London, 1880; pp. xxvii, 340. 3d ed., London, 1890; pp. xxvi, 382. 4th ed., London, 1905; pp. xxx, 437. 5th ed., London, 1912; pp. xxxiv, 470. German translation of the 2d ed. by Franz von Holtzendorff, Berlin, 1884; pp. xvi, 374. French translation of the 5th ed. by Goulé, Paris, 1914; pp. xii, 560.

"The author has made himself master of all the learning on the subject; that is, has not only read, but has digested and exercised a critical and independent judgment of all the works and discussions on the subject, and on their plan, purpose, and merits; and has assigned to each its proper place, as a part of the learning on the subject." Review in Law Magazine and Law Review, vi, 229.

"Mr. Westlake has carried condensation to the furthest limit that can be reached without sacrifice of sense. But sense he has never sacrificed. He has gone through the whole topic of Private International Law on its civil side. It is true that he has limited himself almost exclusively to English decisions, giving but slight notice to the cognate publications of jurists of the continent of Europe, and notice even slighter of cognate publications in the United States. But what he has done, he has done admirably, and, so far as his object is concerned, with entire success. For his object was to give, in a small compass, such rules in private international law as are authoritative in England. And this he has done. The English edition [of 1879], which is now before us, contains within 330 pages a series of succinct propositions, giving the present English law on the topic to which they relate, and sustaining each proposition by all the pertinent authorities. That this is done drily there can be no question. But it is done not only with great analytical force, but with singular precision of style." Francis Wharton in So. Law Rev. N. S. vi, 682.

See also a Review of the 5th ed. by A. V. Dicey in Law Quarterly Review, xxviii, 341. The first chapter of the 2d edition is published in a French translation by Ernest Nys in Rev. dr. intern. xii (1880), 23–46.

WHARTON, FRANCIS. *A Treatise on the Conflict of Laws, or Private International Law,* including a comparative view of Anglo-American, Roman, German and French Jurisprudence. Philadelphia, 1872; pp. xxxii, 758. 2d ed., Philadelphia, 1881; pp. xvii, 847. 3d ed. by George H. Parmele, 2 vols., Rochester, 1905; pp. ccxxiv, xxvii, 1830.

A review by Charles Brocher, *De la crise qui s'opère actuellement dans le droit international privé et de l'ouvrage récemment publié sur ce sujet par M. Francis Wharton,* may be found in Revue de législ. ancienne et moderne, v (1875), 557–570.

"Is not only calculated to bring before its reader a full view of German jurisprudence, but is richer in detail than is the work of Judge Story. It has the advantage also of a better analysis, of clear subdivisions; sometimes of a more satisfactory exposition of the authorities, and not rarely of more comprehensive philosophical discussion." von Bar in Alb. .L. J., xii, 232.

"A most careful examination of the author's division of the questions involved in the Conflict of Laws fails to disclose anything remotely resembling a plan which he has followed. . . . While the editor of this new edition has done his work with zeal and ability, no amount of editing can overcome the defects inherent in Wharton's Conflict of Laws." Harvard Law Review, xix, 75.

§ 7. French Authors, including French-speaking Swiss and Belgian Authors.

ARMINJON, PIERRE, and SHELDON-AMOS, MAURICE. *Problèmes juridiques et questions pratiques de droit commercial et de droit international privé.* Cairo.

ARNTZ, E. R. N. and WESTLAKE, JOHN. *Principes généraux en matière de nationalité, de capacité, de force obligatoire des lois.* Règles d'Oxford. Rapport à l'Institut de droit international. Annuaire de l'Institut, iv (1880), 190–262.

AUBRY, J., professor at the University of Rennes.

De la notion de territorialité en droit international privé. Clunet, 1900; pp. 689–704; 1901, pp. 253–273, 643–671; 1902, pp. 209–243.

AUDINET, EUGÈNE, professor in the University of Aix.

Principes élémentaires du droit international privé à l'usage des étudiants en droit. Paris, 1894; pp. 620. 2d ed., Paris, 1906; pp. 692.

A standard students' text-book.

Principios de derecho international privado. Spanish tr. by Barutell, 2 vols., Madrid, n. d.; pp. 372, 365.

BARD, ALPHONSE. *Précis de Droit international: droit penal et privé.* Paris, 1883; pp. 369.

An excellent short summary of the law.

BARDE, LOUIS. *Théorie traditionelle des statuts ou principes du statut réel et du statut personnel d'après le droit civil français.* Bordeaux, 1880.

A work based on the old theory of statute personal and statute real. "His thesis is, that 'statute personal' means the law which creates status and capacity of persons, while 'statute real' means the law which creates the juridical position of property. . . . The opponents of the juridical ideas which he obstinately defends will be obliged to recognize the merit of this interesting plea for the traditional view." Clunet, 1880, 635.

BARILLIET, THOMAS. *Études de droit international privé.* Revue pratique, xv (1863), pp. 141–163, 521–557; xvi (1864), pp. 551–574.

BARTIN, ÉTIENNE, professor in the University of Lyons.
Études de droit international privé. Paris, 1899; pp. 284.

Three articles, dealing in general with the impossibility of eliminating conflicts of law. The articles are entitled: The theory of qualifications [on the meaning of international agreements] in private international law; the conflict between legislative provisions in the field of private international law; the theory of the *renvoi;* the provisions of public order; the theory of fraud on the law; and the idea of international community.

De l'impossibilité d'arriver à la suppression définitive des conflits de lois. Clunet, 1897; pp. 225–255, 466–495, 720–738.

A careful examination of French and foreign jurisprudence, with a view to determining the trend of thought and the ultimate possibility of unity on various disputed questions of the conflict of laws.

BASILESCO. *Études de droit international privé.* Paris, 1884.

BERTAULD. *Conflit des lois françaises et des lois étrangères.* Questions pratiques et doctrinales du Code civil. Paris, 1867–1869.

BOEUF, HENRI and BOUTAUD, E., advocates at the Court of Appeal of Paris.
Résumé de droit international privé; on trouve à la fin du volume: des Tableaux Synoptiques, servant de Memento pour l'examen. Paris 1906; 2d ed., 1907. 4th ed., Paris, 1912; pp. 343 (30).

A student's book for review and preparation for examination.

BOURDON-VIANE, G., and MAGRON, H. *Manuel de droit international privé,* avec indication et solution des questions posées aux examens en 1882 et 1883. Paris, 1883; pp. 396. 2d ed., Paris, 1897.

A mere crammer's book for examination, but with a clear analysis and terse form of statement which give it some little value for an American student.

BROCHER, CHARLES, professor at the University of Geneva. *Théorie du droit international privé.* Revue de droit international, iii (1871), 412–439, 540–567; iv (1872), 189–229; v (1873), 173–168, 390–420.

A complete and valuable treatise, not altogether superseded by his later works.

Nouveau traité de droit international privé au double point de vue de la théorie et de la pratique. Geneva, Basle, Lyons, Paris, 1876; pp. 454.

An excellent and standard treatise, crowned by the Academy of Legislation of Toulouse. The Preface was first printed in Revue de droit international, viii (1876), 35–59, under the title *Nouvelle étude sur les principes fondamentaux du droit international privé,* and reprinted, Paris, 1876. On this work see: Bressolles, Joseph. *Questions de droit international à propos du traité de droit international privé offert à l'Académie de Legislation* [de Toulouse] *par M. Charles Brocher:* Toulouse, 1884. *Des bases théoriques du droit international privé.* Clunet, 1878; pp. 225–235. *Cours de droit international privé suivant les principes consacrés par le droit positif français.* 3 vols., Paris and Geneva, 1882–85; pp. 460, 436, 369.

A careful treatise, by a distinguished author, based on the provisions of the French code. An extract from this book was published in Clunet, 1881, 5–19, under the title *Étude sur les principes généraux consacrés par le Code civil français comme bases du droit international privé.*

See further: Olivi, L.: *Carlo Brocher e la scuola italiana di diritto internazionale privato* Archivio guiridico, xvii, pt. 1.

For an obituary notice of Professor Charles Brocher see L. T. lxxvii, 364.

BROCHER DE LA FLÉCHÈRE, HENRI, professor in the University of Geneva.

Des principes naturels du droit international privé. Rev. dr. intern. xvii (1885), 313–331.

CALVO, CHARLES. *Le droit international théorique et pratique,* précédé d'un exposé historique des progrès de la science du droit des gens. 3d ed., complétée; Vol. II (dealing with private law), Paris, 1880; pp. xxix, 634. 4th ed., revue et complétée; Vol. II (dealing with private law), Paris, 1887, pp. xxiii, 624. 5th ed., revue et complétée par un Supplément; Vol. II (dealing with private law), Paris, 1896; pp. xxiii, 624.

The excellent qualities of Calvo's book are fulness and completeness of treatment, clearness, and great richness of illustrative cases. By birth a South American, and by profession a diplomat, he had a wider field of knowledge than most writers on the subject. His work is of the greatest value as a collection of precedents from all parts of the world.

The earlier editions contained no discussion of private international law.

Manuel de Droit International public et privé conforme au programme des facultés de droit. 2d ed., Paris, 1884; pp. xxxiv, 422. Pages 198–258 deal with private international law. 3d ed., Paris, 1892. Greek tr. by Stephen Papafrangon, 1893.

This is a mere elementary manual. The so-called first edition, which was an English translation, published under the name of Edward M. Gallaudet, the translator, New York, 1879, contains nothing about private international law.

Dictionnaire de droit international public et privé. 2 vols., Berlin and Paris, 1885; pp. 517, 374.

A valuable work, in the form of a digest, on international law.

CHAMPCOMMUNAL, J. *Le conflit des lois personnelles.* Revue de dr. int. pr. v (1909), 536–544; vi (1910), 57–74, 712–731.

DAIREAUX, ÉMILE. *Étude sur les principes de droit international privé dans la république argentine* à propos d'une réforme des lois qui y regissent la constitution de la famille. Paris, 1885; pp. 22.

An address. Extract from the Bulletin of the Society of Comparative Legislation.

DARRAS, A., and LAPRADELLE, A. DE. *Répertoire de droit international privé et de droit penal international.* Vol. I: Abandon-Brevets. Paris, 1914.

The first volume of an elaborate digest of the law, which promises to be of the greatest value.

DEMANGEAT, CHARLES. *Introduction.* Force obligatoire du droit international en dehors et au-dessus de la loi positive. Necessité pour le jurisconsulte de connaître les lois positives de son pays, les lois étrangères et le droit international. Où faut-il chercher les règles du droit international? But du Journal. Clunet, 1874; pp. 7–16.

Introduction to Clunet's Journal de droit international privé.

DESPAGNET, FRANTZ, professor in the University of Bordeaux.

Précis de droit international privé. Paris, 1886; pp. 629. 2d ed., Paris, 1890. 3d ed., Paris, 1899; pp. 791. 4th ed., Paris, 1904; pp. 847. 5th ed., by Charles de Boeck. Paris, 1909; pp. xii, 1250.

A summary of the law, with references to authors and to jurisprudence.

L'enseignement du droit international privé en France. Clunet, xvii (1890), 786.

De l'avenir du droit international privé. Rev. de dr. int. pr., ii (1906), 5–22, iii (1907), 481–494.

DONNEDIEU DE VABRES, H. *De l'impossibilité d'arriver à une solution rationelle et définitive des conflits de lois.* Clunet, 1905, 1231–1244.

L'évolution de la jurisprudence française en matière de Conflit des Lois. Paris, 1905; pp. 644.

The author divides the history of doctrine in France since 1804 into three periods: 1, 1804–1840, the reality of law; 2, 1840–1874, the autonomy of the will; 3, 1874–1904, the personality of law.

DUBOIS, ERNEST, professor in the University of Nancy.

La statistique et le droit international privé. Clunet, 1877, pp. 511–515.

Du conflit des lois françaises et des lois étrangères. Paris, 1861.

DURAND, LOUIS, advocate of the Court of Appeal of Lyons.

Essai de Droit international privé, précédé d'une étude historique sur la condition des étrangers en France et suivi du texte de tous les traités intéressant les étrangers. Paris, 1884; pp. 820.

Saggio di Diritto internazionale privato. Translated into Italian by Diodato Lioy, with an introduction by Francesco Paolo Contuzzi. Naples, 1887; pp. 495.

"Work crowned by the catholic faculty of law of Lyons and by the Academy of Legislation at Toulouse."

The first part is a learned essay on the treatment of foreigners in France from Celtic times; the second, an essay on private international law, which is treated philosophically. An appendix contains treaties of interest to foreigners.

FOELIX, E. *Traité du droit international privé ou du conflit des lois de différentes nations en matière de droit privé.* Paris, 1843; pp. 618. 2d ed., Paris, 1847. 3d ed., edited by Charles Demangeat, 2 vols., Paris, 1856; pp. viii, 486, 520. 4th ed., the same, 2 vols., Paris, 1866; pp. 512, 536.

Tratado de derecho internacional privado, 3d ed., translated by the directors of the Revista General de Legislacion y Jurisprudencia. Madrid, 1858; pp. 435.

Tratado de derecho internacional privado, traducido con notas y amplificaciones sobre la legislacion española. 2 vols. Madrid, 1877.

Trattato di diritto internazionale, 2d ed., translated into Italian by P. Borelli and B. Montuoro; Naples, 1870; pp. xxxvi, 527.

This carefully written treatise, based on the doctrines of the statutists and especially of Huber, and greatly influenced by Story, remained for half a century the standard French treatise. The editor took a fundamentally different view of the principles of the subject from that of M. Foelix.

FOIGNET, R. *Manuel élémentaire du droit international privé.* Paris, 1907. 4th ed., Paris, 1914; pp. 384.

FOLLEVILLE, DANIEL DE, professor in the University of Lille, and Dean of the Faculty of Law in the University of Douai.

Leçon d'introduction à un cours de droit international privé. Lille, 1880, Paris, n. d.; pp. 59.

Spanish tr. by Candido Emperado y Felez. *Introducion a un curso de derecho internacional privado,* Saragossa, 1887.

FOUCHER, VICTOR. *Introduction to private international law.* American Jurist, xx (1838), 33.

An English translation of the prolegomena of a manual of the subject "about to be published."

HAUS, E. *Du droit privé qui régit les étrangers en Belgique,* ou du droit des gens privé, considéré dans ses principes fondamentaux et dans ses rapports avec les lois civiles des Belges. Ghent, 1874; pp. 455.

A treatise on the conflict of laws in so far as it applies to foreigners in Belgium, with reference to many decisions, Belgian and French.

JOLLIVET, G., and WILHELM, A. *Le Droit international privé résumé en tableaux synoptiques.* Paris, 1886; pp. 75.

A mere cram-book for examinations.

LAINÉ, ARMAND, professor in the University of Paris. *Introduction au droit international privé, contenant une étude historique et critique de la théorie des statuts et des rapports de cette théorie avec le Code civil.* 2 vols.: pp. xxi, 425, 434. Paris, 1889–1892.

The standard history of the subject.

Contains a careful analysis of the doctrines of writers of the early Italian, French and Dutch schools. Vareilles-Sommières says (i, 6 *n*): "This is one of the best written and strongest works that French jurists have produced for a long time. We do not agree with all its doctrines, but we admire its erudition, precision, clearness, and style, which is of unusual purity."

An excellent account of the work of Professor Lainé is given by his successor, Professor Pillet: L'Œuvre de M. Lainé, in Revue de droit international privé, v, 1.

Introduction au Revue de Droit international privé et de Droit penal international. Paris, 1905; pp. 20.

Extract from the first number of the *Revue.*

Rôle, fonction et méthode du droit comparé dans le domaine du droit international privé. Congrès international de droit comparé, procès-verbaux des séances et documents, i, 327.

Le droit international privé dans ses rapports avec la théorie des Statuts. Clunet, xii (1885), 129–143, 259–265.

LAURENT, F., professor in the University of Ghent.
Droit Civil International. 8 vols., Brussels and Paris, 1880–81; pp. 702, 564, 694, 636, 640, 734, 623, 517.
Diritto civile internazionale, translated into Italian by Marghieri. Milan, 1888.

A diffuse and choleric, but interesting treatise on the law. The author is an enthusiastic disciple of the Italian school, and dedicates the work to Mancini. The first volume is devoted entirely to the history of the subject, and before the work of Lainé it was the principal historical examination.

"One cannot read it without feeling a lively sense of admiration, respect and gratitude for the treasures of labor and of knowledge which are gathered here. It is not only considerable in itself: it answers exactly to the needs of the present time. . . . The work will certainly remain a witness of the past and a starting-point for the future." Charles Brocher in Revue de droit international, xiii (1881), 531. See this whole review, entitled Étude sur le traité de droit civil international, publié par M. Laurent, et sur les principes fondamentaux du droit international privé, Rev. de dr. intern. xiii, 531–570. See also a brief résumé of the first volume by Professor Brocher, Le droit international privé, Clunet 1880, 279–292.

"Permeated with the vivacity, the zeal, the freshness, and the occasional paradox, which belong to a successful and brilliant lecturer. Authorities are rarely cited — usually only when the object is to criticise. There are none of the notes which make our American treatises at once so cumbrous and so indispensable. There is no division into the compartments of sections, each with its accompanying summary; there are no locks to regulate the stream: it flows on untrammelled by such artificial assistance. Sometimes the current may be but slow; sometimes, on the other hand, it pours in swollen torrents; but in whatever condition it is found, it is strong and instinct with life. . . . He is one of the leading and most enthusiastic propagandists of a new school of jurisprudence." — Francis Wharton in 6 So. Law Rev. N.S. 680.

The gist of the first volume of the treatise was published under the title Études sur le droit international privé in Clunet, 1878, pp. 309–344, 421–446, 1879; pp. 5–21.

LEHR, ERNEST. *Du principe de la réciprocité ou de l'assimilation aux nationaux.* Rev. dr. intern., vol. 12 (1880), pp. 108–111.

LERAY. *Exposé élémentaire des principes du droit international privé.* Paris, 1901; pp. 48.

LEVY, EMMANUEL, professor at the University of Lyons. *Sur le droit international privé.* (Questions de dr. int. privé, Paris, 1913, n. 360.)

LIONCOURT, ROUGELOT DE. *Du conflit de lois personnelles françaises et étrangères.* Paris, 1883; pp. 307.

Crowned by the faculty of law of Caen and by the Academy of Legislation of Toulouse.

A general study of the conflict of laws as to personal status.

MAILHER DE CHASSAT, A. *Traité des Statuts:* (lois personnelles, lois réelles) d'après le droit ancien et le droit moderne, ou du droit international privé, considéré comme conséquence ou reproduction, dans le sens individuel, du droit international public; plus expressément: de la nationalité et de ses modifications diverses ou de la personnalité et de la réalité considérées comme faits de souveraineté des puissances entre elles, et ayant pour objet les affectations individuelles et les dévolutions de biens, soit à l'intérieur, soit à l'extérieur des États. Paris, 1845; pp. 462.

An examination of the theories of the statutists. He treats their distinctions as inapplicable to international conflicts of law. The work is careful, ingenious, original and able.

MANCINI, P. S., professor in the University of Rome. *De l'utilité de rendre obligatoires pour tous les États, sous la forme d'un ou de plusieurs traités internationaux, un certain nombre de règles générales du droit international privé,* pour assurer la décision uniforme des conflits entre les différentes législations civiles et criminelles, Clunet, 1874, pp. 221–239, 285–384. Also in Rev. dr. intern. vii, 329, 361; Bull. de l'Institut (The Hague) 1, 36.

MOREL. *Esquisse de droit international public et privé.*

PELLERIN, PIERRE. *A digest of cases decided in France relating to private international law.* London, 1913; pp. 134.

A translation of about 100 French decisions, with notes and an index.

PERROUD, JEAN, *Chargé de conférences* in the University of Paris.

Des conséquences d'un changement de la loi personnelle. Clunet, xxxii (1905), 292–306.

PICARD, EDMOND. *Le droit et sa diversité nécessaire d'après les races et les nations.* Clunet, xxviii (1901), 417–423.

PILLET, ANTOINE, professor at Grenoble and at Paris.

Étude sur les sources du droit international privé. Clunet, xviii (1891), 5–37.

Le droit international privé considéré dans ses rapports avec le droit international public. Paris, 1892; pp. 36.

Spanish translation by Nicolas Rodriguez Aniceto, Salamanca, n. d., under the title *El derecho internacional privado, considerado en sus relaciones con el derecho internacional publico,* Salamanca, n. d.; pp. 87.

A brochure reprinted from the Revue pratique de droit international privé, 1892, Pt. II, 105–140.

Le droit international privé, sa définition, son origine rationnelle, son domaine, ses conditions générales et son but. Clunet 1893, pp. 5–24; pp. 318–331.

Intended as an introduction to the next work.

Le droit international privé. Essai d'un système général de solution des conflits de lois. Clunet, xxi (1894), 417–435, 711–754; xxii (1895), 241–259, 500–517, 929–952; xxii (1896), 5–30.

A series of brilliant essays by which Professor Pillet's general reputation was made. In it he states and develops his theory that the extent of application of a rule of law is determined by the social need which the law is intended to solve; if it is for the benefit of an individual its application is universal, if for the public good it is applicable locally.

Droit international privé, année 1904–05. Résumé du Cours de M. A. Pillet. Paris [1905]; pp. 391.

A report of the author's university lectures on the subject.

Principes de droit international privé. Paris and Grenoble, 1903; pp. xii, 586.

Professor Pillet's fundamental theory is an original one, carefully worked out in this volume. He is to be regarded as the foremost theoretical writer in France at the present day. The work was elaborately reviewed by Maurice Bernard, Principes de droit international privé, Clunet, xxxi (1904), 769–785; xxxiii (1906), 647–671, 1064–1072; xxxiv (1907), 56–69. Cited as Pillet.

De la nature des règles d'origine législative relatives à la solution des conflits de lois. Revue de dr. int. pr. v (1909), 790–799.

PITOIS. *Principes de droit international privé.* Paris, 1895. 3d ed., Paris, n. d.; pp. 62.

POLITIS, N. *Le droit international privé en Grèce.* Paris, 1908.

ROGUIN, ERNEST, professor in the University of Lausanne.

Conflits des lois suisses en matière internationale et intercantonale; commentaire du traité franco-suisse du 15 juin 1869. Lausanne, 1891; pp. 920.

A treatise based on the laws and jurisprudence of Switzerland and France. The decisions of Swiss courts are cited at large in the text, which is interesting as showing the operation of the law in a federation of states legally independent.

La Règle de Droit: analyse générale, spécialités: souveraineté des États, assiette de l'impôt, théorie des statuts, système des rapports de droit privé. Lausanne, Paris, Leipzig, 1889; pp. 431.

A philosophical consideration of legal conceptions which are fundamental in the conflict of laws, including a discussion of the theories of the statutists.

ROLIN, ALBÉRIC, professor in the University of Ghent.

Principes du droit international privé et application aux diverses matières du Code civil (Code Napoléon). 3 vols., Paris, 1897; pp. 818, 615, 573.

"The author knows, on every question, all the theories which have been suggested, and discusses them with the sagacity of a man of good judgment, versed in affairs as well as in jurisprudence. . . . I have only eulogies to offer on fundamental matters." E. Lehr in Revue de droit international, xviii, 699.

STOUFF, L. *Étude sur le principe de la personnalité des lois depuis les invasions barbares jusqu'au* XXe *siècle.* Paris, 1894; pp. 102.

A careful historical study; first published in the Revue bourguignonne de l'Enseignement supérieur, Vol. 4.

SURVILLE, F., professor in the University of Poitiers.

De la personnalité des lois envisagée comme principe fondamental du droit international privé. Clunet, 1889, pp. 528–538.

SURVILLE, F., and ARTHUYS, F., professors in the University of Poitiers.

Cours élémentaire de droit international privé, conformé au programme des facultés de droit: droit civil, procédure, droit commercial. Paris, 1890; pp. 602; 2d ed., Paris, 1895; pp. 636; 3d ed., Paris, 1900; 4th ed., Paris, 1904; 5th ed., Paris, 1910.

The best known and most widely used student's text-book.

VALERY, JULES, professor in the University of Montpellier.

Manuel de droit international privé. Paris, 1914; pp. 1391.

A very well-written and original manual, worth examination.

VAQUETTE, T. *Cours résumé de Droit international privé.* Paris, 1884; pp. 501.

An elementary text-book for students.

VAQUETTE, T. and BALLEUR, A. Memento de Droit international privé, permettant au candidat de revoir les matières la veille de l'examen. Paris, 1883; pp. 70. 2d ed., 1887; 3d ed., 1902.

A mere cram-book for examination.

VAREILLES-SOMMIÈRES, LE COMTE DE, dean of the Faculty of Law at the Catholic University of Lille.

La synthèse du droit international privé. 2 vols., Paris, 1897; pp. xxxix, 420, 414.

A singularly original, well-reasoned and careful work, which will repay careful study. He holds the theory of vested rights, and his work is therefore one of especial interest to an American scholar. See also: La synthèse du droit international privé (Clunet, 1900, pp. 5, 258); a summary by the author. *Lainé, A.* Considérations sur le Droit international privé à propos d'un livre récent; la *Synthèse du Droit international privé,* de M. le *Comte de Vareilles-Sommières; Paris,* 1900: an extract from the Revue critique de législation et de jurisprudence, xxviii (1899), 613–623, xxix (1900), 20–46, 83–93, 216–227, 350–374, 614. Un conflit sur les conflits: Revue critique, xxix (1900), 385–404, 599–611; xxx (1901), 85–109, xxxi (1900), 184–196, 383–400, 477–490, a reply by the author to M. Lainé's criticism.

VAUGEOIS. *Du rôle et de la formation du droit international privé.* Caen, 1884.

VINCENT, RÉNÉ. *Derecho internacional privado.* Los extranjeros ante los tribunales franceses. Trad. de G. Condé. Havre, 1889.

VINCENT, RÉNÉ, and PÉNAUD, ÉDOUARD, advocates at the Court of Appeal of Paris.

Dictionnaire de droit international privé; législation, doctrine, jurisprudence françaises. Paris, 1888; pp. 951. *Revue* de l'année 1888: Paris, 1889; pp. 128; 1889: Paris, 1890; pp. 140. *Revue pratique de droit international privé.* See Periodicals, § 94.

A digest of the French law through 1887, with annual supplements.

VISSCHER, CHARLES DE. *Des fondations en droit international privé,* à propos de la fondation de Niederfullbach. Paris, 1913.

WEISS, ANDRÉ, professor in the University of Dijon and of Paris.

Traité élémentaire de droit international privé. Paris, 1886; pp. 996. Second edition, Paris, 1890; pp. 898.

A one-volume practical treatise, crowned by the Institute.

Traité théorique et pratique de droit international privé. 5 vols.: Paris, 1892, 1894, 1898, 1901, 1905; pp. 756; xix, 916; xlviii, 641; 718; xxxix, 902. 2d ed., 6 vols., Paris, 1907, 1908, 1912, 1912, 1913, 1913; pp. xl, 844, xxxviii, 749, lxxv, 761, 757, xlvi, 710, 355 and App. 516.

A careful and thorough work, with full citation of authorities; treatises, monographs, jurisprudence, legislation, treaties. Clear and concise; the standard practical work on the Conflict of Laws in the French language. Cited as Weiss.

Manuel de droit international privé, à l'usage des étudiants des facultés de droit. Paris, 1895; pp. 640. 2d ed., Paris, 1899; 6th ed., Paris, 1909; 7th ed., 1914; pp.

xxix, 726. 5th ed., translated into Spanish by Estanislao S. Zeballos, 2 vols., Paris, 1911–12; pp. 576, 740.

"Not a scientific work; it is addressed to students."

Zeballos' Spanish translation is however a serious piece of work, especially valuable for the comparison of European and American doctrines.

Rôle, fonction et méthode du droit comparé dans le domaine du droit international privé. Report to the Congrès international de droit comparé. Bull. Soc. Législ. Comparée, 1900, pp. 417–424.

Questionnaire sur le droit international privé soumis à la commission de révision du Code civil. Rev. de dr. int. pr. iii (1907), 641–653: also in Bull. de la Société d'études législatives, 1907, 494.

ZIX. *Du conflit des lois françaises et des lois étrangères.* Lyons, 1861.

§ 8. **German Authors.** — This section includes not only authors within the present empire, but German-speaking authors in Austria and Switzerland.

ALEF, F. *De diversorum statutorum concursu eorumque conflictu.* In his *Diebus Academicis,* No. 4. Heidelberg, 1840.

"Alef has something original about all his writings. He has a lively style. But his rhapsodical method does not really bring him to a consistent conclusion." Schäffner, 9.

BAR, LUDWIG VON, professor at the University of Göttingen.

Internationales Privat- und Strafrecht. Hannover, 1862; pp. xviii, 616. 2d ed. entitled *Theorie und Praxis des internationalen Privatrechts;* Hannover, 1889; 2 vols., pp. xl, 660, xvi, 719.

International Law, private and criminal, translated into English by G. R. Gillespie. Edinburgh, 1883; pp. xxxii, 766. 2d ed., Edinburgh, 1892; pp. xlvi, 1162.

This is by far the best book by means of which an American lawyer can make himself familiar with the prevailing doctrine of the European writers on Private International Law. The scope of the second edition is very broad, including the law of patents, copyrights, and industrial property; the translation is an excellent one; and Professor von Bar is the most distinguished exponent of the German school of private international law. "If the learned reader buys this book he will have his reward when he has read it." Law Quarterly Review, viii, 342.

The second edition is reviewed in Zeitschrift für internationales Privat- und Strafrecht, i (1891) 34–48, 190–204 by Kloppel, under the title, Die leitenden Grundsätze des internationalen Privatrechts. Gillespie's second edition is cited as Bar.

Lehrbuch des internationalen Privat- und Strafrechts. Stuttgart, 1892; pp. xvi, 360. Japanese tr. by Miyada, 1899.

A student's book; learned and helpful.

Du conflit entre la loi du domicile et la loi de la nationalité. Translated into French by Héron de Villefosse. Clunet, 1895, pp. 22–31..

Internationales Privatrecht (reprinted from Holtzendorff-Kohler's Encyklopädie der Rechtswissenschaft). n. p. n. d.; pp. 45 [1904].

An admirable summary. An earlier edition is translated by Professor Weiss, Esquisse du droit international privé. Clunet, 1887, xiv (1887), 257–273; 1888, xv (1888), 5–16, 441–447.

Internationales Privatrecht (reprinted from Die Kultur der Gegenwart: Systematische Rechtswissenschaft). Berlin and Leipzig, 1906. pp. 144–161.

A new summary, an entirely different one from the preceding.

BARAZETTI, CAESAR, professor in the University of Heidelberg.

Das Internationale Privatrecht im Bürgerlichen Gesetzbuche für das Deutsche Reich. Hannover, 1897; pp. 123.

An examination and criticism of the provisions (or lack of provisions) for private international law in the first draft of the civil code.

Die technischen Ausrdücke für die verschiedenen verwandten Kollisionsarten römischer Gesetzesnormen und für die damit verwandten Begriffe, wie sie in der Theorie des internationalen Privatrechts vorkommen. Zeitschrift für internationales Privat- und Strafrecht, viii (1898), 273–292.

BARON, JULIUS. *Peregrinenrecht und Ius Gentium.* Leipzig, 1892; pp. 40.

A Festschrift.

BEER, LUDWIG. *Neue Entwicklungsstufen des internationalen Privatrechts.*

Bloch, Alfred, and Frank, Felix. *Normen über die internationalen Rechtsbeziehungen auf dem Gebiete des Zivil- und Strafrechtes und über den Rechtshilfeverkehr mit dem Auslande.* Vienna, 1910; pp. 1119.

A collection of treaties, statutes, decisions, official correspondence, etc. bearing on the subject.

Böhm, Ferdinand, judge of the Court of Appeal.
Die räumliche Herrschaft der Rechtsnormen (örtliche Statutenkollision) auf dem Gebiete des Privatrechtes einschliesslich des Handels-, Wechsel- und Konkursrechtes. Nach Theorie und Rechtsprechung, unter besonderer Berücksichtigung der Entscheidungen der obersten deutschen Gerichtshöfe, zum Handgebrauche für die Praxis. Erlangen, 1890; pp. ix, 237.

An admirable collection of German authorities, especially judicial decisions, with extracts from the opinions.

Bogeng. *Internationales Privat- und Civilprozessrecht.* Berlin, 1908.

Braam. *De legum nostrarum civilium cum legibus peregrinis conflictu.* Groningen, 1821.
An inaugural dissertation.

Cohn, Georg, professor in the University of Zürich.
Ueber international-gleiches Recht. Vortrag gehalten in der juristischen Gesellschaft in Wien am 18 März 1879. Vienna, 1879; pp. 26.

Address before the Bar Association of Vienna. Also published in Juristische Blätter, 1879, pp. 233–236, 245–247, 257–259.

Cybichowski, Sigismund, professor in the University of Lemberg.
Die Bestandteile des internationalen Privatrechts. Zeitschr. f. intern. P. und ö. Recht., xx (1910), 367–398.

Ehrlich, Eugen, professor in the University of Czernowitz.
Internationales Privatrecht. Deutsches Rundschau, 1906, p. 419. *Les tendences actuelles du droit international privé.* French translation by Robert Caillemer. Paris, 1909; pp. 24. Reprinted from Rev. de dr. int. pr. vol. 4 (1908) pp. 902–924.

A study of the topic in Professor Ehrlich's characteristic manner, with the purpose of discovering the actual present condition and tendency of the law.

ESCHER, CARL, professor at the University of Zürich. *Das schweizerische interkantonale Privatrecht auf Grund des Bundesgesetzes betreffend die civilrechtlichen Verhältnisse der Niedergelassenen und Aufenthalter* (vom 25 Juni 1891). Zürich, 1895; pp. vi, 287.

An inaugural dissertation. A discussion of Swiss legislation on inter-cantonal relations. The author examines criticisms previously made on former laws and projects for codification, and comments on the federal code of 1891. The authorities on the Conflict of Laws oftenest cited are Huber and von Bar.

FINK. *Die Prinzipien des internationalen Privatrechts und die Vorbehaltklausel.* (Zeitschrift f. intern. Privatrecht, xxiv (1914), p. 138.

HABICHT, HERMANN. *Internationales Privatrecht nach dem Einfürungsgesetze zum Bürgerlichen Gesetzbuche.* Berlin, 1907; pp. vi, 254.

Prepared for publication, after the author's death, by Max Greiff. A consideration of the provisions about private international law in the introduction to the German civil code.

HÄLSCHNER. *De legum quae ad jus privatum pertinent vi et auctoritate quam obtinent extra civitatis fines.* 1851.

HAUSS, AUGUSTUS FRIDERICUS CHRISTIAN GEORG. *De principiis a quibus pendet legum sibi contrarium auctoritas,* si quae variorum locorum constitutiones colliduntur, ob singularem causae, de qua agitur, indolem et naturam, in primis de usu regulae "Locus regit actum" recte determinando. Göttingen, 1824; pp. 62.

This learned thesis considers first the whole subject, which is regarded as a question of contemporary public law. The entire subject is then reduced to four rules for solving conflicts of law: 1, the rule of autonomy of the will; 2, the application of the local law; 3, if that is not applicable, then a necessary application of the foreign law; 4, as to things in a foreign territory subject to the foreign jurisdiction, the laws of that territory govern. The author next considers the maxim "locus regit actum," and determines its meaning and its limits.

HOFÄKER. *De efficacia statutorum in res extra territorium sitas.* (In his *Opuscula*). Stuttgart, 1804; pp. 181–230.

JETTEL, EMIL. *Handbuch des internationalen Privat- und Strafrechtes, mit rücksicht auf die Gesetzgebungen Oesterreichs, Ungarns, Croatiens, und Bosniens.* Vienna and Leipzig, 1893; pp. xv, 344.

The greater part of this volume is taken up with a consideration of the foreign treaties and the constitutional provisions as between the different parts of the Austro-Hungarian empire, especially with regard to judicial procedure and to crime. General principles are stated only in summary form.

KAHN, FRANZ. *Ueber Inhalt, Natur und Methode der internationalen Privatrechts.* Jena, 1899; pp. 87.

Reprinted from Jherings Jahrbücher, vol. 40. An extremely valuable consideration of the nature of private international law, which is distinguished from the law of foreigners, the law of nations and the ordinary private law. His conclusion is that private international law is "national law with an international method." Reviewed by von Bar, Archiv für öffentliches Recht, vol. 15, p. 1. "Den vortrefflichen Aufsatz." Niemeyer, Methodik, 2.

Rôle, fonction et méthode du droit comparé dans le domaine du droit international privé. Paris, 1900; pp. 11.

A report presented to the International Congress of Comparative Law. Found also in a Bull. Soc. Legisl. Comparée, 1900, 406–416. See also: Chausse, *Observations sur le rapport de M. Kahn relatif au rôle, à la fonction et à la méthode du droit comparé dans le domaine du droit international privé.* Congrès international de droit comparé. Paris, 1900.

Bedeutung der Rechtsvergleichung mit Bezug auf das internationale Privatrecht. Zeitschrift für internationales Privat- und Strafrecht (1900), 97–105.

Gesetzeskollisionen: ein Beitrag zur Lehre des internationalen Privatrechts. Jherings Jahrbücher, xxx, 1.

Die einheitliche kodifikation des internationalen Privatrechts durch Staatsvertrage. Leipzig, 1904.

KLEIN, PETER, Privatdozent in the University of Königsberg.

Die Revisibilität des Internationalen Privatrechts. Zeitschrift für intern. Privat- u. öffentl. Recht, xiii (1903),353–365.

Internationalrechtliche Privatrechtseinheit. Zeitschr. für intern. Privat- u. öffentl. Recht, xvi (1906), 1–33.

Abhandlungen aus dem internationalen Privatrecht. Arch. für burgerliches Recht, xxvii (1906), 252–282; xxix (1906), 92–116, 311–384.

Three articles on the following special subjects:

I. Die Rück- und Weiterverweisung im internationalen Privatrecht.

II. Die Bedeutung des Völkerrechts für das international Privatrecht unter besonderer Berücksichtigung des Rechts der neuen Haager Staaten Konferenzen.

III. Die Lehre vom *ordre public.*

KOHLER, JOSEF, professor in the University of Berlin.
Völkerrechtliche Studien. Zeitschr. f. Völkerrecht u. Bundesstaatsrecht, vi (1912), 89–124.

KRASNOPOLSKI, HORAZ, professor at the University of Prague.
Staatsangehörigkeit oder Domizil? Oesterr. Zentralblatt für die jurist. Praxis, xxv (1907), 3–22, 193–216.

An interesting discussion of the controversy between the Italian nationalist school and the jurists who still place the seat of personal law at the domicil.

KRUG, AUGUST OTTO. *Das internationale Recht der Deutschen.* Uebersichtliche Zusammenstellung der zwischen verschiedenen deutschen Staaten getroffenen Vereinbarungen über die Leistung gegenseitiger Rechtshülfe. Leipzig, 1851; pp. 74.

A collection of the laws and treaties of the German states, before the time of the Empire, which involved questions of private international law.

MANITIUS, CARL ERNST GUSTAV. *De iurium quae ex diversorum territoriorum legibus ducuntur collisione, ex iure germanico communi spectata habita iuris borussici ratione.* Breslau, 1833; pp. 39.

A doctoral dissertation.

MARCUSEN, WOLDEMAR, professor in the University of Berne.
Innerstaatliches und überstaatliches internationales Privatrecht. Zeitschrift für internationales Privat- und Strafrecht, x (1900), 257.

MEIER, DIDERICUS. *De conflictu legum diversarum in diversis locis obtinentium.* Bremen, 1810; pp. 70.

"Very clearly written, though but short." Schäffner, p. 11.

MEILI, FRIEDRICH, professor in the University of Zürich.

Die Kodifikation des internationalen Civil- und Handelsrechts: eine Materialiensammlung. Leipzig, 1891; pp. 151.

A collection of the codes and treaties of the various states preceded by a bibliography.

Die Doctrin des internationalen Privatrechts. Zeitschrift für internationales Privat- und Strafrecht, i (1891), 1–23, 135–170.

Geschichte und System des internationalen Privatrechts im Grundriss. Leipzig, 1892; pp. viii, 209.

An excellent syllabus of the subject, with numerous extracts from the old authors, from legislation, and from treaties.

Ueber das historische Debüt des internationalen Privatrechts. Zeitschr. f. int. Privat- und Strafrecht, ix (1899), 1.

Das wissenschaftliche Problem des internationalen Privatrechts. Oesterreichisches Centralblatt für die juristische Praxis, xv, 193–222.

Das internationale Privatrecht und die Staatenkonferenzen im Haag. 1900.

Das internationale Civil- und Handelsrecht auf Grund der Theorie, Gesetzgebung und Praxis. 2 vols. Zürich, 1902; pp. xix, 405, viii, 391.

International Civil and Commercial Law, as founded upon theory, legislation, and practice. Translated and supplemented with additions of American and English law by Arthur K. Kuhn. New York and London, 1905; pp. xxvii, 559.

A learned treatise, full of quotations from many authors and of statutes from all states. The translation furnishes a useful key to European writers for American lawyers.

Cited as *Meili;* if without volume number, the English translation is cited.

Die moderne Fortbildung des internationalen Privatrechts. Zürich, 1909; pp. 35.

A paper read before the Bar Association of Berlin.

Grundriss zu Vorlesungen über das internationale und interkantonale Auslieferungsrecht. Zürich, 1910; pp. 29.

Syllabus of the subject, with bibliography.

Die Hauptfragen des internationalen Privatrechts. Zeitschrift für Völkerrecht u. Bundesstaatsrecht, iv (1910), 161–207; reprinted, Breslau, 1910; pp. 58.

Die Zukunft des internationalen Privat- und Strafrechts. Zeitschrift f. Völkerrecht und Bundesstaatsrecht, i (1907), 113–158.

MEILI and HITZIG, F. *Festschrift zu Ehren von Ferdinand Regelsberger.* Zürich, 1907.

MUHEIM. *Die Principien des internationalen Privatrechts im schweizerischen Privatrechte.* Altdorf, 1887.

MUTZNER. *Das Postulat eines internationalen Gerichtshofes für Streitigkeiten aus dem internationalen Privatrecht.* Zeitschrift f. internat. Privat- und öffentl. Recht, xxiv (1914), 78.

NEUBAUER. *Regelung des internationalen Privatrechtes durch Verträge zwischen den einzelnen Staaten.* Zeitschrift für das gesammte Handelsrecht, xxxvi, 397.

NEUMANN, HUGO, Privatdozent in the University of Munich.

Internationales Privatrecht in Form eines Gesetzentwurfs nebst Motiven und Materialien. Ein Beitrag zur Kodifikation des deutschen bürgerlichen Rechts. Berlin, 1896; pp. xvi, 284.

A draft of a code in 34 sections, with reasons at length, and a collection of statutory provisions of all nations.

NEUMEYER, KARL, professor in the University of Munich.

Die gemeinrechtliche Entwickelung des internationalen Privat- und Strafrechts bis Bartolus. Erstes Stück: Die Geltung der Stammesrechte in Italien. Munich, 1901; pp. xi, 313.

A careful and scholarly study of the Roman, Lombard, and other systems of law as they prevailed in Italy in the middle ages.

Partikulare Staatsverträge über internationales Privatrecht. Seufferts Blätter für Rechtsanwendung, lxxi (1906), pp. 333–342.

NIEMEYER, THEODOR, professor in the University of Kiel.

Das in Deutschland geltende internationale Privatrecht. Leipzig, 1894; pp. viii, 109.

The statutory and treaty provisions in the German Empire and its separate states which deal with conflicts of laws.

Zur Methodik des internationalen Privatrechtes. Leipzig, 1894; pp. 39.

An essay on the positive nature of the rules of private international law: "not exclusive but positive."

Das internationale Privatrecht im Entwurf eines bürgerlichen Gesetzbuchs. Berlin, 1896; pp. 44.

An examination of the provisions in the draft of the German code.

Vorschläge und Materialien zur Kodification des internationalen Privatrechts. Leipzig, 1895; pp. xiv, 282, 140.

A study of the laws of various states, extracts from writers on the subject, etc., bearing on the codification of private international law.

Das internationale Privatrecht des bürgerlichen Gesetzbuchs. Berlin, 1901; pp. viii, 222.

Deals entirely with the provisions and interpretation of the German civil code.

NIPPOLD, OTFRIED, professor in the University of Berne.

Internationale Rechtseinheit. Blätter für vergleich. Rechtswiss. 1906, 65–80.

PFEIFFER, L. *Das Princip des internationalen Privatrechts.* Stuttgart, 1851; pp. 79.

PÜTTER, K. Th., professor in the University of Greifswald.

Das praktische europäische Fremdenrecht; nebst einem Anhang zur Kritik der fremdenrechtlichen Bestimmungen des preussischen Strafgesetz-Entwurfs. Leipzig, 1845; pp. 212.

A treatise on the conflict of laws as applied to the rights of foreigners within the state, with an appendix containing a criticism of the project for a Prussian criminal code. A work well-esteemed in its day, though not of much value now to an American lawyer.

ROHS, E. *Zur Revisibilität des internationalen Privatrechts.* Zeitschr. f. intern. u. ö. R. xiv (1904), pp. 59–63.

Das Prinzip der "wohlerworbenen Rechte" im internationalen und intertemporalen Privatrechte. Zeitschrift für internat. Privat- und öffentliches Recht, xiv (1904), pp. 362–369.

Einführung in das internationale Privatrecht. Bonn, 1911; pp. 47.

An introduction to the study of the law, in which many of the fundamental conceptions of the subject are critically examined. No authorities are cited.

SAVIGNY, FRIEDRICH CARL VON, professor in the University of Berlin.

System des heutigen römischen Rechts, vol. 8: Berlin, 1849; pp. xii, 540. Translated into Spanish by Jacinto Mesía and Manuel Poley, vol. 6, Madrid, 1879; pp. 119–461. *A treatise on the Conflict of Laws*, translated into English by William Guthrie. 2d ed., Edinburgh, 1880; pp. 567.

This work on the Conflict of Laws is part of Savigny's great work on modern Roman law. It is the starting-point of a school of thought; as such, it has been fully discussed, § 64.

In the second English edition are contained, in an Appendix, the important discussions on the Conflict of Laws from the works of Bartolus, Dumoulin, Paul Voet, and Huber.

The first edition, in Guthrie's translation, is reviewed in the Journal of Jurisprudence, xiii, 134.

"Savigny has done much to clear away the confused notions which met the student on the threshold of the subject. . . . The style of Savigny is a model of precision and clearness. Each sentence has its purpose, each word its distinct meaning and proper place. The translation faithfully reflects these good qualities, and will enable the attentive reader to judge whether our estimate of the merits of the author is exaggerated. The chief difficulty lay in representing the abstract ideas and technical terms, which, though familiar to German lawyers, have sometimes no precise representatives in English. This difficulty Mr. Guthrie has in almost every instance successfully overcome." Æneas Mackay in Journal of Jurisprudence, xiii, 137, 143. Guthrie's second edition is cited as Savigny.

SCHÄFFNER, WILHELM. *Entwicklung des internationalen Privatrechts.* Frankfort, 1841; pp. 213.

Esplicazione del dritto privato internazionale. Translated into Italian by Michele Tenore. Naples, 1859; pp. 185.

A learned consideration of the theories of others, as well as a statement of the author's own.

SCHMID, REINHOLD, professor in the University of Berne.
Die Herrschaft der Gesetze nach ihren räumlichen und zeitlichen Grenzen im Gebiete des bürgerlichen und peinlichen Rechts. Jena, 1863; pp. vi, 204.

SCHOLLER. *Fragen internationalen Privatrechts in der Uebergangszeit.* Kosmodike, 15 juill. 1900.

SIEBER, J., professor in the University of Berne.
Das Staatsbürgerrecht im internationalen Verkehr, seine Erwerbung und sein Verlust. 2 vols., Berne, 1907; pp. xx, 618, 410.

A historical sketch of the doctrines of nationality in the different countries, together with the legislation of every country bearing on the question.

STRISOWER, LEO, professor in the University of Vienna.
Die italienische Schule des internationalen Privatrechtes.

Published in Gerichtshalle, Vienna, March 10–31, 1881, Nos. 20–26.

TITTMANN. *De competentia legum externarum et domesticarum in definiendis potissimum juribus conjugum.* Halle, 1822.

VESQUE VON PÜTTLINGEN, JOHANN. *Handbuch des in Oesterreich-Ungarn geltenden internationalen Privatrechtes, mit besonderer Berücksichtigung des Staats- und Völkerrechtes.* 2d ed., Vienna, 1878; pp. xv, 660.

A treatise which examines foreign laws and especially the laws and judicial decisions of Austria-Hungary.

WÄCHTER. *Ueber die Collision der Privatrechtsgesetze verschiedener Staaten.* Archiv für die civilistische Praxis, xxiv (1841), pp. 230–311; xxv (1842), pp. 1–60, 161–200, 361–419.

A series of articles which forms a complete and important treatise on the subject. See also *L' opera di Giorgio von Wächter nel diritto internazionale privato.* Atti del Reale Istituto Veneto, ix, 527.

WERTHEIMER, LUDWIG. *Jahrbuch für den internationalen Rechtsverkehr,* 1912–13. Munich, 1912.

A review of the private international law of the year. Articles by various authors, with bibliography. In an appendix is a vocabulary, in German, English, French and Italian, which will prove useful to an American lawyer in translating German legal terms.

WÖRNER, GERHARD. *Kollisionsnormen zum Versicherungsvertrag.* Zeitschr. f. i. u. ö. R. xiii (1903), 366–373.

WOLF, P. *Zur Rechtsprechung des Bundesgerichts auf dem Gebiete des internationalen und des interkantonalen Privatrechts.* Basle, 1896; pp. 12.

Brochure reprinted from Zeitschrift für schweizerisches Recht, xxxvii (1896), pp. 20–31.

WORMS, STEPHEN. *Die Schaffung eines einheitlichen internationalen Privatrechtes.* Vienna, 1909.

ZITELMANN, ERNST, professor in the University of Bonn. *Internationales Privatrecht.* 2 vols. Leipzig, 1897; 1898, 1903, 1912; pp. xxi, 408, 1025.

A very able work, the latest German work on the subject. Unlike von Bar, however, his conclusions are not based at all upon decided cases. The work is criticised by von Bar in Archiv für öffentliches Recht, xv, 1.

Artikel 7 bis 31 des Einführungsgesetzes zum bürgerlichen Gesetzbuch für das Deutsche Reich; nebst sämtlichen Entwürfen. Leipzig, 1908; pp. 49.

A comparison, in parallel columns, of the various stages through which the articles of the German civil code passed, from the first proposal until final enactment, with notes.

§ 9. **Dutch Authors.** — Among the Dutch authors I have included Jitta, although his works are published in French.

ASSER, T. M. C., professor in the University of Amsterdam. *Schets van het internationaal privaatregt.* Haarlem, 1880; pp. vi, 182.

Das internationale Privatrecht. German translation by Max Cohn. Berlin, 1880; pp. 140.

Eléments de droit international privé ou du conflit des lois; translated, completed, and annotated by Alphonse Rivier, professor in the University of Brussels. Paris, 1884; pp. iv, 297.

Derecho internacional privado, by Asser and Rivier, translated from the French, with Introduction and notes by Joaquín Fernandez Prida, professor in the University of Santiago. Madrid [n. d.] pp. 298 (1909).

Elemente de Drept international Privat sau Conflictul legilor, Roumanian translation by George E. Schina, Bucharest, 1895; pp. xiii, 252.

Asser's work, in Rivier's translation and with his additions, is one of the important treatises on the subject. It is, however, only a summary consideration of the doctrines of the Conflict of Laws. The original work was reviewed by H. J. Hamaker. De grondslag van het internationaal privaatrecht, 634–683.

Droit international privé et droit uniforme. Rev. dr. intern. vol. 12 (1880), pp. 5–22. Reprinted, Brussels, 1880; pp. 18.

De Vos, L. *Het internationaal privaatrecht in het ontwerp van burgerlijk wetboek voor Belgie.* Brussels, 1897.

Dolk, Willem. *Internationaal Privaatrecht:* I. *Personenrecht.* II. *Zakenrecht.* Utrecht, 1880, 1882; pp. 107, 46.

Two essays, which include a summary of the doctrines of the most important modern writers, and a statement of the author's own views in the form of rules.

Hamaker, H. J., professor in the University of Utrecht.

Das internationale Privatrecht, seine Ursachen und Ziele. Translated into German by Otto Mühlbrecht. Berlin, 1878; pp. 31.

Aard en doel van het internationaal privaatrecht. Leiden, 1878.

Inaugural dissertation on the establishment of the first Chair of Private International Law in Holland. "The essay gives in brief the fundamental principle of international private law in a clear form" is the translator's criticism.

Jitta, Josephus, professor in the University of Amsterdam.

La méthode du droit international privé. The Hague, Paris, Brussels and London, 1890; pp. vii, 499.

Metodo de derecho internacional privado, Spanish translation by J. F. Prida, Madrid, 1905; pp. 524.

Das Wesen des internationales Privatrechts, German translation in Archiv für öffentliches Recht, xiv (1899) 301–327.

This original and remarkable work has been considered at length above, § 67. See a criticism by von Bar, Archiv für öffentliches Recht, xv (1900) 1–49, under the title *Neue Prinzipien und Methoden des internationalen Privatrechts;* and a reply by Jitta, *Alte und neue Methoden des internationalen Privatrechts,* in the same volume, pp. 564–581. See also a review of Jitta's theories by T. Baty, entitled *Modern* jus gentium, Juridical Review, xx, 109–120.

Le droit commun international comme source du droit international privé. Paris, 1910; pp. 16.

Reprinted from Revue de droit international privé, vol. v (1909), pp. 485–500.

JITTA and RUTGERS. *L'influence de la Belgique et de la Hollande dans le développement du droit international privé.* Questions prat. de dr. intern. privé, 1913, p. 89.

KOSTERS, J., professor in the University of Groningen.

Het karakter van het internationaal privaatrecht. Groningen, 1908; pp. 44.

An inaugural dissertation.

MEIJERS, E. M. *Bijdrage tot de Geschiedenis van het internationaal Privaat- en Strafrecht in Frankrijk en de Nederlanden.* Haarlem, 1914; pp. 99, xxxvi.

A carefully written history of the doctrines of French and Dutch authors and courts in the early Middle Ages.

TIEOBEL VAN DEN HAM, M. G. *De Kracht van Buitenlandsche Vonnissen in het internationaal Privaatrecht.* Utrecht, 1890.

§ **10. Italian Authors.** — This section includes Italian-speaking authors of Dalmatia.

ANZILOTTI, DIONISIO, professor in the Royal Institute of Social Sciences, Florence.

Studi critici del diritto internazionale privato. Rocca S. Casciano, 1898; pp. 313.

Three essays, entitled: A page in the history of civil codification in Germany; national laws in international affairs; the question of the *renvoi*, and the conflicts between legislative provisions with respect to private international law.

La codificazione del diritto internazionale privato. Florence, 1894; pp. 85.

Reviewed by Alessandro Corsi, Unificazione o codificazione del diritto internazionale privato. Revista italiana delle scienze giuridiche, xviii (1894), 367–390.

AUDISIO, G. *Juris naturae et gentium privati et publici fundamenta.* Naples, 1853.

BAISINI, JACOPO. *Studii di diritto civile internazionale,* leggi, trattati, dottrina e giurisprudenza, dei diversi stati sul godimento dei diritti civili sulla cauzione "judicatum solvi" e sul patrocinio gratuito sulla esecuzione dei giudicati, provvedimenti, ed atti stranieri sulle rogatorie, citazioni e notificazioni giudizarie, con proposte di riforma. Milan, 1892; pp. 326.

A work published under the auspices of the Italian Society of Authors. Devoted entirely to procedural questions.

BIANCHI, F. S. *Principii di Diritto internazionale privato.* 1914.

BUZZATO, GIULIO CESARE, professor in the University of Pavia.

Trattato di diritto internazionale privato secundo le convenzioni dell' Aja. 1907.

CATELLANI, ENRICO, professor in the University of Padua.

Il diritto internazionale privato e i suoi recenti progressi. 3 vols. Turin, 1883, 1885, 1888; pp. 334, 240, 1028. 2d ed., 1895. 3d ed., 1902.

The history of the modern doctrines, followed by an elaborate treatise, in which the entire subject is treated theoretically and practically. A chapter of the second edition, under the title *Il diritto internazionale privato nel sistema del diritto internazionale* was printed in Il Filangierei, xvii (1892), 284–289; reprinted in pamphlet form. Milan, 1892; pp. 6.

Il diritto internazionale privato nell' antica Grecia. Rome, 1892; pp. 245–297.

Extract from "Studi e Documenti di Storia e Diritto" for 1892.

Del conflitto fra norme di diritto internazionale privato. Venice, 1897; pp. 75.

Le droit international au commencement du xxe siècle. Japanese translation by Ninagawa and Kafuku. Rev. dr. intern. japon, 1903, numbers 14, 171.

CAVAGLIERI, ARRIGO, professor in the University of Padua.

Diritto internazionale privato e diritto transitorio. Verona, Padua, 1904; pp. 123.

A philosophical examination of the relations between the principles regulating the conflicts of laws in space and in time.

La teoria dei diritti acquisiti in due recenti opere di diritto internazionale privato. Pisa, 1905; pp. 82.

A criticism of Vareilles-Sommières' *La Synthèse du droit international privé* and of Pillet's *Principes de droit international privé.*

L' elemento consuetudinario nel diritto internazionale privato. Appunti critici. Padua, 1908; pp. 130.

A study of the part which the traditional element has played and is likely in the future to play in the development of private international law.

CIMBALI, EDUARDO, professor at the University of Catania.

Di una nuova denominazione del cosidetto diritto internazionale privato, e de' suoi effetti fondamentali. Milan, 1892. 2d ed., Rome, 1893; pp. 111.

An exhaustive and acute consideration of the proper name to be given to this branch of law, reprinted from Spedalieri (No. 7, Sept. 1892) with a lengthy polemical correspondence with several Italian professors of law. Reviewed by Frantz Despagnet: D'une nouvelle dénomination de ce qu'on appelle droit international privé et de ses effets fondamentaux. Clunet, 1898, pp. 5–22.

CONTUZZI, FRANCESCO P., professor in the University of Naples.

La codificazione del diritto internazionale privato; commento agli articoli 6–12 disposizioni preliminari, articoli 3–15 codice civile, art. 58 codice di commercio e relativi articoli 105, 107, 941, 950 procedura civile. Naples, 1886; pp. 97.

A study of the possibility of reducing the principles of private international law to a code.

Diritto internazionale privato. Milan, 1890; pp. 391.

A student's manual.

DIENA, GIULIO, professor in the University of Siena.

I diritti reali considerati nel diritto internazionale privato. Turin, 1895; pp. 458.

A complete treatise on that portion of the conflict of laws which has to do with property; with copious references to treatises and to decided cases.

Sui limiti all' applicabilità del diritto straniero. Prolusione al corso di diritto internazionale letta nell' Università di Siena il dì 13 Gennaio 1898. Turin (Rome, Milan, Florence) 1898; pp. 31.

A learned introductory lecture, with references to decided cases as well as to treatises.

De la rétroactivité des dispositions législatives de droit international privé. Clunet, 1900, pp. 925–940. Also in German: *Die rückwirkende Kraft des internationalen Privatrechts.* (Zeitschr. für intern. Privat- und Strafr. 1900, 353.)

Principi di Diritto internazionale. Parte Seconda; diritto internazionale privato. Naples, 1910; pp. 455.

The second volume of a general work. A short general treatise on the topic.

ESPERSON, PIETRO, professor in the University of Padua.

Movimento giuridico in Italia e nel Belgio sul Diritto internazionale privato. Florence, 1870; pp. 36.

A review of the current thought of the so-called Italian school.

FEDOZZI, PROSPERO, professor in the University of Padua.

Revista critica di giurisprudenza controversa in materia di diritto internazionale privato. Modena, 1898; pp. 30.

Reprint from the Archivio giuridico.

FIORE, PASQUALE, professor in the University of Naples.

Elementi di diritto internazionale privato: manuale ad uso degli instituti di scienze politiche e sociali e degli instituti tecnici superiori. Florence, 1869. 2d ed., Florence, 1874; pp. xiii, 643. 3d ed., Rome, 1889; pp. xiii, 643. 4th ed. 5th ed., 1897; pp. xiii, 643. 6th ed., Turin, Milan, Rome and Naples, 1905.

An elementary treatise. The later editions are reprinted from the plates of the early editions.

Diritto internazionale privato, o principii per risolvere i conflitti tra le leggi civili, commerciali, giudiziarie, penali di stati diversi. 3d ed., 4 vols., Turin, 1888, 1889, 1901, 1903; pp. 540, 583, 579, 668. 4th ed., 4 vols. Turin, 1907–15; pp. 541, 583, 579, 668.

Le droit international privé. Translated into French by Pradier-Fodéré, Paris, 1875; pp. xliv, 728. 2d ed., translated into French by Charles Antoine. 3 vols. Paris, 1890, 1891, 1903; pp. 595, 613, 644. 3d ed., from the 4th Italian ed., by Charles Antoine, 4 vols., Paris, 1907.

Derecho internacional privado, translated by A. García Moreno, with introduction and appendix by D. Cristino Martos. 2 vols., Madrid, 1878; pp. 375, 360. 2d ed. of the translation, 3 vols., Madrid, 1888–9; pp. 394, 416, 427.

This is called the third edition of the preceding work. Its title however is new, and the work enormously amplified, becoming a large practical treatise, the principal work on this subject by one of the best known Italian writers. This is the standard Italian work at present.

Questioni di diritto sue casi controversi esaminati e discussi. Turin, Milan, Rome, Naples, 1904; pp. 652.

Solutions of controverted questions in the following topics: succession; nationality; gifts; foreign sentences; crime; marriage; status; foreign judgments; wreck; dowry; jurisdiction of courts.

Statuto personale e statuto reale. In Il digesto italiano, vol. 22², pp. 432–456.

A complete essay upon the theory of statutes from the modern point of view.

FOCHERINI, ATTILIO. *Problemi di diritto internazionale privato per uso degli studenti in giurisprudenza e degli allievi alla carriera consolare e diplomatica.* Carpi, 1913; pp. 81.

One hundred and forty-two problems in various topics of private international law, with references to authorities for their solution.

FUSINATO, GUIDO, professor in the University of Turin.

Il principio della scuola Italiana nel diritto privato internazionale. Bologna, 1885.

Introduzione ad un corso di diritto internazionale. Parte seconda. Diritto internazionale privato. Lanciano, 1885. 2d ed., Turin, 1897.

Questioni di diritto internazionale privato. Turin, 1884.

GABBA, CARLO FRANCESCO, professor in the University of Florence.

Introduzione al diritto civile internazionale italiano. Rome, 1906; pp. 46.

A theoretical discussion of the articles of the Italian code bearing on private international law. See also: Brusa, Emilio, *Les idées de M. le professeur C. F. Gabba sur la théorie générale du droit international privé.* Rev. de droit intern. et de leg. comp., 1906, p. 518.

Criterio fondamentale del gius civile internazionale. Rivista di diritto intern., i (1906), 8–15.

GEMMA, SCIPIONE, professor at the University of Bologna.

Propedeutica al diritto internazionale privato, da un corso libero tenuto nella R. Università di Bologna nell' anno 1897–98. Bologna, 1899; pp. 123.

Introductory lectures in a university course, in which the author considers the fundamental conceptions and sources of the subject.

L' autonomia scientifica e didattica del diritto internazionale privato. Studi Senesi, xxvi (1909), pp. 1–20.

GRASSO, GIACOMO, professor in the University of Genoa.

Principii di diritto internazionale, pubblico e privato. Florence, 1889; pp. 332. 2d ed., 1890. 3d ed., Florence, 1896; pp. 332.

A student's or popular manual, of which the last one hundred pages are devoted to private international law.

GUARINI, GIOVANNI BATTISTA, Privatdozent in the University of Rome.

Applicabilità delle norme di diritto internazionale privato contenute in una legge straniera. Rome, 1900; pp. 266.

The force of foreign law is first studied historically and then the present condition of jurisprudence, legislation and doctrine is examined. There is a good collection of decisions, mostly from Clunet and the Zeitschrift.

LAGHI, FERDINANDO, professor in the University of Parma. *Il diritto internazionale privato nei suoi rapporti colle legg. territoriali.* Bologna, 1888; pp. 340.

An historical introduction, the theory of territorial laws, and the law of persons are considered in this volume.

LOMONACO, GIOVANNI, professor in the University of Naples. *Trattato di diritto civile internazionale.* Naples, 1874; pp. 302.

A treatise in which considerable space is given to an examination of Italian jurisprudence.

LOZZI, CARLO. *Introduzione al codice civile e al diritto internazionale privato.* Saggio teoretico e pratico. 2d ed., Venice, 1880; pp. 354.

The last hundred pages of the essay constitute a brief statement of some of the principles of private international law.

MACRI, GIACOMO, professor in the University of Messina. *Teorica del diritto internazionale.* Messina, 1883. Vol. 1, pp. 624.

The last 150 pages of the first volume form a concise treatise on the fundamental doctrines of private international law.

MANCINI, P. S. *Della nazionalità come fondamento del diritto delle genti.* 1851.

MARINONI, MARIO, professor in the University of Florence. *La natura giuridica del diritto internazionale privato.* Rivista di diritto internazionale, vii, fasc. 3.

MARIOTTI, GAETANO, professor in the University of Sassari. *Diritto internazionale pubblico e privato.* Sassari, 1877.

MAURO, MARIO DE, professor at the University of Catania. *Questioni di diritto internazionale privato.* Catania, 1876.

MILONE, FILIPPO, professor in the University of Naples. *Saggio di studi intorno i principi e le regole del diritto privato internazionale.* Bologna, 1871; pp. 46.

A rather elementary essay with citation of German, French and English authors. First printed in the Archivio Giuridico, vii (1871), 518–563.

NORSA, EMILIO, professor in the University of Padua.
Le conflit des lois et l'unification internationale. Milan, 1885.

OLIVI, LUIGI, professor in the University of Modena.
Della retroattività delle norme giuridiche in diritto internationale. Il Filangieri, 1893, p. 65.
Also in French: *De la rétroactivité des règles juridiques en droit international.* Rev. dr. intern. xxiv (1892), 553–569.
And in Spanish, translated by Jerónimo Vida: *De la retroactividad de las reglas juridicas en derecho internacional.* Rev. gen. legisl. y jurisprud., 1893, 401.
Manuale del diritto internazionale pubblico e privato. Milan, 1902; pp. 935. 2d ed., Milan, 1911; pp. 964.

One volume in a general "Library of Science." The last Book (about 300 pages) is devoted to private international law.

OTTOLENGHI, GIUSEPPE, professor in the University of Turin.
Sulla funzione e sull' ufficio delle norme interno di diritto internazionale privato. Milan, 1912.

PAPPAFAVA, VLADIMIR. *Il diritto internazionale privato, delineazioni storico-giuridiche.* Zara, 1884; pp. 58.

A rather popular treatment; extract from the Annuario Dalmatico, vol. 1.

Des vicissitudes du droit international privé dans l'histoire de l'humanité. Brussels, Paris, Philadelphia, Grenoble, 1884; pp. 48.

A short history of doctrine. Extract from the "Revue catholique des institutions et du droit."

PIERANTONI, AUGUSTO, professor in the University of Rome.
Il diritto civile internazionale nella codificazione francese ed italiana. Naples, Rome, Milan, 1881; pp. 44.

A history of legislation and of the decisions of the courts interpreting it.

Per la codificazione del diritto internazionale civile mediante trattati. Discorsi pronunciati in Senato nelle tornate 8 e 12 Aprile 1905. Rome, 1905; pp. 71.

Speeches in favor of the ratification of the Articles agreed upon at the Hague Conference of 1902.

ROCCO, NICCOLA. *Dell' uso e autorità delle leggi del regno delle due Sicilie considerate nelle relazioni con le persone e col territorio degli stranieri.* Naples, 1837; pp. 545. 2d ed., Naples, 1842. 3d ed., Naples, 1858–9; 3 vols: pp. 369, 479, 477.

Iannuzzi. *Niccola Rocco:* Discorso necrologico con brevi cenni sull' esplicamento storico del diritto privato internazionale. Naples, 1877.

The earliest of the modern Italian works on the subject.

ROSSI, VITTORIO DE. *Studii di diritto internazionale privato in relazione alla legge italiana. . . .* Pubblicazione fatta per il congresso giuridico internazionale di Torino. Leghorn, 1880; pp. 207.

Essays on the hypothecary system in its relations to international law; the right of reciprocity and retorsion; the juridical position of foreigners before the Italian law; questions of international civil procedure; questions of international maritime law; bankruptcy in its relations to international law.

SAREDO, GIUSEPPE, professor in the University of Rome.

Saggio sulla storia del diritto internazionale privato; introduzione al trattato dei conflitti delle leggi nei rapporti di diritto internazionale privato. Florence, 1873; pp. 137.

Largely concerned with the history of the treatment of foreigners.

Trattato delle leggi, dei loro conflitti di tempo, di luogo, della lora interpretazione e applicazione. Florence, 1871.

TAHMARO, GENNARO. *Dell' uniformità legislativa nel diritto internazionale privato.* Naples, 1913.

TRILLO, A. *Compendio di diritto privato internazionale, fatto secondo il metodo di P. Fiore.* Naples, 1891; pp. 22.

§ 11. Spanish and Portuguese Authors, including Ibero-Americans.

ALCORTA, AMANCIO, professor in the University of Buenos Ayres.

Curso de derecho internacional privado. 3 vols., Buenos Ayres, 1887–1890; pp. viii, 447, 520, 447.

An elaborate and valuable treatise on the subject from the South American point of view.

ALGARA, J. *Lecciones de derecho internacional privado.* Mexico, 1899.

El derecho internacional privado en la República mexicana. Mexico, 1898; pp. 14.

ANDRADE, VIEIRA PINTO DE. *Direito internacional e possival chegar entre as nacões civilisados a unidade legislativa no direito civil e no commerciale, especialmente maritimo?* Em caso affirmativo, que principios poderiam servir de base a essa unificacão. (O Mundo legal e judiciario, 1891, p. 108.)

ARCAYA, PEDRO MANUEL. *Proyecto de ley de aplicacion del derecho internacional privado.* Caracas, 1915; pp. 25.

ASPIROZ, MANUEL. *La liberté civile comme base du droit international privé.* Mexico, 1896; pp. 55.

French translation of an article entitled *La libertad civil como base del derecho internacional privado.* El Derecho (Mexico), 1896, July 29 and August 8; also published in Boletin oficial de la secretaria de relaciones exteriores, vol. 2, p. 205.

BEVILACQUA, CLOVIS, professor in the University of Recife.

Principios elementares de direito internacional privado. Bahia, 1906; pp. 368.

BRAVO, EMILIO, president of the Supreme Court of Spain.

Derecho internacional privado vigente en España. 3 vols., Madrid, 1886; pp. 272, 276, 272.

Written from the point of view of the lawyer and judge. Doctrine, legislation, and treaties in every country having relations with Spain are considered.

BUSTAMANTE Y SIRVÉN, ANTONIO DE, professor in the University of Havana.

Programas de las asignaturas de derecho internacional público y derecho internacional privado, precedidos de la exposición del plan y metodo de los mismos. Madrid, 1891; pp. 242.

This is a syllabus of a course of university lectures. The greater part of it is occupied with private international law.

Tratado de derecho internacional privado. Vol. 1: Nociones preliminares: Historia del derecho positivo: Historia del derecho cientifico. Havana, 1896; pp. 550.

An original and suggestive work. The first volume (which is the only volume yet published) contains a preliminary discussion of the subject and a history of the law, together with an excellent bibliography.

Le leggi di ordine privato nel diritto internazionale. Rivista di dir. intern., iii (1908), 3–30.

CALANDRELLI, ALCIDES, professor in the University of Buenos Ayres.

Questiones de derecho internacional privado. 2 vols., Buenos Ayres, 1911, 1913; pp. 408, 396.

Collected essays upon some fundamental principles; the *régime* of property and capacity to acquire it, with the Argentine legislation; introduction to a course on private international maritime law; capacity to contract marriage, with the Argentine legislation; intervention of consuls in successions, with the Argentine legislation; with a prologue, and an appendix, containing the conclusions of various international conventions.

La Codificación del derecho internacional privado. Buenos Ayres, 1913; pp. 51.

CALVO, CARLOS. See § 87.

CARRIÓ, V. M. *Apuntes de derecho internacional privado: conteniendo los tratados vigentes celebrados por la república oriental del Uruguay desde su independencia hasta nuestros días, el programa de la materia en la facultad de derecho, notas bibliográficas y varios apéndices complementarios del curso.* Montevideo, 1911; pp. xii, 626.

An excellent treatise, containing a short summary of the theories of various authors, a study of the conflicts of civil, commercial, penal, and procedural law, followed by an appendix containing the Acts of the Congress of Montevideo, treaties of the Republic of Uruguay, bibliography, etc.

CASTAÑEDA, TIBURCIO PEREZ. *Historia y crítica de la antigua doctrina de los estatutos y principios que los sustituyen en el derecho internacional moderno.* Madrid, 1891; pp. 154.

Awarded the gold medal by the Bar Association of Havana in 1889. The greater part of it is a history of the doctrine.

CASTRO Y CASALEIZ, A. DE. *Estudios de derecho internacional privado.* Madrid, 1901.

CONDE Y LUQUE, RAFAEL, professor at the University of Madrid.

Oficios del Derecho internacional privado. 2 vols., Madrid, 1901, 1907; pp. 577, 423. 2d ed., vol. 1, Madrid, 1910; pp. 419.

A thoughtful and elaborate treatise, giving an original conception of the subject. Part I deals with the author's conception of this topic, its nature, origin, and characteristics, and its sphere of action, which in the author's opinion is to accomplish three distinct *offices:* to create juridical personality in a foreigner, to attach civil rights to him, and to determine what law rules his rights. The author examines his authorities with care, but in his choice of authorities he appears to be limited almost entirely to those which have appeared in the French language. "The first systematic and fundamental treatise on private international law published in Spain." Olivart, Bibliography.

DA VEIGA, DIDIMO. *Constituindo o direito internacional privado, em sua essencia,* o conjuncto das reglas juridicas que dominam as relacões individuães da sociedate internacional, alcanca na area de sua accão a parte processual correspondente? Comprehendese no direito internacional privado o direito penal internacional? O Direito, vol. 107, pp. 427–430.

FABRÉS, JOSÉ CLEMENTE. *La legislación de Chile con relacion al derecho internacional privado.* Santiago, 1892.

FALÇÃO, FERNANDES. *Do Direito internacional privado.* Coimbre, 1868.

FALCON Y OZCOIDI, MODESTO, professor in the University of Barcelona.

Conflictos de derecho internacional privado. Revista de los tribunales, xxiii, nos. 1 and 2.

FERNANDEZ PRIDA, JOAQUÍN professor in the University of Seville, of Valladolid, and of Madrid.

Fundamentos del derecho internacional privado; conferencias pronunciadas en el Ateneo y sociedad de excursiones de Sevilla. Vitoria, 1888; pp. 95.

Lectures on the general conceptions of private international law delivered to an audience of cultivated laymen.

Derecho internacional privado. Valladolid, 1896; pp. 318.

Intended as an introduction to a more extended work. The general conception, sources, and fundamental principles of the subject are considered. The first chapters are a complete revision of his earlier work.

Estudios de derecho internacional publico y privado. Madrid, 1901; pp. 311.

A collection of essays, of which the last three discuss our subject; they are entitled respectively the conception, the relation and the codification of private international law.

GALLARDO Y MARTINEZ, A. *El derecho interregional español y el código civil.* Madrid, 1893.

GESTOSO Y ACOSTA, LUIS, professor in the University of Valencia.

Apuntes para un curso de derecho internacional privado. Valencia, 1892; pp. 410 and index.

Lectures delivered to students. A brief history and an elementary consideration of the law.

Curso elemental de derecho internacional privado, civil, mercantil, y procesal. Valencia, 1900; pp. 632.

A second edition of the preceding book.

GOMEZ, NICOLÁS LOPEZ R., lecturer in the University of Valladolid.

Lecciones elementales de derecho internacional privado. 2d ed., Valladolid, 1904; pp. 490.

An elementary book.

GUIMARÃES PEDROSA, ANTONIO LOPES, professor in the University of Coimbra.

Introducção ao estudo do direito privado internacional. Coimbra, 1878.

HEYDRICH, R., and GONZALEZ BENARD, A. *Lecciones de Derecho internacional privado desenvueltas con arreglo al Programa de enseñanza del Dr. D. Antonio S. de Bustamente.* Havana, 1893.

MARÍN, JOSÉ GASCÓN. *Programa de derecho internacional privado.* Saragossa, 1900; pp. 14.

A bare list of headings covered in lectures on the subject.

MARTÍNEZ, ALFONSO PÉREZ. *Los conflictos interregionales según las disposiciones contenidas en el título preliminar del Código Civil.* Madrid, 1906; pp. 37.

A reprint from the Revista de Derecho internacional y política exterior.

MIÑANA Y VILLAGRASA, EMILIO. *Derecho internacional privado* (contestaciones al programa para oposiciones á notarías determinadas y al cuerpo de aspirantes al notariado). Madrid, 1904; pp. 294.

An elementary book for notaries.

MOLINA, VICTOR M. *El Derecho internacional privado, y el Codigo civil argentino.* Buenos Ayres, 1882; pp. 238.

A collection of the articles of the code which bear on Private International Law, with elementary comments.

MONSEGUE, SYLLA J. *El derecho internacional privado en la Republica Argentina. Apuntaciones bibliograficas.* Buenos Ayres, 1896.

OCTAVIO, RODERIGO, professor in the University of Rio de Janeiro.

A codificacão do direito internacional privado. Rio de Janeiro, 1910.

OLIVARES BIEC, VICENTE, professor at the Central University, Madrid.

Caso de subsistir en España varias legislaciones civiles, como debe aplicarse á las relaciones de unas con otras la doctrina de los Estatutos: estado actual de esta cuestión después del Congreso jurídico Español celebrado en Madrid en 1886. Madrid, 1887; pp. 46.

A pamphlet of no great importance.

Tratado en forma de código del derecho internacional en sus relaciones con el civil, mercantil, penal y de procedimientos; precedido de la exposición de sus motivos y adicionado con algunos apéndices tomados de disposiciones de nuestro derecho, jurisprudencia del tribunal supremo y convenios internacionales mas importantes. Madrid, 1879; pp. 312, xxiv. 2d ed., Madrid, 1886.

A summary statement of principles, followed by a project for a code, with appendices.

OLIVART, R. DE DALMAU, MARQUES DE. *Manual de derecho internacional publico y privado;* extractado y traducido de las obras de Calvo (Carlos), Bar (L. de), Neumann (Barón de) etc., con extensas notas y un bosquejo del derecho internacional privado español. Madrid, 1886; pp. 851.

A learned compilation, with a comparison of the scope of public and private international law, bibliographies, references to standard treatises, etc.

OTEIZA. *Estudios de derecho internacional privado.* Revista gener. de legisl. lxvi (1886), 217; lxviii, 5–7.

PALOMEQUE, ALBERTO. *Los fueros de Cataluna ante los tribunales nacionales.* Montevideo, 1893; pp. 40.

PIMENTA BUENO, JOSÉ ANTONIO. *Direito internacional privado e applicação de seus principios com referencia ás leis particulares do Brazil.* Rio de Janeiro, 1863; pp. 335.

A short elementary statement of doctrine, abstracted from Foelix and others, followed by a consideration of the Brazilian legislation.

PRATS, BELISARIO. *Derecho civil internacional.* Revista de derecho y jurisprudencia, Montevideo, vol. 4 (1889), pp. 49–64.

RAMIREZ. *Código de los extranjeros. Diccionario de derecho internacional publico y privado de la Republica mexicana.* Mexico, 1870.

RAMIREZ, GONZALO, professor in the University of Montevideo. *Proyecto de código de derecho internacional privado y su commentario.* Buenos Ayres, 1888.

SEGOVIA, LISANDRO. *El derecho internacional privado y el congreso sud-americano de Montevideo.* Buenos Ayres, 1889; pp. xiii, 277.

A valuable theoretical discussion of the topics considered at the Congress of Montevideo.

SEIJAS, R. F. *El derecho internacional hispano-americano publico y privado.* Caracas, 1884, vol. 1, pp. 548.

This work is full of examples drawn from the history of Spanish America. The last half of the first volume discusses a few topics of private international law.

TELL Y LAFONT, G. A. *Notas sobre la teoría de los estatutos en la antigua jurisprudencia catalana.* Barcelona, 1887; pp. 38.

Extract from Revista de la España Regional, ii, 213. A study of the old law of the Spanish province.

TORRES CAMPOS, MANUEL, professor in the University of Granada.

Principios de derecho internacional privado o de derecho extraterritorial de Europa y America en sus relaciones con el derecho civil de España. Madrid, 1883; pp. 325.

An excellent general treatise on the history and present condition, in Spain and abroad, of private international law.

Elementos de Derecho internacional privado. Madrid, 1887; pp. 218. 2d ed., Madrid, 1893; pp. 515. 3d ed., Madrid, 1906; pp. 549.

An excellent student's treatise, divided into Lectures, with a source-note at the beginning of each lecture, but little additional citation.

Estudios de derecho internacional privado; continuación de los elementos de esta ciencia. Madrid, 1891; pp. 132.

A few lectures omitted in the first edition of the Elementos. They are contained in the second edition.

Bases de una legislación sobre extraterritorialidad: estudios sobre el derecho internacional privado bajo los puntos de vista del derecho constituído y del derecho constituyente. Madrid, 1896; pp. 440.

This work received a prize from the College of Advocates of Madrid. It contains, first, an examination of the legal doctrine of extraterritoriality in general, and in various modern nations; the legislation; the statistics of emigration; diplomatic action, etc.

TRÍAS, JUAN DE DIOS, professor in the University of Barcelona.

El derecho inter-regional según el artículo 15 del código civil. Barcelona, 1889; pp. 24.

A short pamphlet article.

Programa de las lecciones de Derecho internacional privado según las explicaciones del catedrático de la expresada asignatura en la Universidad de Barcelona. Barcelona, 1895; pp. 17.

Syllabus of a course of lectures at the University.

Estudios elementales de derecho internacional privado con aplicación especial al derecho español. Preliminares: Barcelona, 1898; pp. 59. Vol. I: Barcelona, 1910; pp. 129.

Student's treatises, with adequate references to general treatises.

VERDIA, LUIS PEREZ, professor in the University of Guadalajara.

El principio de la nacionalidad en el derecho internacional privado. Mexico, 1895.

Tratado elemental de derecho internacional privado. Guadalajara, 1908; pp. 359.

An elementary but scholarly work, with a useful bibliography at the beginning of each chapter.

ZAVALA, FRANCISCO J., professor in the University of Jalisco. *Elementos de derecho internacional privado o sea conflictos de derecho civil, comercial, de procedimientos y penal entre las legislaciones de diversos países.* Guadalajara, 1886. 2d ed., Mexico, 1889; pp. 322. 3d ed., entitled *Compendio de derecho internacional privado,* Mexico, 1903; pp. 360.

An elementary treatise, to which is appended a commentary on the Mexican Law of Foreigners.

ZEBALLOS, ESTANISLAO S., professor in the University of Buenos Ayres.

Conférence inaugurale du cours de droit international privé faite à la faculté de Buenos Aires, le 2 avril 1902. Buenos Ayres, 1902; pp. 21.

An address to a general audience.

Codification of private international law. Buenos Ayres, 1907.

Justicia internacional positiva; conferencias dadas en la Facultad de Derecho y Ciencias Sociales de la Universidad de Buenos Aires en el curso intensivo de derecho internacional privado (derecho privado humano), 1910. Madrid and Valencia [1911]; pp. 225.

A short-hand report of university lectures, developing the author's theory of the Private Law of Humanity. An original and interesting work.

L'enseignement de droit international privé en Europe et en Amérique. Bulletin argentin de droit international privé, 1904, p. 289.

(See also *Ante,* § 87, under WEISS.)

§ 12. **Authors of other Nations and Languages.**

FEDERSPIEL, H., honorary docent at the University of Copenhagen.

Den internationale Privatret i Danmark. Copenhagen, 1909; pp. xvi, 416.

FERENCZY, ARPAD, professor in the University of Budapest.

Conflict of Laws in Hungary (Conference of the International Law Association at Budapest, 1908). Budapest, 1908.

A nemzetkozim maganjog kezikonyve (handbook of private international law). Paris and Budapest, 1911.

GIURCULESCU, I., AND ARONESCU, I. *Drept international privat;* intocmit pentru studentii facultatei de drept. Bucharest, 1906; pp. 83.

An elementary manual for students.

KAZANSKY, PETR JEVGENIEVIC, professor in the University of Odessa.

Principes généraux de droit international privé, translated from the 3d Russian edition by E. Delhumeau, Paris, 1910; pp. 39.

The first edition, in Russian, was published in Odessa, 1904. A mere elementary summary of the subject.

KRČMÁR, JAN, professor at the University of Prague.

Úvod do mezinárodního práva soukromého (introduction to private international law). Prague, 1906; pp. 304.

A learned treatise, with copious references to the authorities. In Bohemian.

MARTENS, FRIEDRICH VON, professor in the University of St. Petersburg.

Völkerrecht. Das internationale Recht der civilisirten Nationen. German translation from the Russian by Carl Bergbohm. Vol. II: Berlin, 1886; pp. 273–447: Das internationale Privatrecht.

Traité de droit international. Translated from the Russian by Alfred Léo. Vol. II. Paris 1886; pp. 391–505; Vol. III. Paris, 1887; pp. 1–124. Du droit international privé *and* criminel.

Tratado de Derecho internacional publico y privado. Spanish translation, with prologue and notes by J. Fernández Prida: Vol. II. Madrid [1894] pp. 262–368, Vol. III. Madrid, n. d. pp. 1–115; Derecho internacional privado *and* criminal.

An adequate treatise, based in general upon juristic sources, but sometimes discussing actual cases.

REUTERSKIÖLD, KARL LUDVIG AUGUSTUS AXEL, professor in the University of Upsala.

Handbok i svensk privat internationell rätt (process-, utlämnings-, straff- och privaträtt). Upsala and Stockholm, 1912; pp. vi, 214.

A short treatise, with good bibliography and references to authorities, and with frequent citations of decisions. In Swedish.

Föreläsningar öfver privat internationell rätt. 1909.

RUNDSTEINA, SZYMONA. *Kodyfikacyja prawa Miedzynarodowego prywatnego w Niemczech.* Studyjum dogmatyczne. (The codification of private international law in Germany.) Warsaw, 1901; pp. 153.

A commentary upon the provisions of the German Civil Code bearing upon private international law. In Polish.

STREIT, GEORGIOS, professor in the University of Athens.

Systema idiotikon diethnous dikaion. (System of private international law.) Vol. 1. Athens, 1906; pp. 452.

A learned treatise with copious references to the literature of the subject, and a good bibliography. This volume contains Book I, Dogmatic Introduction; Book II, History of Private International Law; Book III, Attempts at Codification. In Greek.

Idiotikon diethnous dikaion essagoge enarkteros paradosis en toi ethnikoi panepistemioi. Athens, 1895; pp. 35.

Dikononikoi Kanones tes epharmoges tou allodapou dikaiou. Athens, 1895; pp. 24.

SYNNESTVEDT, MAGNUS. *Le droit international privé de la Scandinavie.* Paris, 1904; pp. xiv, 331.

This work contains a rather summary treatment of the conflict of laws, with reference to treatises, decisions, legislation and treaties of the Scandinavian countries.

TERAO, TORU, professor in the University of Tokio. *Treatise on private international law.* In Japanese.

§ 13. **Articles on the Law of particular Countries.**

1. AMERICA.

a. The United States.

Mitteilungen aus der internationalrechtlichen Praxis der Vereinigten Staaten. Zeitschrift f. intern. Recht, xxii (1912), 412.

b. Spanish-America.

BELGARANO, NESTOR M. *Le droit international privé dans l'Amérique coloniale.* Bulletin argentin de droit international privé, 1905, p. 525.

CALANDRELLI, A. *Le droit international privé au point de vue sud-américain.* Clunet, xxxvi (1909), 1004.

STOERCK, FELIX. *El derecho internacional americano.* Revista de los tribunales, Aug. 13 and 20, 1898.

TORO. *El derecho internacional americano.* Revista del foro, 1899, no. 3.

(1) Argentine.

DAIREAUX, E. *Étude sur les principes de droit international privé dans la République Argentine, à propos d'une réforme des lois qui y régissent la constitution de la famille.* Paris, 1885.

(2) Brazil.

LEITE, SOLIDONIO. *Le projet de Code civil du Brésil et le droit international privé.* Rev. dr. int. pr. iii (1907), pp. 377–383.

(3) Chili.

FABRES, J. C. *Le droit international privé dans la législation du Chili.* Clunet, xiv (1887), 133, 291; xv (1888), 482.

(4) Colombia.

GRILLO, MAXIMILIANO. *Resumen historico del derecho*

internacional privado y dispociones de esta ciencia contenidas en la legislación de Colombia. Anales de jurisprudencia. Colombia, 1897, pp. 97, 161.

Uribe, A. *Le droit international privé dans la législatiòn colombienne.* Rev. de dr. int. pr. vii (1911), 316.

(5) Cuba.

Bernard, Alfr. Gonz. *Derecho internacional privado. Principios fundamentales consignados en nuestro código civil.* Revista del Foro, La Havane, 1894.

Bustamante y Sirvén, A. *El derecho internacional en la legislacion de la isla de Cuba durante el año de 1894.* Revista del foro, January and February, 1895. *Durante el año de 1895.* Revista del foro, 1896, pp. 375, 506. *Durante el año de 1896.* Revista del foro, January and February, 1897.

(6) Nicaragua.

Glay. *Principios de derecho internacional privado aceptados en el novísimo código civil nicaraguense.* Revista de legislacion universal, 30 May, 1904.

(7) Venezuela.

Rivas, C. *Le droit international privé et pénal du Venezuela.* Rev. de dr. int. pr. Paris, viii (1912), 5.

2. Asia.

Arminjon, E. *Le droit international privé et droit interne principalement dans les pays de l'Islam.* Clunet, xxxix (1912), 698, 1025; xl (1913), 34, 435, 812.

Niemeyer. *Das internationale Privatrecht im Japanischen Civilgesetzbuch.* Zeitschrift für Internationales Privat- und Strafrecht, xi (1901), 197.

Yamada, Saburo. *Le droit international privé au Japon.* Clunet, xxviii (1901), 632.

3. Europe.

a. Austria-Hungary.

Klein, P. *Zur Revision des internationalen Privatrechts des österreichischen B. G. B.* Oesterr. Zentralblatt f. die juristische Praxis, iii, no. 4.

POLLATSCHEK. *Ueber internationales Privatrecht, insbesondere mit Rücksicht auf Oesterreich.* Juridische Rundschau, v, no. 5.

SCHWARTZ, J. *Die örtliche Herrschaft der materiellen Privatrechtsnormen nach ungarischem Rechte.* Juristische Blätter, xxiv, 217.

TRIGANT-GENESTE. *Le droit international privé en Bosnie et Herzégovine.* Clunet, xviii (1891), 776.

b. Belgium.

ANON. *Revision du code civil belge: droit international privé.* Rev. dr. intern. xviii (1886), 444.

DE VOS, L. *Het internationaal privaatrecht in het ontwerp van burgerlijk wetboek voor Belgie.* Brussels, 1897.

LAINÉ, A. *Étude sur le titre preliminaire du projet de code civil belge.* Bull. Soc. legisl. comparée, 1890, 315, 383, 449, 525.

c. England.

DICEY, A. V. *Private international law as a branch of the law of England.* The law quarterly review, v (1890), 1; vi (1891), 113. Translated into German. *Internationales Privatrecht als Bestandtheil des englischen Rechts.* Zeitschr. für internat. Privat- und Strafr. ii (1892), no. 2.

HENDERSON, ROBERT C. *The recent development of private international law in England.* (American Law Review, xxxiv, 386.)

WESTLAKE, J. *La doctrine anglaise en matière de droit international privé.* Clunet, viii (1881), 312; ix (1882), 5. Rev. dr. intern. xiii (1881), 435; xiv (1882), 285.

d. France.

DE LESPINASSE. *Du conflit des lois étrangères avec les lois françaises en ce qui touche le droit privé.* Rev. judiciaire du Midi, v, 25.

Des rapports de droit international privé avec la France extra-continentale. Clunet, viii (1881), 373–386.

DEJAMME, J. *Les dispositions de la nouvelle loi militaire française qui touchent au droit international.* Clunet, xxxii (1905), 612.

DESPAGNET. *La théorie des statuts dans le code civil.* Rev. critique, 1884, p. 487.

DONNEDIEU DE VABRES, H. *L'art. 3 du code civil et la jurisprudence française de 1804 à 1904.* Rev. de dr. int. pr. ii (1906) 829.

HORN. *Das internationale Privatrecht in Frankreich.* Zeitschrift d. intern. Anwalts-Verbandes, ix, nos 3–7.

LAINÉ, A. *Le droit international privé en France, considéré dans ses rapports avec la théorie des statuts.* Clunet, xii (1885), 129, 249; xiii (1886), 146; xiv (1887), 21.

LAURENT, F. *Exposé et critique des principes généraux en matière de statuts réels et personnels d'après le droit français.* Rev. dr. intern. i, 244–272.

PIERANTONI, A. *Il diritto civile internazionale nella codificazione francese ed italiana.* Il Filangieri, 1881, p. 264.

SURVILLE. *Jurisprudence en matière de droit international privé.* Revue critique, lx (xl N. S.), 193, 218.

TRIGANT-GENESTE, J. *La nouvelle loi française du 21 mars 1905 et le droit international privé.* Rev. de dr. intern. privé, i (1905), 97.

e. Germany.

BARAZETTI, CAESAR. *Erörterungen auf dem Gebiete des internationalen Privatrechts im Bürgerlichen Gezetzbuch für das Deutsche Reich.* Zeitschr. für internat. Privat- und Strafr. viii (1898), 118.

EDELMANN, HEINRICH. *Der grundsätzliche Standpunkt des deutschen Bürgerlichen Gesetzbuchs im internationalen Privatrecht.* Zeitschr. für internat. Privat- und Strafr. viii (1898), 295.

HIRSCHFELD, I. *The German code and private international law.* Law Quarterly Review, xvi (1901), 88.

JITTA, J. *Die Kodifikation des internationalen Privatrechts im Entwurfe eines bürgerlichen Gesetzbuchs für das Deutsche Reich vom Standpunkt eines Ausländers.* Jahrbuch der internat. Vereinigung für Vergleich. Rechtswissenschaft, ii, 55.

Bepalingen van internationaal-privaat-rechtelijken aard in het Ontwerp van een Burgerlijk Wetboek voor het Duitsche Rijk, 2e Lesing. Rechtsgeleerd Magazijn, 1896, p. 130.

KEIDEL, J., and TRIGANT-GENESTE. *Le droit international privé dans le nouveau code civil allemand.* Clunet, xxv (1898), 867; xxvi (1899), 17, 239.

LAURENT, F. *Le droit international privé dans le second projet de code civil allemand.* Rev. dr. intern. xxvii (1895), 327.

MOMMSEN, FR. *Wie ist in dem bürgerlichen Gesetzbuch für Deutschland das Verhältniss des inländischen Rechts zu dem ausländischen zu normiren?* Archiv für civilistische Praxis, lxi (1879), 149.

ROLIN, A. *Étude sur les dispositions du droit international privé du Code civil de l'Empire allemand, comparées avec celles de certains projets récents et de certaines lois.* Rev. dr. intern. xxx (1898), 188.

SACHS. *Les arrêts de la Cour suprême commerciale de Leipzig en matière de droit international privé.* Rev. dr. intern. vi, 230–246, 404–418.

STERNBERG, MORIZ. *Das Uebereinkommen zur Regelung einiger Fragen des internationalen Privatrechtes Nr. 85 R. G. B.* Juristische Blätter, Aug. 20, 1899.

GEMMA, S. *Norme di diritto internazionale privato contenute nella legge d' introduzione al Cod. civ. tedesco.* Rivista di diritto internazionale, 1899, p. 76.

f. Greece.

POLITIS, N. *Le droit international privé en Grèce.* Clunet, xxxv (1908), 5, 406.

g. Italy.

ESPERSON. *Le droit international privé dans la législation italienne.* Clunet, vii (1880), 245, 337; viii (1881), 206; ix (1882), 154, 270; x (1883), 263; xi (1884), 168, 251, 365, 604.

SETTI, AUG. *Die international-rechtlichen Bestimmungen im neuen italienischen Strafgesetzbuch.* Zeitschrift für internationales Privat- und Strafrecht, i (1891), 24–31.

h. Netherlands.

Note di dottrina e giurisprudenza olandese in materia de trattati internazionali normativi nel diritto internazionale privato. Riv. di dir. internazionale, ii, no. 6.

Godefroi, F. *Le droit international privé au parlement hollandais.* Clunet, xxv (1897), 369.

Jitta, J. *La jurisprudence des cours et tribunaux des Pays-Bas en matière de droit international privé.* Rev. de dr. int. pr. ix (1913), 43.

i. Roumania.

Flaischlen, George. *Quelques points de droit international privé roumain dans la jurisprudence roumaine.* Rev. dr. intern. xxxviii (1906), 751.

k. Russia.

Challandes, Leo. *Aus der jüngsten Kassationspraxis des Russischen Senats in Fragen des internationalen Privatrechts.* Zeitschrift für internationales Privat- und öffentliches Recht, xiii (1903), 65–86.

Lehr, E. *De la force obligatoire de la législation civile russe au point de vue du droit international.* Clunet, iv (1877), 205–210.

l. Spain.

Audinet. *Le droit international privé dans le nouveau code civil espagnol.* Clunet, xviii (1891), 1106.

Castille y Abril, Ant. de. *Anales de derecho internacional: El derecho internacional privado, según el titulo preliminar del código civil espagnol vigente.* Revista general de legislacion y jurisprudentia. Sept. and Oct. 1906.

Torres y Aguilar, Salvador de. *Le droit international privé suivant la législation espagnole.* Clunet, vi (1879), 27–40.

Torres Campos (tr. by Louis Périé). *Le droit international privé en Espagne.* Rev. prat. dr. intern. 1892, Pt. 2, p. 45.

m. Switzerland.

Barazetti, C. *Einige Bestimmungen des Vorentwurfs*

zum ersten und zweiten Teil des schweizerischen Civilgesetzbuchs (Personen- und Familienrecht), die für das internationale Privatrecht Interesse bieten. Zeitschr. für internat. Privat- und Strafr. ix (1899), 304.

CATELLANI. *Il diritto internazionale privato nel codice civile svizzero.* Rivista di diritto intern. iii, 1–3.

KAUFMANN. *Die Neuerungen im internationalen Privatrecht der Schweiz.* Zeitschrift f. internat. Recht, xxii (1912), 447.

LAINÉ, A. *Étude concernant la loi fédérale suisse du 25 juin 1891 sur les rapports de droit civil des citoyens établis ou en séjour.* Bull. Soc. législ. comparée, 1894, pp. 128, 209.

LEHR, E. *Le droit international privé dans la législation suisse.* Rev. de dr. int. pr. vii (1911), 241.

MARCUSEN, W. *Das internationale Privatrecht des schweizerischen Entwurfs eines Civilgesetzbuches.* Zeitschrift für internationales Privat- und Strafrecht, x (1901), 37.

REICHEL. *Die Stellung des internationalen Privatrechts im System des Zivilgesetzbuches.* Zeitschrift des bernischen Juristenvereins, xlix, no. 8.

ROSSEL, VIRGILE. *L'art. 6 de la loi fédérale sur les rapports de droit civil.* Journ. des Tribunaux (Lausanne), Sept. 16, 1893.

SCHLATTER. *Zur Regelung der Statuten-Kollision in der Schweiz.* Zeitschrift für internationales Privat- und Strafrecht, ii (1892), 452.

Das schweiz. Bundesgesetz betr. die zivilrechtlichen Verhältnisse der Niedergelassenen und Aufenthalter vom 25 Juni 1891. Zeitschrift für vergleichende Rechtswissenschaft, 1892.

§ 14. Periodicals.

CLUNET, ÉDOUARD. *Journal de droit international privé.* Paris, 1874– (42 volumes to 1915).

Tables générales du journal de droit international privé, augmentées de plusieurs répertoires et de nombreux documents concernant le droit international, 1874–1904. 4 vols., Paris, 1905–06.

This is the oldest and most important periodical which deals with private international law alone. Like all such periodicals, it contains articles, decided cases, statutes, and treaties from all parts of the world, reviews, etc. It furnishes in itself a sufficient treatise on the European law.

The Tables include a copious bibliography of public and private international law which has formed one of the principal sources of the present bibliography. The author is glad here to acknowledge his great indebtedness to the publication.

The Journal will be cited in the following pages as Clunet.

DARRAS, A. *Revue de droit international privé et de droit pénal international.* Paris, 1905– (10 volumes through 1914).

The later volumes are edited by A. de Lapradelle. This is another excellent periodical of the same general scope as Clunet.

HORN. *Nouvelle revue pratique de droit international privé.* Paris, 1905– (11 volumes to 1915).

This work follows the general lines of the other periodicals, with less pages and with a larger proportion of space devoted to the decisions of courts.

LAFONT, ERNEST, and LAGARDELLE, HUBERT. *Questions pratiques de droit international privé.* 6 numbers, Paris, 1913.

VINCENT, RÉNÉ. *Revue pratique de droit international privé.* 2 vols., Paris, 1891–92.

This is a continuation of the author's Dictionnaire, q. v. It includes jurisprudence, legislation, treaties, and miscellany.

ZEBALLOS, E. *Bulletin argentin de droit international privé.* 2 vols., Buenos Ayres, 1903–10.

Zeitschrift für internationales Privat- und Strafrecht. Leipzig, 1890– (26 volumes to 1915).

The only German periodical devoted to this subject. Cited as Zeitschrift, or by the title in full or abbreviated.

§ 15. Collections of Cases.

BEALE, JOSEPH HENRY, professor in Harvard University. *A selection of cases on the Conflict of Laws.* 3 vols., Cambridge, 1900–1902; pp. xviii, 489, xv, 548, xviii, 548. Vol. 1, 2d ed., Cambridge, 1907; pp. 19, 553.

About 400 American and English cases, and 70 foreign cases translated into English; with a Summary of the Conflict of Laws at the end of the third volume.

A shorter selection of cases on the conflict of laws. Cambridge, 1907; pp. 828.

About 230 cases selected from the preceding collection.

DWYER, JOHN W., instructor in the University of Michigan.
Cases on Private International Law. Ann Arbor [1899]; pp. viii, 509. 2d ed., entitled *Leading Cases on Private International Law,* Chicago, 1904; pp. xii, 599.

About 40 cases, and a few extracts from text-books, to illustrate a course of lectures in the University. The second edition contains 20 more cases than the first.

LORENZEN, ERNEST G., professor in the George Washington University and in the University of Minnesota.
Cases on the Conflict of Laws, selected from the decisions of English and American Courts. St. Paul, 1909; pp. xxi, 784.

About 200 American and English cases, with occasional notes on European law. An excellent collection.

NELSON, HORACE. *Selected Cases, Statutes and Orders illustrative of the principles of Private International Law as administered in England,* with a commentary. London, 1889; pp. xxiii, 483.

A collection of English cases on the subject, with a commentary which is substantially an annotation of the English cases and statutes.

§ **16. Suggested Collection for Public Law Library.** — A Bar Library, or other public law library of more than merely local importance, should be able, at an expense of about five hundred dollars, to secure a small library dealing with the subject, which would be sufficient for ordinary purposes of study.

For historical study, and the first-hand consultation of the most important early authors, the books recommended are Beale's *Bartolus,* Guthrie's translation of Savigny's *Conflict of Laws,* which contains in an Appendix the text of several early authors, and D'Argentré's *Commentaries,* important for an American or English student and obtainable only in the original.

Most of the general works in the English language should be included. Foreign works of importance are almost all in French, or translated into English. No collection of that size can be complete, however, without Zitelmann's treatise and the *Zeitschrift für internationales Privat- und Strafrecht,* both of which can be had only in the original German. Bustamante's work is so interesting that it has been included, although it has not been translated from the Spanish. The important journals and collections of cases are of course included, since they furnish the great body of material necessary for a lawyer's study of a question in the Conflict of Laws. The list of about 125 volumes recommended follows:

Bar, *Private International Law,* 2d ed., Gillespie's tr.
Beale, *Cases on the Conflict of Laws,* 3 vols.
Bustamante, *Tratado de derecho internacional privado.*
Clunet's *Journal de droit international privé,* 42 vols. to date, with Tables, 4 vols.
D'Argentré, *Commentaries,* 2 vols.
Darras, *Revue de droit international privé,* 10 vols. to date.
Darras and Lapradelle, *Répertoire de droit international privé,* publication begun.
Dicey, *Conflict of Laws,* 2d ed.
Fiore, *Le droit international privé,* Antoine's French translation, 3 vols.
Foote, *Private International Jurisprudence.*
Jitta, *La méthode du droit international privé.*
Lainé, *Introduction au droit international privé,* 2 vols.
Laurent, *Droit civil international,* 8 vols.
Lorenzen, *Cases on the Conflict of Laws.*
Meili, *International civil and commercial law,* Kuhn's tr.
Minor, *Conflict of Laws.*
Pillet, *Principes de droit international privé.*
Rattigan, *Private International Law.*
Rorer, *American Interstate Law.*
Savigny, *Conflict of Laws,* Guthrie's tr.
Story, *Conflict of Laws,* 8th ed.
Surville and Arthuys, *Cours élémentaire du droit international privé.*
Valery, *Manuel de droit international privé.*

Vareilles-Sommières, *La synthèse du droit international privé*, 2 vols.

Weiss, *Traité théorique et pratique de droit international privé*, 5 vols.

Westlake, *Private International Law*, 5th ed.

Wharton, *Conflict of Laws*, 3d ed., 2 vols.

Zeitschrift für internationales Privat- und Strafrecht, 25 vols. to date.

Zitelmann, *Internationales Privatrecht*, 2 vols.

§ 17. **Suggestions for Private Library.** — A lawyer whose practice includes questions of the Conflict of Laws (which must include most American lawyers) should have in his own private library the best English and American books, and a few foreign books on the subject. He should certainly have Clunet's Journal, with the Tables, since this would make accessible to him all the foreign decisions on the subject. Such a library would consist of about sixty-five volumes, and would cost somewhat less than two hundred dollars. A list follows:

Bar, *Private International Law*, Gillespie's tr.

Beale, *Cases on the Conflict of Laws*, 3 vols.

Clunet's *Journal de droit international privé*, with Tables, 46 vols. to date.

Darras and Lapradelle, *Répertoire de droit international privé*, publication begun.

Dicey, *Conflict of Laws*, 2d ed.

Lorenzen, *Cases on the Conflict of Laws.*

Minor, *Conflict of Laws.*

Story, *Conflict of Laws*, 8th ed.

Weiss, *Traité théorique et pratique de droit international privé*, 5 vols.

Westlake, *Private International Law*, 5th ed.

Wharton, *Conflict of Laws*, 3d ed., 2 vols.

A TREATISE ON THE CONFLICT OF LAWS

BOOK I. INTRODUCTORY

CHAPTER I

SCOPE AND NAME OF THE SUBJECT

§ 1. Definition of the subject.
2. Other definitions.
3. Practical necessity for this branch of law.
4. Preliminary topics for investigation.
5. Whether criminal law is included in the subject.
6. Public international law how far included.
7. Comparative law how far included.
8. Sources of private international law.
9. The use to be made of authorities of various kinds.
10. The method of treatment outlined.
11. Names proposed for the subject.
12. Criticism of names indicating conflict.
13. Criticism of names suggesting international character.
14. Difficulty of finding appropriate name.
15. Reasons for adopting the name "Conflict of Laws."

§ **1. Definition of the Subject.** — The branch of the law called for convenience *THE CONFLICT OF LAWS* deals primarily with the application of laws in space.[1] Whenever a question is raised of applying to a juridical situation the law of one or of another country, the question so raised must be settled by the principles of the Conflict of Laws. Thus when parties married in one state are living together in another, when property situated in one state is to be transferred in another, when a contract is made in one state to

[1] A similar topic, *The Application of Laws in Time* (Zeitliche Gränzen, Savigny 49), has received no name; and though it makes use of similar principles it is not usually regarded as sufficiently important for separate treatment. Its general principle is that of the non-retroactivity of laws.

be performed in another, or when suit is brought in one state for breach of an obligation arising in another, a juridical situation arises where the law applicable might be in doubt; and this doubt is settled by the principles of the Conflict of Laws.

As Bustamante well shows,[1] the question presents itself in a two-fold aspect: what law created a certain right; or, what right could a certain law create. The older writers confined themselves to the first phase of the question; while the later writers tend more and more to fix their minds on the second.

Perhaps this distinction may be made clearer by a few illustrations. Suppose John appears in the state of New York with a horse, having ridden into the state from Massachusetts. Thomas appears from Massachusetts and makes a claim upon the horse, founding his claim upon a transaction in Massachusetts. The older writers would have asked, by what law are the rights of Thomas in the horse to be judged? The later writers would be more likely to ask, did the law of Massachusetts, under which Thomas claims his right, have power to create it? Or suppose John makes an agreement in New York, fails to perform it, is sued upon it, and sets up the defence that he is an infant by the law of Massachusetts, his domicil: it might be asked, by what law is his capacity to be determined; or, on the other hand, does the law of Massachusetts have the power to make him incapable in New York.

This distinction might be thought merely verbal, and dismissed as of no importance. But the way in which the subject is put may indicate a fundamentally correct or incorrect conception of the principles underlying the subject, as will hereafter be seen. The older form seems to rest upon the theory that the applicability of law to the facts of the case may properly be determined as of the moment of litigation. The more modern form, on the other hand, is the natural expression of the principle, which seems indisputable, that the applicability of law to the juridical facts must be determined as of the time of their occurrence. Some proper law must have governed the juridical situation at the moment of its occurrence; the effort of the court is to determine what that law was; and that is a question of the power of some particular law to extend to and rule the juridical situation.

[1] Bustamante, 95.

§ 2. **Other Definitions.** — Definitions of the subject of our study are almost as numerous as the authors who have written upon it. No attempt will be made to repeat all the definitions which have been proposed. They may roughly be divided into three classes.

First: Definitions which emphasize the solution of the conflict of two laws, either of which in the nature of things might be applicable. Such is the definition of Asser:[1] "The body of the principles which determine what law is applicable either to the juridical relations between persons belonging to different states or to acts done abroad, or in short in all cases where it is a question of applying the law of one state within the territory of another." The definition of Bar[2] is of the same sort: "Private international law determines the applicability of the legal systems and the jurisdiction of the agencies — the courts and magistrates — of different states in private legal relations." So Foelix:[3] "The body of rules by which are judged the conflicts between the private law of different nations." Story:[4] "The jurisprudence arising from the conflict of the laws of different nations in their actual application to modern commerce and intercourse." Pillet:[5] "The science which creates juridical regulations for international relations of a private nature."

Second: Definitions which emphasize the difference in nationality of the subjects of the rights involved. Such is Fiore's definition:[6] "The science which establishes the principles for resolving conflicts of laws, and for regulating the mutual relations of the subjects of different states." Similar definitions are those of Torres Campos, Pedroza, and de Martens.

Third: Definitions which emphasize the limitation of legislative jurisdiction. Such is another definition of Pillet.[7] "A system of conciliation, destined to fix the rational limits of the respective legislative jurisdiction [of national laws] in all cases where international commerce has resulted in creating a conflict between their principles." Savigny[8] describes the subject as "the local limitations of the authority of the rules of law." Rolin[9] defines it as "The body of rules which define the rights of foreigners, and the respective

[1] § 1. [2] § 1, p. 1. [3] p. 2. [4] p. 9. [5] Principes, 7.
[6] p. 3. [7] Principes, 123. [8] p. 45. [9] i, 12.

jurisdictions of the law of different states so far as private rights are concerned." Bustamante[1] has a similar definition: "The body of principles which determine the limits in space of the legislative jurisdiction of states, when it is applied to juridical relations which might be submitted to either jurisdiction"; or more concisely, "The science which limits legislative capacity in space."

The curious may be interested in further essays at definition.

"That department of national law which arises from the fact that there are in the world different territorial jurisdictions possessing different laws."[2]

"That branch of the law of a country which relates to cases more or less subject to the law of other countries."[3]

"That portion of the law of each state which determines the conditions in accordance with which legal relations are governed by the principles of some other system of law."[4]

"Principles . . . governing the extra-territorial operation of law or recognition of rights."[5]

"The law which has to do with foreigners."[6]

"The law which, having determined nationality, regulates the relations of States so far as concerns the juridical condition of their respective subjects, the efficacy of the judgments of their courts and of the official acts of their officers, and especially the conflict of their laws."[7]

"The body of rules applicable to the solution of the conflicts which may arise between two sovereignties with regard to their respective private laws, or to the private interests of their citizens."[8]

"The rules which should be followed in the conflict of private laws of different states."[9]

"The branch of law which is concerned with private legal relations which contain a foreign element."[10]

"An aspect of private law which involves such juridical relations between individuals as transcend the sphere of national law."[11]

"The legal principles which determine which of several objective private laws of different places are to be applied to a certain private legal relation: the legal principles, in other words, which relate to

[1] i, 10. [2] Westlake, 1. [3] Wharton (3rd ed.), i, 2.
[4] Harrison in Clunet, 1880, 540. [5] Dicey, 3.
[6] Vareilles-Sommières, i, xxx. [7] Lainé, i, 17.
[8] Weiss, Manuel, xxx. [9] Despagnet, 19.
[10] Valery, 3. [11] Jitta, Méthode, 50 (slightly condensed.)

the applicability in space of private law; the rules for the application of law in space."[1]

§ 3. **Practical Necessity for this Branch of Law.** — International commerce created the necessity for some principle of law which should protect the interests and give effect to the undertakings of the foreigner. As foreign commerce has increased, this necessity has increased with it; and now that our whole manner of life is based upon exchange of products between nations, a body of legal principles to regulate international juridical relations is as supremely needed as a similar body of principles to give effect to ordinary contracts or protect ordinary property. International commerce is necessary to modern civilization; and "international commerce would be impossible if there did not exist a law which has for its object and effect to favor the international extension of human activity."[2] International trade could not be carried on as has now become necessary unless the trader could be assured that he would not be placed absolutely at the mercy of the vagaries or unknown requirements of the local law, but would find a well-established body of law to protect his rights. This body of law is the Conflict of Laws, of which an eminent German author eloquently says: "It protects and assures the peaceable intercourse of private persons in different nations. In this way, therefore, it maintains the threads, — which, fine as they are, still together will sustain great things, — on which the exchange of goods and of ideas, the mutual respect of nations, and therefore the maintenance of peace, depend."[3]

§ 4. **Preliminary Topics for Investigation.** — While, however, the local application of laws is the principal part of this topic, the difficulties raised cannot be fully solved without a study of certain other legal principles which underlie the solution. In considering how a conflict of laws shall be solved, it is necessary first to study with some care the nature of law; and to delimit the jurisdiction of the various laws which are alleged to apply. The first of these topics is generally dealt with under the title Jurisprudence; the second, under that of Public International Law, or the Law

[1] Zitelmann, i, 1. [2] Pillet, 5. [3] Bar, Preface, xi.

of Nations. It is necessary next to study the nature of Rights, of Acts, and of Remedies, since they are involved in every juridical situation, and a knowledge of their real nature is essential if we would determine the power of law over them. This study also is usually relegated to the science of Jurisprudence, and is thought quite unnecessary as a preparation for the practice of law. Finally, as rights of personal status, according to the Common law, depend upon domicil, it is necessary to study with some care the international conception of domicil; again, a topic of International Law, since the meaning of the legal term is fixed by the general consent of nations, and cannot be changed at the will of a single nation.

§ **4a. The Nature of Law as a necessary preliminary study.** — The necessity of studying the nature of law has already been indicated. The lawyer engaged merely in the practice of a single positive law will not find this necessary, and will even ignore its value. For him, the law is contained in the statute-books and the reports of his own state; or if he studies other sources, it is only to supplement these authoritative books with less important learning. He need not trouble himself with inquiries as to the nature of law; he is only concerned with its content. But if he is obliged to step outside the narrow circle of his own positive law, and take into consideration another law, it at once becomes necessary, in order that each should take its proper place with relation to the other, that their nature should be more fully apprehended. A consideration of the nature of law thus becomes essential; and it at once appears that the word is used, and indeed has been used and understood by every lawyer, in more than one sense. This ambiguity must be removed before the mutual relations of domestic and foreign law can be scientifically determined.

§ **4b. The Limits of Jurisdiction as a necessary preliminary study.** — If we are to apply laws in space, we should first of all delimit the space to which each law is applicable; and as law-giving is a function of sovereignity, this amounts to fixing the limits of jurisdiction. So obvious a proposition seems hardly worth argument; yet few writers on the subject have included this topic in their works. The result has been that many authors have assumed without discussion and proof some untenable theory of sovereign power and extent of legislative jurisdiction upon which their respective doctrines of the conflict of laws have been based.

§ 4c. Rights, Acts and Remedies as necessary subjects for preliminary study. — If we are to judge the effect of law upon juridical relations — rights, acts, and remedies — we must first study with care the nature of these conceptions; since the effect of the law must depend upon the nature of the relation to be established. Many works on the Conflict of Laws show the detrimental effect of vagueness in conception of the nature of juridical relations. This vagueness is especially dangerous in the states of the European continent where the same word — ius, droit, Recht — serves to designate law itself and a right created by the law. When vagueness of conception is added to ambiguity of meaning, such errors may be expected as we shall find existent in the works of certain continental writers.

The study of these juridical relations is an exact and a practical study; and it seems necessary to a clear knowledge of the municipal law, as well as of the conflict of laws. Many lawyers are inclined to regard studies of this sort as merely academic and unpractical, to call them jurisprudence, and under that term to dismiss them as of no value in the actual practice of the profession. What has already been said must show the fallacy of such notions.

§ 4d. Nationality and Domicil. — The subject of nationality forms a considerable part of every European treatise on Private International Law. In Weiss's monumental work, for instance, it occupies one of the five volumes. This is necessary in any system where, as in the systems of the Italian and modern French schools, personal rights are based upon nationality. The common law does not base personal rights upon nationality, but upon domicil. It is therefore entirely unnecessary, in an American book upon the Conflict of Laws, to consider nationality at all.

The common law, as will be seen, bases personal status upon the law of the domicil. It is therefore necessary in an American book to substitute the study of domicil for that of nationality.

§ 5. Whether Criminal Law is included in the Subject. — A question has been raised and much discussed whether the conflict of criminal laws is to be included in the general subject.[1] On the one hand it is argued that criminal law is a portion of the public law, and therefore properly belongs with Public rather than with Private International Law — an argument which a little savors of verbalism, for surely

[1] For reasons against this inclusion, see Asser, § 1, p. 5; Despagnet, 14–16; Renault, 26; Rolin, i, 16 *et s.*; Zitelmann, i, 28. For reasons in favor, see Bustamante, 17; Lainé, i, 11 *et s.*

it is not a proper function of the Law of Nations to determine the punishability of an individual for an act done abroad. On the other side it is pointed out that the interests concerned are solely individual, and should be determined by that branch of international law which concerns individual rights. Professor Weiss follows a middle course, and segregates all questions of conflict of criminal laws and procedure under the title of "Droit international criminel." [1]

The truth is, as often happens, both sides are partly right. Those writers who have considered questions of criminal law have usually included in their discussion two distinct topics: punishment for foreign crime, and extradition. The former is clearly a question in which individual rights are chiefly concerned, and is therefore a proper topic of the Conflict of Laws. Extradition, on the other hand, is a process which depends entirely upon the existence and interpretation of treaties between nations, and the only rights directly involved are those of the nations parties to the treaties. Furthermore, the questions which arise have no relation whatever to those considered in the Conflict of Laws. It seems, therefore, that the consideration of extradition should be left to the Law of Nations, while the topic of jurisdiction over crime should form part of the Conflict of Laws; and that course will be pursued in this work.

§ 6. **Public International Law How Far Included.** — As has been seen, some portions of public international law are necessarily included in the scope of this topic. The whole great subject of Jurisdiction is purely international, and so is the topic Domicil.

Besides these, other topics of the Law of Nations are often included in the discussion. The subjects of Nationality and Naturalization are usually examined by European authors; [2] and this is for them a necessary study, because, as has been seen, rights of personality, according to the codes of most European states, are based upon nationality instead of upon domicil. This doctrine has never been extended by statute to a country governed by our Common law. For

[1] Traité élémentaire, xxxiii.

[2] *e.g.* Foelix, Weiss (who devotes the first volume of his longer work to this subject), Laurent, Rolin, Fiore, Bar.

this reason, as well as because the topics are thoroughly discussed in works on Public International Law, they will not be examined in this work.

Another question, which is commonly included in the Law of Nations but is often also included in works on Private International Law, is the Legal Condition of Foreigners;[1] although, as has been pointed out, there is no conflict possible as to the rights of foreigners because no possible law can be applied to these rights except the law of the country in which they are enjoyed.[2] The question is one of much importance in France and other European countries where civil rights are not regularly extended to foreigners; but in England and America, where all civil rights are now and, with very few exceptions, have long been extended to foreigners, the topic is of no practical importance. It is therefore omitted entirely from our discussion.

§ 7. **Comparative Law How Far Included.** — It is often difficult and sometimes impossible, in dealing with a question of the conflict of laws, to avoid considering the nature of one or both of the national laws between which the question arises; and some authors have in fact considered such a study as a legitimate part of the subject.[3] Thus for instance the principal "Journal of Private International Law," Clunet's, discusses comparative law as well as the conflict of laws.

Strictly speaking, this is no part of our subject. Yet it is often convenient and useful to point out differences in national laws, and this course will sometimes be taken in this work. But all statements of foreign law must lie under suspicion, since an author is dealing with a subject unfamiliar to him, and subject to rapid change. In the words of Bar,[4] "So quickly do laws alter in our own times, every general work upon international law must be taken, as traders say, 'with errors excepted,' and any lawyer who consults the book for the practical purpose of some particular case

[1] Foelix, Weiss (whose second volume is devoted to this subject), Pillet, Laurent, Rolin, Fiore, Bar.

[2] Pillet, 28.

[3] Laurent, for instance, frequently discusses and compares national laws.

[4] Preface, viii.

should be warned to apply to legal specialists for information as to the law of the country in which he happens to be interested."

§ 8. **Sources of Private International Law.** — In enumerating the sources of such a subject as the Conflict of Laws it is necessary to bear in mind that " law " for this purpose has a double meaning. The exact significance of this phrase will be examined later. For the present it is enough to speak, in language common in European works, of the theoretical and the positive law. Theoretical law, as the name indicates, is the body of principles worked out by the light of reason and by general usage, without special reference to the actual law in any particular state. Positive law is the law as actually administered in a particular country.

The sources of the theoretical law are, speaking generally, the opinions of authors and universal custom, *i.e.*, the consensus of civilized states solving the same question in the same way. The study of the legislation and of the decisions of the courts of particular states is of importance only in so far as it results in finding a general agreement upon a proposition of law. As Foelix well says,[1] " Nations recognize no supreme judge with power to decide, according to abstract and philosophical principles of law, the disputes to which conflicts of different national laws may give rise" ; and it is, therefore, useless to look for any more authoritative source of the theoretical law than will be found in the pages of standard works.

The positive law, on the other hand, is based on actual written sources ; treaties, legislation and the decisions of courts, as well as the tenets of the theoretical law.[2] It is a branch of the ordinary private law of each country, and is based upon the same sources as general law.

Besides these two kinds of law recognized by authors generally there is a third sort of law, which is neither merely theoretical nor is it the positive law of any one state. The common basis of the law of the countries of continental Europe is the Roman law. These countries have as a common element a system of law, called by us " civil law," which is equally authoritative in each, but cannot be called

[1] Preface to 2nd ed.

[2] Rolin, i, 132, 137; Despagnet, 38.

positive law in any one state. England and America have a similar common element, the so-called "common law." The doctrines of this system of law are authoritative in each state whose law is based upon it; and the decisions of courts of all such states are important evidences of the law. It follows therefore, that in Europe the "jurisprudence" of each civil-law state may be treated as a source of private international law; while with us any opinion of any common-law court is equally a source of knowledge of the principles of the Conflict of Laws.

§ 9. **The Use to be Made of Authorities of Various Kinds.** — In our law, courts and lawyers have given in general far less attention to the opinions of learned authors than to those of courts. For this preference for the decided case the reason currently given is that the opinion of a Court is based upon a careful argument by counsel in a case where each was not merely striving for victory, but was also responsible for the interests of a client. Argument of counsel, in turn, was based upon a thorough and professional examination of the authorities, that is, upon the experiences of well-trained judges through several centuries. A legal author usually writes without hearing argument and without the responsibility of counsel or judge. As a result, his hobbies may influence his opinion.

Following the common practice of lawyers, the greater part of this work will be based primarily upon the decisions of the courts in every common-law country.

But even in England and America the opinions of careful authors are only relatively neglected. Each carries weight according to his reputation among lawyers. Of all who have written on topics of the common law, no one in modern times stands higher than Story; and his opinions are freely cited in court. More recent, but already accepted as authoritative, is Professor Dicey's "Conflict of Laws"; and the other English and American authors are more than respectable.

To one who follows the current attitude of our courts with care, it is clear that they are tending more and more to regard the works of writers on law as of persuasive authority. Many causes contribute to this tendency. The very multiplication of jurisdictions whose law is based upon the system of the common law leads naturally to the citations in the courts of one state of the decisions of the courts of another. Such decisions are of course not precedents, authoritative statements of the particular law of the state in whose courts they are cited; their force is that only of their intrinsic merit as statements by lawyers in high judicial position of their understanding of the common law. But the great number of American judges detracts from their commanding position as expounders of legal principle; while the wide vogue of many legal treatises gives them an artificial authority as commonly used depositaries of legal knowledge, quite out of proportion to their intrinsic merits as profound or original discussions. As a result the opinions of legal authors are coming to have an influence upon current legal opinion not altogether out of proportion to the decisions of courts.[1]

For these reasons, use will be made in this treatise of the opinions of authors of standard American and English treatises on the conflict of laws. Foreign authors will be cited freely to show the foreign law. In particular, a few books will be habitually used, not because they are of greater authority than those less cited, but partly because they are better adapted for the particular purpose, and partly because it is desirable to confine citations generally to a few books which may be more easily procurable by one wishing to follow out the citations.

For the same reason the decisions of foreign courts will be cited. The reports of foreign courts are very numerous, but not easy of access to English or American lawyers. A great display of erudition might be made by citing cases from a great number of foreign publications; but this again would be valueless for most readers. Fortunately almost all the foreign cases which it will be at all necessary to cite may be found in Clunet's "Journal of Private International Law," commonly cited as "Clunet," which from the beginning of its publication, in 1874, has contained at least a full abstract of every important case on our subject decided in France, and most of those in other European countries. Sets of this periodical are obtainable without much difficulty,

[1] See on this point an article by J. H. Wigmore in 9 Ill. Law Rev. 529 (1915).

and it should be possible to verify references to it in any law library of even moderate size.

Little use will be made of foreign legislation, since there will be no effort to develop the positive law of any particular foreign state.

§ 10. **The Method of Treatment Outlined.**—The method of treating the subject of Conflict of Laws in this book will be as follows.

After an introduction, dealing with the nature, history, and bibliography of the subject, the general nature of law, of legal rights and of jurisdiction will be considered. This will be followed by a detailed theoretical study of legal rights, in which an attempt will be made to establish the time and place in which legal rights come into existence, the legal effect of acts, and the limits of merely remedial action. As a result of this study, a theoretical conclusion will be reached as to the law by which these rights, acts, and remedies should be governed. The remainder of the work will be devoted to a careful study of the positive common law of England and America. The analysis and arrangement of the law adopted in the theoretical study will be followed in this practical part. No claim will be made that the author has accomplished the impossible feat of collecting all the cases from common-law jurisdictions. This is more than commonly difficult in the subject of Conflict of Laws because neither the current American digest nor the latest American encyclopedia has an article on the Conflict of Laws. All that can be truly asserted is, that the author has included such cases as after a diligent search he has found applicable; and that he believes he has considered cases enough to be sure of the actual condition of authority. At the end of each chapter, where it has seemed desirable, a section has been added dealing with the foreign law on the subject covered by the chapter.

§ 11. **Names Proposed for the Subject.**—A considerable number of names have been proposed by different authors for the subject here named "Conflict of Laws." Its principles were first discussed at length in one portion of a general work on "Statutes": a word which, as will be seen, meant then what we should now call the ordinances of a local governing body, such as a city or a county. Eventually these principles came to be treated by themselves, under some name indicating conflict or collision of laws: Conflict of Statutes,[1] or Conflict of Laws.[2] As the important aspect of the subject, at least on the continent of Europe, shifted from contrariety of local laws to difference in national laws, a process which will be described later, a tendency grew to mark the international character of the subject in its name;[3] and Private International Law[4] or some variant of it[5] came to be accepted by a majority of authors. A few exceptional names have been proposed.[6] The names suggested fall, with almost no exception, into two classes: those suggesting a conflict, and those laying stress on the international character.

§ 12. **Criticism of Names Indicating Conflict.** — Professor Harrison, in a series of striking articles in Clunet's "Journal of Private International Law,"[7] says that "Conflict of Law" is "a metaphor and a very false metaphor." Bustamante also disapproves the term,[8] saying, "The laws of different sovereigns do not contend with one another for the mastery. Each one keeps within its sphere of operation, and only asserts its power in a foreign country when the law of that country commands or permits it. In practice a conflict is impossible." Bar regards the expression as too narrow.[9] "A conflict of laws is not caused by the difference of the laws which may possibly be applied to any particular case, but arises only when the legal systems of different states, differing among themselves, all claim that a particular case shall be submitted to their own jurisdiction."

On the other hand, Lainé[10] asserts that the expression is correct, that it involves no notion of struggle, but merely that where two laws are in question one must yield, and it

[1] Paul Voet. [2] Huberus, Story, Savigny, Bar, Dicey.

[3] Hertius, Wächter.

[4] Foelix, Pillet, Calvo, Fiore, Zitelmann, Westlake.

[5] Civil international law; Weiss. Private Law of Nations: Haus. International private law: Holland, Jurisprudence.

[6] The law of foreigners (Fremdenrecht), von Pütter. Extraterritorial recognition of rights; Holland's Jurisprudence. Extraterritorial law; Torres Campos. Intermunicipal law: Harrison (Clunet, vii (1880), 537). The private law of foreigners, Cimbali.

[7] Clunet, 537. [8] p. 18. [9] § 6, p. 7. [10] i, 9.

is for the law to settle which one shall yield. He cites as analogous the similar phrase, conflict of jurisdiction.

The phrase is coming to be rather commonly applied (as it properly applies) to only one portion of the subject; that portion which determines which law of two possible laws governs a certain relation in question. Thus Professor Pillet [1] divides his work into three parts: 1. The Condition of Foreigners; 2. The Conflict of Laws; 3. The Effect in other Countries of Juridical Acts. This narrow use is doubtless the more correct. The phrase Conflict of Laws exactly applies to only a portion of the principles usually dealt with under the title.

§ 13. Criticism of Names suggesting International Character. — The adoption of the name "private international law" was no doubt a result of the great stress laid upon nationality in the Code Napoléon. The local laws disappeared from France; all conflicts came to be differences between the laws of different nations, and therefore, to French authors, took on an international character. Any principles settling differences in national laws seemed at once to be established by some super-national power. This idea was strengthened by the fact that most of the nations with which France came into contact were governed by a single system of law, derived from that of Rome; and lawyers trained in the same system of law naturally developed almost identical principles, not only in the books they wrote, but also in their courts. This seemed to confirm the idea of an international sanction.

There was little criticism of the name until rather lately.[2] Vareilles-Sommières [3] is one of the strongest of the critics. Zitelmann says,[4] "The expression Private International Law is ill-constructed, inconvenient and ugly."[5] Jitta's view is worth detailed notice. Private International Law is in no sense, he says, a branch of the law of nations, since nations as such have no part in it. In this name, "international" is used in a different sense from its sense in the title "public international law." In the phrase "private international law" the word means having extra-national elements, as in the phrase "international society."

[1] p. 27. [2] See Bustamante, 33–35.
[3] i, xv. [4] i, 1. [5] Méthode, 35–40.

§ 14. **Difficulty of finding Appropriate Name.**—The truth is, as has been seen, the subject has elements of various sorts, national and international: topics where the solution of conflicts of law is the subject of discussion, and others where the nature of law and the bounds of international jurisdiction are in question. In the beginning, the subject was a disquisition on the nature of law and its application; then the solution of conflicts became important; finally its supreme effort is to set bounds to the jurisdiction of nations. Some portions of the law are purely international; the portion in which conflicts are considered has no international element. It is not possible therefore in a single phrase to present the whole content of this branch of the law. Even though a satisfactory, because comprehensive phrase might be found, it would probably be open to the objection that it "hints too plainly at a particular theory of the subject."[1]

§ 15. **Reasons for adopting the Name "Conflict of Laws."**—Since no name yet proposed is exactly accurate, it becomes necessary to use a name not quite what one would choose, or to try one's hand at inventing a better. The latter course is not at all desirable. To be accurate the term must be long and clumsy; inexcusable vices in a proper name. It is far better to use a term not in itself satisfactory, if it is concise and so sanctified by use as to have become unambiguous. "A title which is not strictly correct does little harm, so soon as it is generally known what is to be understood by it"; for "in all such questions the point is not simply absolute correctness, but also handiness."[2] In this dilemma we choose the term which came first into use, and was made familiar to Anglo-American ears by Story's great book, and by the later works of Wharton, Dicey and Minor. One can do no better, in explaining his choice of this title, than quote the wise and witty words of Vareilles-Sommières:[3] "The warlike expression 'Conflict of Laws' is used to describe the pacific work of settling by fixed bounds the line of separation between two legislative jurisdictions. The only conflict is among the legal authors who are doing this

[1] Bar, § 6, p. 8. [2] Bar, § 6, pp. 7, 8. [3] i, xviii *n.*

work. Yet since the expression is consecrated by good use and is simple we may well make use of it." [1]

In opposition to the view here expressed, that accuracy of terminology is not, upon the whole, of extreme importance, see the opinion of Cimbali,[2] who has written an interesting and ingenious book to prove the contrary. The false designation of the subject, he says, has caused us to lose sight of an entire new field of study in international law: to wit, the law governing private transactions of states. He has not succeeded in convincing other jurists of the importance of his objection.

[1] Compare also the language used by Zitelmann, directly after his criticism of the term "Internationales Privatrecht" (i, 1): "It is fixed in international usage, and so firmly settled that it cannot be misunderstood."

[2] Di una nuova denominazione del cosiddetto diritto internazionale privato.

CHAPTER I

HISTORY OF THE CONFLICT OF LAWS

§ 21. Identity of law in the Roman world: the *ius gentium*.
22. Roman law following the edict of Caracalla.
23. The rules of the Corpus Juris.
24. The barbarian incursions: personal tribal law.
25. The early middle ages: the law and the statutes.
26. Bartolus.
27. Baldus and the successors of Bartolus.
28. The contribution to doctrine of the early Italian school.
29. The later middle ages: the coutumes.
30. The French statutists of the 16th century: Dumoulin.
31. Argentré.
32. Guy Coquille and other writers of the early French school.
33. The Dutch statutists of the 17th century.
34. Huber.
35. The later French statutists of the 18th century.
36. Boullenois and Bouhier.
37. Summary of the doctrines of the statutists.
38. The beginning of modern law: Livermore.
39. Story.
40. The influence of Story on European thought.
41. Summary of this history.
42. Efforts to unify the law: international conferences.
43. Efforts to unify the law: comparative study.

§ 21. Identity of Law in the Roman World: the *Ius Gentium*. — The history of the Conflict of Laws, as an actual branch of modern civilized law, goes no further back than the later law of Rome. The law of the states which preceded Rome have left no mark on the modern law and their study is of no historical importance.[1] The law of the Roman republic took no account of foreigners, and ignored their law. The Romans guarded their own law as a sacred possession for themselves and their children, not to be cheapened by extending it to foreigners. Yet, as foreign conquest and foreign commerce increased, it was impossible to leave

[1] An exhaustive study of the condition of foreigners and foreign law at an earlier time may be found in Catellani, i, 12–45 (oriental states); 46–107 (Greece); Laurent, i, 99–134.

their conquered subjects or foreign traders without the protection of any law. Rome could not take the enlightened step which England took, eighteen centuries later, in extending to its conquered subjects in India the benefit of their own law, while retaining for Englishmen their birthright, the common law. Instead of this, the Roman lawyers invented a uniform system of law of their own for dealing with non-Romans, the *Ius Gentium*, a part of the Roman law, administered as such by Roman judges. The Roman lawyer never dreamed of learning the law of the non-Roman and applying it in specified cases: in other words, he had no conception of such principles as are now included in our topic.[1]

§ 22. **Roman Law following the Edict of Caracalla.** — With the edict of Caracalla, however (A. D. 212), this situation was changed. Every person who could receive any recognition at the hands of the law became, by this edict, a Roman citizen, entitled to the *ius civile*. In Ehrlich's happy phrase,[2] "The Roman law then became, in a sense at least, the territorial law of the Roman empire. The principle of territoriality thus entered the law, for the first time in juridical history." But the habits and thoughts of a race cannot be changed by a mere scrap of paper; and the habits of thought about legal matters which the nations cherished before the edict continued thereafter. Though proud of its position as Roman, each province must nevertheless continue in the practice of such of its own laws as really controlled the actions of daily life. These old laws, abolished in theory as laws, continued effective as local customs; and every Roman governor must reckon with the local custom of his province, until in the slow process of time and education it became merged in the imperial law.[3]

Provincial law, then, under the guise of local custom, came for the first time into conflict with the civil law of Rome; and rules became necessary for the solution of these

[1] For a discussion of the beginnings of the topic among the Romans, see: Foelix, 4; Despagnet, 186; Catellani, i, 108; Bustamante, 239; Bar, § 10, p. 12; Meili, i, § 15, p. 69; Foote, xxiv; Story, 2. See also Huberus, ii, lib. i, tit. 3, s. 1; Meili, Int. Civil and Com. Law (tr. Kuhn), 53–58.

[2] In Rev. de dr. int. pr., iv (1908), 904.

[3] Catellani, i, 165–196.

conflicts. The jurisconsults of imperial Rome wrote opinions, and the Emperors sent down rescripts to solve such conflicts; and in the end a considerable body of doctrine became embodied in the Corpus Juris.

§ 23. **The Rules of the Corpus Juris.** — The texts of the Corpus Juris created a body of doctrine as to the conflict of laws which may be briefly summarized as follows.

1. Jurisdiction

The power of the provincial official was bounded by the limits of his province. Within his province, however, he had full jurisdiction over all persons within the province for their acts there done, and also over persons born in the province and over persons there domiciled, though the question at issue might be an act done outside the province.

Dig. i. 18. 3. The *praeses* of the province has a right of *imperium* over the men of his own province only, and he has the right only while he is in the province; if he leaves it he becomes a private person. Sometimes he has *imperium* even over outsiders, if they commit any active offense. (Monro's tr.)

Dig. ii. 1. 20. An officer who exercises jurisdiction outside his local limits may be disobeyed with impunity. (Monro's tr.)

Dig. xlviii. 22. 7. § 13. If one agrees with this opinion, that whoever commits a crime in a province may be banished by the ruler of that province, it will happen that a man so banished must keep away from three provinces as well as from Italy: namely, that in which he committed the offense, that in which he was domiciled, and his native province. And if he is found to have different native provinces, owing to his own condition and that of his father or relatives, we say that he is consequently banished from even more provinces.

Cod. iii. 15. 1. It is well known that prosecutions for crimes should be instituted where they were committed or initiated, or where the accused are found. (Auth. *qua in provincia.* In whatever province one commits a delict, or is prosecuted for money or crimes, whether with respect to lands, or boundaries, possession, property, or mortgage, or any other matter, there let him be subject to the law. Nov. lix. c. 1. pr.)

Other passages often referred to upon this point are: Dig. xlviii. 22. 7. §§ 1 and 10; Cod. i. 3. 10; Cod. iii. 24. 1.

These and the later cited passages from the Corpus Juris may be found in Beale's "Bartolus on the Conflict of Laws," Appendix.

2. Personal Status

Personal status legally created under another law continues to exist, and is recognized, in so far as it is not inconsistent with the Roman law. The law which properly creates status is the law of the domicil. An incapacity which does not affect personal status has no extra-territorial effect.

Cod. iv. 42. 2. We forbid the transfer to the ownership of anyone in any way whatever of men of Roman race who have been made eunuchs, whether in barbarian or in Roman territory; and the most severe punishment is to be imposed upon those who have dared to do the act. . . . But we grant to all merchants or others the right to buy and sell in commerce, wherever they will, eunuchs of barbarian race, who have been made outside the territory subject to our jurisdiction.

Cod. viii. 49 (48). 1. If the law of the city in which your father emancipated you gave such jurisdiction to the duumvirs that even foreigners might emancipate their sons, what your father did is binding.

Dig. xxvi. 5. 1. The *praeses* of a province may give a tutor only to those who belong to his province or have a domicil there.

Dig. iii. 1. 9. When a man is forbidden to move on behalf of others on some ground which does not entail infamy, and consequently does not deprive him of the right to move on behalf of others in every case, he is only disabled from moving on behalf of others in the province in which the magistrate who pronounced the prohibition was *praeses;* the prohibition does not extend to any other province, though it should bear the same name. (Monro's tr.)

3. Property

The law that governs property is the law of the situs. Thus rights in land are determined by the local custom; and land is taxed in the province where it lies. Property is administered where it is found. A mere *chose in action* however has no situs for this purpose, and must be transmitted to the debtor's domicil for suit.

Dig. viii. 4. 13. § 1. If it is understood that there are stone quarries on your land, no one can hew stone there . . . unless indeed there is a custom existing in those quarries to the effect that, should anyone desire to hew any such stone, he is at liberty to do it, if he first gives the owner of the land the customary payment in consideration thereof. (Monro's tr.)

Dig. l. 15. 4. § 2. He who has an estate in another city ought to declare [his property for taxation] in the city in which the property is; for he should pay the land tax to that city in whose territory his estate lies.

Dig. xxvi. 5. 27. In case of a ward who has property both at Rome and in a province, the praetor may appoint a tutor for the property in Rome, the *praeses* for that in the province. (See also Dig. xxvi. 7. 39. § 3.)

Dig. xxvi. 7. 47. Tutors for Italian property found, at Rome, instruments executed by provincial debtors, which provided that a sum of money should be paid at Rome, or wherever payment was demanded. I asked, where neither the debtors nor any property of theirs was in Italy, whether the collection of the debt belongs to the tutors for Italian property? I answered that if the contract were a provincial one the collection did not belong to them; but it was their duty to give information about the instruments to the tutors to whom the administration belonged.

4. Obligations

An obligation is made where the act on which it rests is done, and in accordance with the law of that place; though upon this point there is some ambiguity in the texts. Damages accrue according to the law of the place of the wrong. A judgment validly rendered abroad is to be performed.

Dig. v. 1. 20. The correct view is that every kind of obligation is to be treated like [one founded on] contract, so that, wherever a man incurs an obligation, it is to be held that a contract was made there, though it should not be a case of a debt founded on a loan. (Monro's tr.)

Dig. xxi. 2. 6. If an estate be sold, the security against defect in title should be given according to the custom of the place where the sale was made.

Dig. xliv. 7. 21. Everyone is supposed to have contracted in that place in which he bound himself to perform.

Dig. xii. 1. 22. A loan of wine was made, and legal proceedings were taken to recover it. . . . I asked to what locality the valuation should refer. He replied that if it had been agreed that restoration should be made at some particular place, the valuation should follow the price at that place. (Monro's tr.)

See also Dig. xiii. 3. 4; xxii. 1. 1.

Dig. xlii. 1. 15. § 1. The Emperor and his father have decided that the *praeses* of a province, if so ordered, shall execute a judgment given at Rome.

5. Acts

The maxim *locus regit actum* is established, both for ordinary acts and for the form of legal documents.

Dig. xxv. 4. 1. § 15. The custom of the place is to be regarded, and the womb should be inspected and the birth of the infant arranged by it.

Dig. xxix. 1. ult. The *rescripts* of the Emperors show that all who are of such a condition that they cannot make a will by military law, if they are seized and die in hostile territory may make a will as they will and can: whether it be the president of the province or anyone else who cannot make a will by military law.

§ 24. The Barbarian Incursions: Personal Tribal Law. — With the incursions of the barbarians and their settlement as conquerors on Roman territory, permanently domiciled there, new principles for determining the application of laws necessarily came into existence. It was no longer possible for the Roman lawyer to ignore a foreign law, when it was the law of his conqueror. The tribal law of the German must now be considered by the lawyer, alongside the Roman law; and the principles adopted for the mutual accommodation of the two systems established some of the doctrines of the Conflict of Laws of the Middle Ages.[1]

The tribal law differed fundamentally from the *ius gentium*, previously applied to foreigners; the latter was Roman law, but tribal law was non-Roman law recognized perforce by Roman lawyers.

The problem was worked out by applying to the Germans their tribal law, while the Romans retained their Ius Civile.[2]

[1] On the development of the subject resulting from the barbarian invasions see: Asser, 7, 5, 2; Bar, 17; Bustamante, 245; Catellani, i, 197; Despagnet, 186; Foelix, i, 11; Meili, i, 72; Rolin, i, 32; Weiss, iii, 126.

[2] Several modern analogies will at once come to mind; the laws of the native races in India, the tribal laws of the North American Indians, and the consular laws in Oriental countries.

So far, it was a conflict of systems rather than of particular laws. Each party was judged in his own courts, according to his own law, and quite in accord with the settled Roman doctrine, *actor sequitur forum rei.*[1] In everything except the actual holding of land, therefore, there was no real conflict of laws; all law was personal in its application, and each man was obliged only according to his own law. Thus arose the "personal law" of the middle ages.

As to the only rights not covered by this system, rights in land, the law applicable was apparently that of the owner; and this was of course a real rule for solving a conflict, but one which had no influence upon the law in subsequent times. The notion of personal law, however, first established during this period, continues in force today.

§ 25. The Early Middle Ages: the Law and the Statutes. — The tribal law gradually became assimilated with the law of the land, or rather, in many parts of the empire, more or less completely absorbed the Roman law; though in theory every part of the empire was during the early Middle Ages governed by imperial law, however much the imperial law of one portion of the empire might differ from that of another portion.[2] But throughout the empire, and especially in Italy, city-states developed, and each of these had its own local ordinances, or *statuta.*[3] These statuta were not only in derogation of the imperial law; they were in conflict with it in many points, and some means had to be found for resolving the conflict.

The principle finally adopted for this purpose was developed from the Code, by the commentators and glossators on the first title of the Code;[4] or rather, it was "founded on texts of Roman law and on the nature of

[1] Savigny, Hist. Roman law (tr. Cathcart), i, 151.

[2] Savigny, Hist. Roman Law (tr. Cathcart), i, 156.

[3] The word *Statutum* appears originally to have been limited to city ordinances; afterwards it was extended to the local law of other subordinate governmental or quasi-governmental bodies, like the French provinces, the medieval gilds, and the religious corporations. The broader use in England, as meaning *lex*, was elsewhere unknown in the Middle Ages.

[4] For the development of our subject by the commentators on the Code, and especially by the "Post-Glossators," see: — Bustamente, 261; Catellani, i, 266; Despagnet, 191; Lainé, i, 93; Laurent, i, 273; Meili, i, 77; Rolin, i, 54; Weiss, iii, 15; Westlake, 16.

things."[1] The point of text upon which the discussion was hung was the very beginning of the Code:[2] "Cunctos populos quos clementiae nostrae regit imperium . . . volumus," etc. The commentary was begun by Accursius, who wrote: "If a Bolognian makes a contract at Modena, he shall be judged by the statute of Modena, though he is not subject to it."

The work of the commentators consisted chiefly in putting and solving cases, as in this example from Accursius. A similar passage may be cited from the *Speculum Juris* of Gulielmus Durantis (1237–1296):[3]

"Suppose a Fleming died at Genoa and there in his will made his wife his heir. According to the custom of Genoa a wife cannot succeed her husband, and so the possessor of the goods refuses to deliver them; but in Flanders there is the contrary custom, and the woman takes. Decide that the woman's case is best in obtaining the inheritance, according to the custom of Flanders, by which she is bound."

§ 26. **Bartolus.** — The principal author of this time was Bartolus of Sassoferrato (1314–1357), a professor of law at Pisa and Perugia, the greatest of the school of post-glossators, so-called, and one of the most distinguished lawyers of the Middle Ages.[4]

The fame of Bartolus, says Savigny,[5] surpasses that of every jurist of the Middle Ages; a fame all the more remarkable because he died at an age when many others are just beginning to be known. And Laurent adds:[6] "The reign of Bartolus was long at the bar and in legal science. Some called him the father of law, others the lamp of law. They said that the substance of truth was found in his works and that advocates and judges could do no better than to follow his opinions."

[1] Lainé, i, 306. [2] Cod. i. 4.

[3] Book 2, Partic. 3, § 5, ver. 2 (ed. 1602, pt. ii, p. 785).

[4] For the influence of Bartolus upon the doctrine of the Conflict of Laws, see: Catellani, i, 327; Lainé, i, 131–163; Laurent, i, 299; Meili, i, 80; Weiss, iii, 15; Beale, "Bartolus on the Conflict of Laws"; Montijn, Aanteekening, etc.; Rattigan, in Journal of Society of Comparative Legislation, N. S., v. 230; Meili in Zeitschr. 1894, 258, 340; 1895, 363, 446. Woolf, in his Bartolus, deals with Bartolus as a political thinker; his bibliography enumerates several works and articles on Bartolus from that point of view.

[5] Geschichte des Römischen Rechts, vi, 136.

[6] Droit civil int. i, 299.

While Bartolus's doctrines were fortified by the writings of his predecessors, as well as by the texts of the Corpus Juris, he found in these sources only the germs of the general principles that he formulated. To him is due the entire credit for discovering and stating a body of principle on the Conflict of Laws which will still repay careful study.[1] The following is an attempt at a summary restatement of these principles.

1. *Contracts.* A contract is governed, both as to its form and as to its intrinsic validity, by the law of the place of the maker; but in all that has to do with performance, including the *préscription libératoire* or discharge by lapse of time, it is governed by the law of the place of performance.

2. *Wrongs.* Torts and crimes are governed by the law of the place of acting.

3. *Wills.* Wills are governed as to their form by the law of the place of making; as to testamentary capacity by the law of the domicil of the testator. A will good by the proper law passes property everywhere, even in a place by the law of which the will is not valid; and conversely, a will not valid by the proper law passes the inheritance nowhere, even in a place to the law of which the will conforms.

4. *Property.* The regulation of property is according to the law of the situs; and this law applies to and determines the validity of any attempted transfer of the property in another place.

5. *Judgments.* Ordinary foreign judgments are freely executed upon property within the state. Penal judgments, however, are not executed in another state, even though they run against property alone. If the judgment has affected the status of the guilty party this status of course remains though he go into another place.

6. *Procedure.* All matters of form of action and procedure are governed by the law of the forum.

7. *Statutes.* A considerable part of his work is devoted to a consideration of the jurisdiction of statutes. In order to appreciate this portion of the discussion, it should be

[1] Bartolus' work on the Conflict of Laws has been translated into English in full, Beale, Bartolus; and a summary in French may be found in Lainé, i, 131–163.

remembered that the condition of medieval Italy was not unlike that of the United States today in this respect: that the ordinary law was a common law, prevailing throughout the whole territory; while each city-state had the power to modify the common law by a statute. His doctrine may be briefly stated as follows.

Statutes regulating the form of an act, or giving official power to an officer, cannot operate beyond the territory; though an act done within the territory, or an official act within the territory, in conformity with the statute, would be valid in its effects outside as well as within the territory.

Statutes regulating dealings with property apply only to property within the territory; but as to such property they apply to dealings outside as well as within the territory.

Statutes regulating the capacity of persons are either favorable or burdensome in their regulations. All provisions for the benefit of a citizen of the state follow him wherever he goes; unfavorable restrictions apply within the state only.

Punitory statutes apply to crimes committed within the state by any person, citizen or stranger. As to citizens acting outside the state, the statutes apply if their terms expressly so provide, otherwise not. As to acts done outside the state by a foreigner against a citizen, Bartolus (differing from most of his predecessors) is strongly of opinion that the statutes cannot be made applicable.

As an example of the method of Bartolus, his discussion of the jurisdiction of a state to punish a crime committed beyond its borders upon its citizen may be quoted:

"Sometimes a foreigner offends a citizen beyond the territory of the city, and a statute provides that the foreigner should be punished here; would this be valid? It has been held so, just as a layman offending a clerk is tried in the ecclesiastical court. Moreover, everyone, even a stranger, is subject to the jurisdiction of the place in which a crime is committed.

"Now if the crime is committed in a place subject to the city, upon the person of its citizens, the case is clear; but that does not cover this case. In the case put of the offense against a clerk, the reason is that he commits sacrilege, which is an ecclesiastical crime, and therefore pertains to the church. And that phrase above quoted which runs, jurisdiction of the place, etc., I understand to mean, jurisdiction of an immovable thing, like territory, not of a movable or self-moving thing. State the rule thus, therefore; such a statute is not valid, because a city cannot legislate beyond its territory upon persons not subject to it."

One of the most striking things about the work of Bartolus is the modern tone of his opinions, though his conclusions are based on reasoning that is medieval in form. So far was his philosophy of the subject in advance of the capacity of his successors, that from the time of the earliest French writers until a few years ago many of his suggestions were misunderstood and ridiculed.

The point on which his doctrine was most seriously criticised by the early French school was his distinction between statutes which apply to a thing and statutes which regulate personal capacity. Having stated his general principle, Bartolus thus put the case on the solution of which he has been bitterly attacked:

"A doubt may be raised on some such question as this. It is the custom of England that the eldest son succeeds to all the goods. Now one having goods in England and in Italy dies; the question is, what law governs. . . . Either the provision is made about a *res*, as by these words: 'The goods of decedents shall go to the first-born'; then I should adjudicate as to all the goods according to the custom or statute at the place where the things are situated; for the law affects the things themselves, whether they are possessed by a citizen or a stranger: — or else the words of the statute or of the custom make provision about a person, as by these words: 'The first-born shall be heir'; then either such decedent was not an Englishman, though he had possessions there, in which case such a statute does not affect him and his sons, because a provision about persons does not affect foreigners, as was said above: or such decedent was English; and then the first-born succeeds to the goods which are in England, and to the others he succeeds at common law, according to what the said doctors say; because either this is said to be a statute which deprives the younger sons, in which case, since it is odious, it does not affect goods situated abroad, as was proved above, or you call the statute permissive in removing an obstacle so that the younger sons may not interfere with the elder, and that is the same, as has been said."

This distinction of Bartolus between a statutory provision *in rem* and one *in personam*, differentiated by the mere order of the words, has been attacked by his successors as a mere verbal difference. It is at most, as Lainé points out,[1] an unfortunate illustration of a distinction which was one of the most original and ingenious discoveries of the great master; a discovery which his contemporaries could not make, and his successors for five hundred years failed to understand. Yet the distinction is a necessary one; a statute might well be interpreted either as determining personal status or as affecting the inheritance of property. The very question which Bartolus was discussing arose in North Dakota in 1899, and the same distinction was made.[2]

§ 27. **Baldus and the Successors of Bartolus.** — Baldus, the pupil and immediate successor of Bartolus, was his only successor among the Italian jurists whom it is necessary to mention. Baldus de Ubaldis (1327–1400) wrote voluminously upon all branches of the law; upon the Conflict of Laws principally, like Bartolus, in his comment upon the law "Cunctos Populos." [3] His chief independent conclusion was as to the status and capacity of persons. Capacity, he thinks, is governed by the law of the domicil, "because it is as if he were a citizen." [4] He however speaks of a "mixed" statute, citing as an example a statute which gives a person testamentary capacity with his father's consent; the consent, he says, is not a matter of capacity, but of form.[5]

In general, the work of Baldus differs little in its conclusions from those of Bartolus. The later jurists of the fourteenth and fifteenth centuries occupied themselves with little more than elaborating the doctrines of Bartolus with new cases.

§ 28. **The Contribution to Doctrine of the Early Italian School.** — A consideration of the work of Bartolus will make it clear that a very considerable body of doctrine was formulated by him, and that if it had been naturally developed it would have given us a well-rounded science. Unfortunately the Renaissance which followed drew the most

[1] i, 158–161. See, among the attacks upon Bartolus for this distinction, Argentré, Art. ccxviii, No. 24; Froland, i, 28–30; Boullenois, i, 20. In defence of Bartolus, Laurent, i, 299–301; Catellani, i, 338 *n.* (5).

[2] Eddie *v.* Eddie, 8 N. D. 376, 79 N. W. 856.

[3] For the work of Baldus see Lainé, i, 166–178; Meili, Int. Civil and Comm. Law, 68.

[4] Comm. Cod. i. 1, § 59.

[5] *Ibid.*

brilliant minds away from the scientific study of law; and the development of doctrine fell into the hands of a class of narrow and formal legists, whose interest centered rather on the distinction between different kinds of statutes than on the more fundamental and important principles. Expressions of Bartolus and Baldus, used by them descriptively only and not as terms of art, were seized upon as containing in themselves the whole gist of the matter; and further discussion of the subject became a struggle to attain the unattainable, namely, a criterion for distinguishing from one another statutes real, statutes personal, and statutes mixed.

It is to be noticed that neither Bartolus nor his Italian successors worked out the artificial system of the later authors, for which they have often been made the sponsors. They did not divide all laws into statutes real and statutes personal; indeed, as has been seen, the treatment of statutes in the works of Bartolus and Baldus forms only a small portion of their doctrine. Nor were the terms statute real and statute personal used by them in their later technical significance. To them, if they used the phrases, they meant statutes relating to things and statutes relating to persons; the terms in themselves possessed no jurisdictional connotation.

§ 29. **The Later Middle Ages: the Coutumes.** — As the scene of the development of law shifted from Italy to France another political condition was found, which materially influenced the doctrines of the Conflict of Laws. France was a confederation of provinces, each with its own law, which was called "custom"; and the customs of northern France retained small traces of the Roman law. The custom of Normandy, for instance, was almost pure Germanic law. On account of this sharp departure from Roman law the custom was no longer regarded as a mere exception to a universal law; the custom was in fact the true and substantially the only law of the land. It is a favorite trick of European modernists in law to speak of the customs as feudal, and of their territorial quality as derived from the feudal system.[1] As a matter of history, it must be clear that it was not the feudal system, but the territorializing

[1] *E.g.*, Laurent, i, 266.

of the tribes that gave territorial character to the customs. The tribal law of the Burgundians became the custom of Burgundy; the tribal law of the Normans settled down into the custom of Normandy. And modern France, made up of its confederated provinces, had as many territorial laws as there were formerly semi-independent provinces.

The "coutumes" of France inherited from the city laws of Italy the name "statuta,"[1] although before the later reception of the Roman law there was no conception of a paramount imperial law from which they derogated. The local law therefore came to be regarded as the proper law, and it ordinarily prevailed in case of conflict. One is tempted to say with Weiss[2] that the territoriality of the customs almost superseded the personality of law; though the statement of Bar[3] that the personal law never absolutely disappeared is quite accurate. In fact, it was as impossible then as it has since been and always must be to disregard foreign laws; and the claims of personal status were always compelling. "The territoriality of law, and justice: there are the two forces whose collision gave rise to the theory of statutes."[4] But since tribality could no longer be the basis of this personal law, and, the provinces not being independent states, nationality was impossible, domicil was substituted for tribality as determining the law of personal relations.[5]

A new element had been brought into the subject by the fact that the provinces of France, though politically parts of a common country, were legally distinct units, and the law henceforth developed as a body of principles regulating the conflict of independent laws. "It was not a conflict between the law of France and of another state, but between two laws, both French; but it was at bottom the same difficulty, and it ought to be solved in the same way. To express the identity of the situation, one may suggest the idea that the different provinces of ancient France, with their customs and their peculiar institutions, guaranteed by the treaties of annexation, were in most respects so many distinct nations."[6]

[1] Guyot's Répertoire de Jurisprudence, *s. v.* Statuts: 1st ed., vol. lix.
[2] iii, 134.
[3] 23–25, § 16.
[4] Lainé, i, 74.
[5] Bar, 21, § 15.
[6] Vareille-Sommières, i, 5.

§ 30. The French Statutists of the 16th Century: Dumoulin. — It has been seen that the "coutumes" inherited from Italy the name "statuta"; and the French writers before the sixteenth century made use of this name to distinguish the subject on which they wrote.[1] They carried out, and applied to the new conditions, the theories of Bartolus as far as wit was given them to understand and follow them.

With the sixteenth century, however, two great lawyers arose in France who developed the traditional view, and put it on a new footing. These two men were Dumoulin and Argentré.

Charles Dumoulin (Molinaeus)[2] was born in the year 1500, and died in 1566. He was a great jurist, whose writings form the beginning of a distinctively French law. He was the connecting link between the early Italians — the school of Bartolus — and the French law.[3] He has been called "the most famous lawyer of France and Germany." He accepted the doctrine of the statute personal, as developed by the Bartolists. His contribution to the development of the law was his doctrine that the law gave all possible scope to the freedom of the will of an actor; from which it followed that a contract, being a legal expression of the freedom of the will, was to be governed by the law to which the parties consented.[4]

The first statement of this doctrine is found in his Commentary on the Code, i. 1.[5] "A statute either speaks of things which have to do with the mere form and solemnity of an act, when we always look to the statute or custom of the place where the act was performed; . . . or it speaks of things which go to the merits of the case and affect the decision; either things which depend on the will of the parties, or things that can be changed by them. In that case the circumstances bearing on the will are to be examined; one of which is the statute of the place where they make their

[1] For the earlier French Statutists, see: Bustamante, 287; Catellani, 381; Lainé, i, 269; Laurent, i, 335, 484, 521; Meili, i, 87; Rolin, i, 67; Weiss, iii, 45.

[2] Lainé, i, 223; Meili, i, 92; Meili, Internat. Civil & Comm. Law, 74; Weiss, iii, 19.

[3] Lainé, i, 225.

[4] *See* particularly the analysis of his doctrine in Weiss, iii, 19.

[5] Conclusiones de Statutis, Works (ed. 1681), iii, 554.

contract, and also the past or present domicil of the parties, and other circumstances. As, where there are differences in measures, if property is sold by measure, or warranted, or measured, the measure which prevails at the place of contracting should not at once be applied, but that of the place in which the property is to be measured and delivered and execution made."

This passage is not of a revolutionary nature; it is obvious that the author has in mind merely the interpretation of the agreement. The idea however was developed and extended so as to cover everything which might be within the power of the parties.

The most important application of this doctrine was to marital contracts, that is, to agreements between the parties to a marriage as to the disposition of the property of the spouses. As to this, Dumoulin invented his celebrated doctrine of tacit consent to the terms of the law under the jurisdiction of which the marriage took place.[1] This was more carefully worked out in one of his opinions.[2] Spouses were married in Paris where community of goods resulted; goods were situated and acquests made elsewhere; what law governed them? It is objected that the law of Paris cannot extend to them. "These objections would be sound if the community of goods were supposed to be caused by force of the custom; but it is not so. It is created by the true consent of the parties; for those who contract in the place of their domicil are supposed by that very fact to contract and agree in accordance with the ways and the notorious custom of that place, unless it is otherwise expressed. . . . And it is to be noted that the custom is not fixed in the contract as public law, or as true binding custom, or by way of law, custom, or statute of public obligation; but as part of the contract, as private and conventional law, willed, laid down and provided by the contracting parties."

§ 31. **Argentré.** — Bertrand d'Argentré (1519–1590),[3] a Breton, lawyer, historian, and man of affairs, broke more completely than Dumoulin from the Italian system, and stated what may be called the distinctive principles of the French statutists. The Bartolists had regarded the statutes of different sorts as being far from exhaustive of the law; many if not most questions were governed by the common

[1] *Ibid.*, 555. [2] Consilia, liii, 3 and 4; Works, ii, 964.

[3] Lainé, i, 310–341; Meili, i, 88; Weiss, iii, 23; De la Lande de Calan, Bertrand d'Argentré; Meili, Argentraeus und Molinaeus, in Zeitschr. v, 363, 452, 554.

imperial law. Argentré, dealing with a "custom" which comprehended every relation of life in its operation, both regarded his statutes (*i. e.*, customs) as comprehending the whole body of law, and placed the principal emphasis on the statute real, the law of the land.[1] The personal statute could not govern, for instance, property beyond the territory; it could only affect the *status* of the person, the *pure* person, to use his phrase. He also admitted the third category of "mixed" statutes, which seems merely to be a method of bringing under the domain of the law of the land transactions in which a relation is established between persons and things.

The doctrines of d'Argentré may best be stated in his own words, especially as he has put them clearly and succinctly. The general principles upon which he proceeds are as follows: [2]

"When it is a question of things affixed in the soil, that is, immovables, or as they are called, matters of inheritance, and different places and situations are assumed for different possessions, and controversy arises as to what law governs with respect to acquiring, transferring, or enforcing rights, it is a principle thoroughly fixed by precedent that that law out of many should be observed which belongs to the place; and its own laws, statutes, and customs should be observed in every place, and whatever customs are accepted concerning things, territory and the limits of power: so that about such things there is no force in any law except that of the territory. So it is provided in the case of contracts, in the case of wills, in the case of all transactions and in the case of places of bringing suit, that nothing may be decided with respect to immovables by private consent against the law of the situs; and it is right that it should be so judged. . . . But it is different with regard to the law of persons; in which are also included movables, because such things are bound by no other law than the person itself, and so they derive their law from the place of domicil. Therefore when the question is about the law of the person or about capacity for civil acts the power is universally that of the judge who judges at the domicil; that is, the one to whom the person is subject, who can so decree in his case that what he determines, adjudges, and ordains about the right of persons shall obtain everywhere the person goes, on

[1] Lainé, i, 337.

[2] Commentaria, Art. ccxviii, glossa 6, §§ 2, 3, 4, 7, 8, 9, 11, 12, 13; Works (ed. 164), i, 647–649.

account of its being, as we say, affixed to the person. . . . The thing may be clearer if examples are given of personal statutes; those, that is, where it is a question chiefly of the right, condition, and quality of persons without consideration of any material thing: as, that one should be declared and held of full age and competent with respect to his acts anywhere who has passed the twentieth year of his age, which is our law, or the twenty-fifth year, which is that of Paris; or when a married woman is made incapable of all power of contracting or obliging herself, and it is claimed that a transaction is therefore not binding; or when those who are subject to the power of another are claimed to be incapable of being legally bound; or when it is provided about children that they should be in the power of the father; or when the administration of property is forbidden to a prodigal.

"Real statutes are, for instance, those which make provision about the method of dividing the inheritance, whether *per capita* or *per stirpes*, or such; even though sometimes it is necessary to inquire into the condition of persons, as, whether they are noble or ignoble, so that the statutes might seem to be mixed. Likewise those which make provision as to the form of transferring property. . . . So of the question whether a legacy may be left in a will to a husband by a wife, because it is a question of immovables and things pertaining to the soil (although it contains a mixed consideration about persons), since the incapacity due to marriage is applied to a thing annexed to the soil; for if it were a question only of movables, it would seem to be personal altogether. So of this question, whether during the existence of the marriage the spouses can transfer things annexed to the soil.

"Examples of mixed statutes occur when by a change of person the rule as to the method of dividing the family inheritance is changed; as when immovables are equally divided because the heirs are pagans. For in the case of the property and estates of nobles the division of property is other and different. Here therefore the condition of the persons alters the judgment as to division of the inheritance.

"Finally, to be personal the question must be purely about the status of persons, without any mixture of immovable things and abstractly from every material thing. For if you legislate thus: he is a minor, because he was born within twenty years, that is personal; but if thus: a minor shall not convey an immovable which is within our territory, that is mixed of real and personal."

"Things which are real or mixed without doubt so pertain to the situs of places and things that they cannot be judged in accordance with any laws other than those of the territory. These are not, to be sure, in force outside the boundaries of the legislator; but conversely, within those boundaries they are not controlled. However unlimited may be the freedom of commerce in contracts, wills, and the doing of business by the Roman law, yet this liberty is limited in this way, that it yields to the customs and laws of the place; . . . for the force of limited power is limited. Whence it follows that if a man has several estates situated in different countries, they are governed, held, transferred, acquired by different customs, laws, and conditions, just as if they were the several estates of several persons; because as often as one and the same thing is governed by more than one law, it is to be taken for several things. One and the same man occupying different magistracies or holding different offices is considered as different persons and as another man than himself, even though he has one and the same body. . . . For every officer, beyond the limits fixed or proper to the office, is a private person; and the jurisdiction and exercise of limited power are limited. So, also, statutes are without effect outside of their own territory, since outside this no one can be terrified, which is the definition of territory; and so the Emperor rightly adds to the phrase 'cunctos populos,' the phrase 'quos clementiae nostrae regit imperium'; although the scholastic writers mix up with this relative phrase many things outside the subject.

"But statutes which are framed in personam are governed by another law; for since persons are hedged in from going outside by no bounds of territory or city walls, and since unlimited freedom of changing their situation is given to them, the statute is to be effective in punishment and to have a location elsewhere, whenever the person desires to take that place for his domicil. Because when anyone acts outside his domicil he is not freed from the laws unless he changes his domicil; from which it happens that a person affected by the law or custom of his domicil in any way whatever is governed by it perpetually, so that he may not free himself by a mere change of place. Wherefore infamy follows in every place a person infamous by the laws of his domicil, and interdiction follows a person interdicted."

§ 32. Guy Coquille and the Other Writers of the Early French School. — The other writers of the early French school, successors of d'Argentré, were numerous and undistinguished.[1] One of his contemporaries, however, is sufficiently important for special mention. Guy Coquille[2] (1523–1603), author of a learned work "De la Coutume de Nivernais," as well as other legal works, was one of the famous French men of law of the sixteenth century. On the subject of the Conflict of Laws he based his doctrine upon a distinction between the *statuta* of Italy and the *coutumes* of France.[3] The *statuta*, he argued, were in derogation of the Roman law, and therefore had a limited application; while the *coutumes* were not merely the local law, but the only law, and had not a limited but an all-powerful application. In this respect, of course, he was in agreement with d'Argentré; but his conclusion was different. D'Argentré's argument had been, substantially, that the local law, being all-powerful, governed everything within the territory except in the case of a status which, having vested elsewhere, could not be altered by change of boundary. Coquille's conclusion was, that since the *coutume* was all-powerful it fixed the rights of persons governed by it so that they could not be affected by other laws. In other words, d'Argentré treated the statute real as the natural operation of legal power; Coquille so treated the statute personal.

"In general, I should say that dispositions and acts, which have their true origin in the human will, ought to be regulated by the custom of the place where the actor is domiciled."[4] "It seems to me that as a general question it is worth while to distinguish and discover whether statutes are personal or real; which I do not understand to depend on the mere husk of words, but on the intention with which the statute was passed; that is to say, the words either with respect to style or meaning are not regarded, but the presumed and apparent purpose of those who have created the statute or custom."[5]

The characteristic achievement of the French school of the sixteenth century was the working out of the theory of a statute real and a statute personal (together with the so-

[1] See a list of them, Catellani, i, 442; Lainé, i, 342–395; Meili, i, 91. See also Lainé, ii, 97; Weiss, iii, 35.

[2] Lainé, i, 297; Weiss, iii, 28. See also Lainé, ii, 388.

[3] Lainé, i, 298.

[4] Works (ed. 1703), ii, 275; qu. 227.

[5] Works (ed. 1703), ii, 211; qu. 131.

called statute mixed). Starting with the conclusions of the Italian school, they developed them, through their application to a state of affairs where there was not merely difference of laws but difference of entire legal systems, into a thoroughgoing body of rules by which it should be possible to determine whether the local or the foreign law applied in each kind of legal relation. One school, that of d'Argentré, leaned toward the law of the land; another, represented by Coquille, was more inclined to the law of the foreign person; Dumoulin laid stress on the autonomy of the will. These doctrines led the jurists who held them to differ as to what laws were statutes real, what were statutes personal; a question upon which the statutists of all centuries have always found themselves unable to agree.

§ 33. **The Dutch Statutists of the 17th Century.** — The scene of legal development in this subject shifted in the 17th century to the Netherlands, where the creation of a confederated nation composed of legally independent provinces had the natural effect of stimulating interest in the Conflict of Laws; just as it had in France a century earlier, and in the United States two centuries later. A society inhabiting a number of federated provinces, each with its own law but united politically and socially into a single people, with constant inter-communication, requires a definitely fixed and workable body of principles for the solution of conflicts of law. The result was a rapid development of the science by a succession of able works.[1]

"It is no longer a question of regulating the spheres of several legislative powers in the same state, — statutes, customs, particular laws, — but of determining the legislative relations of mutually independent states. It is the first time this question has arisen in juridical science. Hitherto, international juridical relations were extremely limited. Foreigners were often submitted to a barbarous *droit d'aubaine*, and a desire to do justice to a foreigner, somehow or other, in accordance with his own law had seldom appeared. But in Holland and Belgium, where the provinces were in fact autonomous states, clinging to their condition of mutual inde-

[1] For an examination of the works of this school see **Bustamante**, 431; Catellani, i, 450; Lainé, i, 401; ii, 95; Meili, i, 95; Rolin, i, 76; **Weiss**, iii, 31; Westlake, 22.

pendence, it was possible neither to apply to the difference of law the Italian theory made with reference only to conflicts between local ordinances, nor to submit to the *droit d'aubaine* residents of other provinces united by community of blood and by ties of confederation." [1]

The earlier writers of importance were Burgundus (1586–1649),[2] Rodenburg (1618–1668)[3] and Paul Voet (1619–1677).[4] Burgundus directed the mind of his successors toward the reality of laws, leaving for the statute personal only questions of personal status and capacity. He parted from the French school in refusing altogether to regard property of any sort as attached to the person of the owner. He denied the accuracy of the maxim "mobilia personam sequuntur." "Goods do not follow the person," he asserted; "persons follow goods"; [5] a witty epigram which contains much good argument.

The work of Rodenburg and of Paul Voet followed in the same line; indeed, Paul Voet proclaimed, forcibly and absolutely, the doctrine of territorial supremacy. "Just as a state which is not subject to another," he says, "is not bound by the custom of the other state, so the statute of one state cannot take effect, expressly or tacitly, in another state." [6]

A greater and more celebrated lawyer was his son, John Voet (1647–1714),[7] of whom Lainé said,[8] "he was the true founder of the Dutch school." Voet's doctrine can be stated fully, though concisely, in his own words.

"No statute, real, personal, or mixed can act of itself beyond the territory of the legislator, nor can it have any effect elsewhere, against the will of the legislator of another place. For since statutes can have no further power than they receive from the legislator who creates them, and the power of the legislator is limited by the bounds of his territory, it is obvious that all force

[1] Eugen Ehrlich, in Rev. dr. int. pr., iv (1908), 910.
[2] Lainé, i, 401–403; Laurent, i, 442–452; Weiss, iii, 31–34.
[3] Lainé, i, 404; Weiss, iii, 34.
[4] Lainé, ii, 97; Laurent, i, 452–457; Weiss, iii, 35.
[5] Lainé, i, 403.
[6] Lainé, ii, 98.
[7] Lainé, ii, 97; Laurent, i, 457–484; Weiss, iii, 36.
[8] Lainé, ii, 388.

of the statutes themselves is shut in and circumscribed by the boundaries of the legislator.[1]

"I think that in the case of all statutes, whether real, personal, or mixed, or however otherwise called or classified, this is the correct rule: that statutes lose absolutely all their power outside the territory of the legislator, nor is the judge of another place obliged, as to things situated in his own territory, by any necessity of law whatever, to follow or approve laws not his own. But here perhaps some careful man may hesitate; if these things are so, how then does the idea happen to be commonly held that in case of successions, testamentary capacity, contracts, and other things, movables wherever situated should be governed by the law of the domicil, and not by the laws of those places in which they are naturally situated? For in accordance with this idea, the jurisdiction of the judge of the domicil appears often to operate beyond the territory of his legislator, upon things dispersed through the several territories of other magistrates whose jurisdiction extends to remote regions stretching toward the rising or the setting sun. . . . But if anyone regards these as legal fictions, alien to that natural reason which alone should be regarded in these cases, I cannot really oppose those who seek one common legislator to introduce and establish such fictions by his law; and yet I believe that this matter is to be ascribed to comity, which one nation manifests to the other, rather than to the rigor of law and the fundamental power which every magistrate has over movables situated in his territory.[2]

"But lest the guaranties of duty and of comity among neighboring nations be vague and uncertain, and often not mutual, and lest that should be denied to one which another had previously obtained by comity, those things which should always be guaranteed are often defined by treaty, or by long-continued customs which have the force of treaty." [3]

§ 34. **Huber.**—The great name of the Dutch school, at least for American scholars, is Huber; and his doctrines require more detailed consideration.

Ulric Huber[4] (1636–1694), professor at the Dutch University of Franeker, compressed in a few paragraphs, in his "Praelectiones Juris Romani et Hodierni," the general principles of the Conflict of Laws, in an essay

[1] Commentariorum ad Pandectas, lib. I, tit. iv, pars ii (de Statutis), § 5.

[2] *Ibid.*, § 11.

[3] *Ibid.*, § 17.

[4] Lainé, ii, 107; Meili, i, 98; Weiss, iii, 37*n*.

entitled "De Conflictu Legum Diversarum in Diversis Imperiis."[1]

"We have found three axioms for solving the subtlety of this most intricate question; which granted, as they seem everywhere to be conceded, appear to point out to us a straight way to the remaining question. They are as follows: I. The laws of any sovereignty have force within the territory of that country, and bind all subjected to it; but not beyond. II. All are considered as subjects of a sovereign who are found within his territory, whether permanently or temporarily there. III. Sovereigns out of comity act so that the laws of each nation, brought into existence within its territory, may hold their force everywhere so far as they do not prejudice the power of the law of another sovereign and his subjects. From which it follows that this is derived not merely from the civil law, but from convenience and the tacit consent of nations. Because as the laws of another nation can have no force directly in another territory, so nothing could be more inconvenient to commerce and international usage than if rights valid by the law of a certain place were at once made void by a different law elsewhere, which is the reason of the third axiom, which like the first seems to be accepted with no doubt. With respect to the second, some persons seem to judge otherwise, when they deny that foreigners are bound by the laws of the place in which they act; we agree that their view is true in some cases, and we shall consider those below. But both the nature of a state and its habit of exercising power over all persons found within the state, as well as the doctrine accepted among almost all nations about arrest of the person proves the correctness of this position: that all found within the boundaries of a state are accepted as subjects. 'One who contracts in another place subjects himself as a temporary subject to the laws of that place' (Grotius, 2, *c.* 11, *n.* 5). For the compulsion of foreigners, with no other cause than that they are found in a place, to submit to mesne arrest, has no other justification than the general principle that a sovereign has power over all who are found within his territory.

"Thence is derived this principle: All acts and transactions, as well in court as out, whether *mortis causa* or *inter vivos*, rightly accomplished according to the law of any particular place, are valid even where a different form of law prevails, by which they

[1] Praelectiones, ed. Macerata, ii, 55; ed. Menck (1707), ii, 23. This passage on the Conflict of Laws may most easily be found by an American scholar, translated into English, in Dallas' Reports, iii, 370*n*.

would be invalid if transacted there. And on the other hand, acts and transactions done in a certain place contrary to the laws of that place, since they are void from the beginning, can nowhere be valid; and this, not only with respect to men who have a domicil in the place of the contract, but even with respect to those who happen to be there at the time: with this exception, nevertheless; if the sovereign of another country would be affected with a serious inconvenience thereby he would not be expected to give use and effect to such acts or business, according to the limitation in the third axiom." [1]

His doctrine as to personal status is as follows: "Personal qualities impressed upon one by the law in a certain place, surround and accompany the person everywhere, with this effect: that everywhere, persons enjoy and are subject to that law which such persons enjoy or are subject to in that other place." [2]

Huber shares with the whole Dutch school the conception of law as a unit, with no distinction of statute and law. His title is "De Conflictu Legum," and from his time, though the "statute personal" continued to form the theme of the lawyers in southern Europe, the title of the subject treated by him was fixed as the *Conflict of Laws*.[3]

Huber's doctrines have never been popular in France. Weiss, who gives large space to forgotten geniuses, dismisses Huber in a note; and Laurent in a section entitled "Jean Voet et Huber" gives to Voet twenty eight pages and to Huber four lines.[4] Yet of all the early authors, Huber's influence has been supreme with the English and American writers. Westlake [5] conjectures that this may be due to the resort of the Scotch advocates to the Netherlands; but this seems mere pedantry. So far as can be discovered, Scotch lawyers had no influence in the statement of the law by Story; and Story, as will be seen, shaped both American and English law. It may be said that the vogue of Huber in America was due in part to the accident of accessibility, but chiefly to the neatness and conciseness of his work and its ready application in a federal republic. His brief pithy paragraphs contained the germs both of Story's principle of vested rights, and of Savigny's doctrine of the proper law applicable

[1] *Loc. cit.*, §§ 1–3.
[2] *Ibid.*, § 12.
[3] Weiss, iii, II.
[4] Laurent, i, 457.
[5] Introd., p. 8.

to a juristic relation. His thought was allied to the Germanic rather than the Romance method of reasoning.

§ 35. The Later French Statutists of the 18th Century. — The French authors of the 18th century, with ideas somewhat modernized but not changed by the writings of the Dutch school, carried forward the work of the early statutists.[1] The two most prominent authors, Boullenois and Bouhier, will be considered below. Out of a cloud of lesser writers one alone, Froland, is worthy of separate mention.[2]

Froland (died 1746) published in 1729 his "Memoires concernans la Nature et la Qualité des Statuts." He accepted, in general, the conclusions of law of the earlier statutists; refusing however to follow in all respects d'Argentré's category of statutes mixed. His service to the growth of the law was not in framing a new theory; it was rather in examining patiently, case by case, the application of the theories of others to the actual facts of daily life, and especially to considering the theories in connection with the decisions of the French courts. In a characteristic passage he states the reasons which led him to this course.

"But are all these definitions, framed in different terms, yet signifying one and the same thing, capable in themselves and sufficient to enable us to recognize the nature and quality of statutes, so that there will be no more difficulty and no more danger of being mistaken in our decision? I fully agree that the statute real is concerned with a thing, the statute personal has to do with the person; and the statute mixed has to do with both thing and person, with those others who allow this third kind. But with all these distinctions the difficulties which I meet hundreds and hundreds of times do not seem yet removed; and my mind, hesitating because it is not sufficiently informed, often does not know what conclusion to reach. In my opinion it is not enough to know that the statute real has to do with the thing, that the statute personal has to do with the person, and that the statute mixed has to do with both thing and person. There is another difficulty much more important to solve; that is, to know when the statute does concern the thing or the person or both: and that, in my opinion, is the question most embarrassing and most difficult to

[1] On the authors of this school see Lainé, ii, 1; Laurent, i, 484; Meili, i, 111; Weiss, iii, 38.

[2] Lainé, i, 417; Laurent, i, 503–508; Weiss, iii, 43.

explain; and it does not appear to me that the old writers who were contented with general definitions have given us very certain rules in this particular." [1]

§ 36. **Boullenois and Bouhier.**—Louis Boullenois (1680–1762),[2] an advocate at the Parlement of Paris, published in 1732 a "Dissertation sur les Questions qui Naissent de la Contrariété des Lois et des Coutumes." After his death, in 1766, was published his "Traité de la Personnalité et de la Realité des Loix, Coutumes ou Statuts," of which the foundation was a translation of Rodenburgh's treatise.

Boullenois was much influenced by the Dutch school, accepting the theory of exclusive territorial power, limited in its operation by the will of each sovereign to allow the operation of foreign laws wherever the requirements of international intercourse called for such derogation from his powers.

Boullenois reduced his doctrines to forty-nine general principles, several of which may be quoted:

"1. The sovereign has the sole right of making laws, and these laws should be executed throughout his dominions.

"4. The sovereign has the right to make laws which shall govern foreigners: first, in respect to property within his sovereignty; second, with respect to the form of contracts made in his territory; third, with respect to suits brought in his courts.

"5. The sovereign may make laws to govern foreigners who are merely passing through his territory, but only with respect to simple police measures made for good order.

"6. In strict law, all laws which a sovereign makes have force and authority only within his own dominions; but the requirements of the general public welfare of nations have led to some exceptions with respect to civil commerce. On this ground the age of majority of the domicil applies everywhere, even with respect to goods situated elsewhere.

"23. The principal direct and immediate subject matter of a statute determines its nature and quality, that is to say, the subject matter makes it real or personal.

"24. The reason for a law should also determine its nature and quality, when this reason is so clear and exactly expressed, that no other reason can fairly be alleged for the law. Thus, the statute which forbids spouses to make mutual conveyances com-

[1] Memoires, i, 54.

[2] Lainé, i, 418; Laurent, i, 492–503; Weiss, iii, 38.

monly passes for real; because although one may say that its reason is to maintain peace between spouses, it is susceptible also of the reason that it preserves the property of each of them for their heirs. But it seems that it should be personal, if it is clear and certain that this defense was given to the spouses alone, in order to give rise to no occasion for trouble and disagreement: yet the authorities are to the contrary. They have considered only the nature of the thing forbidden, and not the reason for it.

"27. Both residents and non-residents are subject to real laws, unless they are expressly confined to residents.

"29. When the statute personal of the domicil is opposed to the statute personal of another place, that of the domicil prevails.

"30. But the statute personal of the domicil which is in conflict with a statute real, whether of the domicil or of any other place, yields to the statute real.

"33. Though movables follow the person and are governed by the law of the domicil, it is not as a personal law, but as the real law of the situs." [1]

During the discussion of these rules he laid down the following principle:

"If in any case it be difficult to distinguish the statute real from the statute personal . . . it is necessary rather to regard the statute real than the statute personal." [2]

John Bouhier (1673–1746) [3] was president of the Parlement of Dijon, and member of the Academy. He published in 1717 his "Observations sur la Coutume du Duché de Bourgogne," in which several chapters were devoted to the Conflict of Laws. Bouhier represented a reaction against the realism of the Dutch school; he derived his inspiration from the theories of Dumoulin, and magnified the statute personal at the expense of the statute real.

Bouhier's principal quarrel with the doctrine of Boullenois was upon the relative importance of the statute real and the statute personal. Accepting the general doctrine that the statute personal was in derogation of the statute real, he differed from Boullenois on the question of the presumption, if there were doubt, as to the reality or the personality of a law. On this point he wrote to Boullenois as follows: [4] "In doubt it is more natural that things

[1] Traité des Statuts, i, 2–11. [2] Traité des Statuts, i, 107.
[3] Lainé, i, 419; Laurent, i, 508–521; Weiss, iii, 41.
[4] Boullenois, Traité des Statuts, i, 107.

should yield to persons, because persons are nobler. Thus, in case of ambiguity in the statute it is much better to interpret it in favor of the person." He admitted that the weight of judicial decision was in favor of the doctrine of Boullenois, but he reprobated this "too blind deference to authority." [1]

The principal points of his doctrine may be stated as follows: "Speaking generally, it is quite indifferent to a nation whether a statute be regarded as real or personal, for what the nation might lose by one interpretation, it would gain on the other hand, so that the total result is equal. That being so, all considerations which should determine the action of the judges in reaching one conclusion or the other are those of public interest, when it is in agreement with the common law and with that equity upon which the principles of this law are based. This is the true clue which should guide us through the labyrinth of these questions." [2]

"First of all we must remember that though the strict rule restrained customs within their own territory, their extension has nevertheless been allowed in favor of public utility and often even of what might be called necessity. . . . So when neighboring people have allowed this extension, they have not regarded themselves as submitting to a foreign law. They have done it only because they have found it to be for their own interest; and in similar cases their own customs have the same power in neighboring provinces. One may say, therefore, that this extension is based on a sort of international law and on comity, by virtue of which different nations are tacitly agreed to allow this submission of custom to custom whenever equity and common utility demand it, unless there is an expressed prohibition of law." [3]

"We attach to the phrase 'reality of customs' the idea of restriction, and to the phrase 'personality of laws,' the idea of their extension. The point is to make a just application of this principle to the different cases which may present themselves. On this point I take the liberty of proposing a few rules.

"1. Every statute which concerns incorporeal and invisible rights should be regarded as personal.

"2. Every statute which is based upon a tacit presumed convention of the parties is personal.

"3. Every statute which imposes a prohibition upon persons submitted to it, for whatever reason, is personal.

"4. Every statute which has to do with the external form of

[1] Observations, ch. xxiii, § 12; Works (ed. 1788), i, 655.

[2] Observations, ch. xxxvi, § 9; Works, i, 820.

[3] Observations, ch. xxiii, § 62; Works, i, 662.

acts and their authentication is personal, so that when the act is done in the forms provided at the place where it is done, it will be executed everywhere." [1]

This last rule will show to what lengths he was carried by his doctrine of judging whether a statute is real or personal by its effects.

§ 37. Summary of the Doctrines of the Statutists. — The statutists studied for the first time the conflict of independent laws, and sought for the particular law applicable to a given case.[2] The best criticism of their doctrine is its impotence. It was powerless to determine the actual affairs of life, because of its failure to develop an accepted rule for the determination of cases as they arose. When the opinions of the various authors are marshalled, as Livermore, for instance, marshalled them, their absolute inability to agree upon details is the most striking feature of their works. As a wise and witty Frenchman has said of them:

" I seem to see skilful masters of the art of fence begin by bandaging their eyes, and then rushing on in the rudest onslaughts, and with the help of a sort of industry resulting from habit and instinct sometimes meeting." [3]

This impotence to lay down a clear body of doctrine is emphasized by the divergence between attempted summaries of their doctrines.

The great French advocate, Merlin says, in his Répertoire, thus:

" There are five principles on the matter of the personality and the reality of statutes which profound jurists have established and proved. They may be stated in a few words.

" The first is, that one should consider as personal every statute which confers on a person a certain status and condition.

" The second, that one should place in the same class permissive statutes conferring capacity in status upon persons, and prohibitive statutes making men incapable in status; because the permission or the defense which they deal with are so to speak only corrollaries of the personal status.

" The third, that a law which forbids a man capable in his status to do a particular act is personal if the object of the act is personal and real if the object is real. Thus, a prohibition to two spouses, of age, that they should not make conveyances one to

[1] Observations, ch. xxiii, §§ 60, 61, 64, 69, 75, 81; Works, i, 662–665.

[2] Jitta, Méthode, 41, 42.

[3] Mailher de Chassat, p. 33.

another is real, because it provides an exception to the general capacity which adult spouses have by their status to dispose of their property, and because its object is real.

"The fourth, that a law which allows a man who lacks capacity by his status to do a particular act is personal if the object is personal, and real if the object is real.

"The fifth, that the statute personal should yield to the statute real in case of a conflict between them."[1]

The doctrines are summed up in six general principles by The Count de Vareilles-Sommières, their latest modern apologist.[2]

"1. As a general rule the custom governs the conduct of all, domiciled or not domiciled, within the territory of the province.

"2. As a general rule, the custom does not govern outside the province the conduct of anyone, domiciled or not.

"3. The statutes or the custom as to status and capacity follow the domiciled and are applied to them in other provinces.

"4. In some particulars, movables should be regarded as situated at the domicil of their owner, and are consequently ruled by the custom of that domicil even though they are in fact upon the territory of other provinces.

"5. The statutes or the customs which interpret or give effect to the will of the parties do not apply to a juridical act done on the territory of the province when the parties have expressly or tacitly incorporated into their act the statutes of another jurisdiction for the purpose of giving effect to their act.

"6. In all matters the form of acts is governed by the custom of the place where they are done."

And again by Lainé.[3]

"The French doctrine presents three principal characteristics.

"First, all laws are divided into two classes, that of statutes real and that of statutes personal, from a double point of view. This division cannot comprehend all laws, and the authors feel this insufficiency without avowing it. To remedy it, they have recourse to three means: 1, they do not altogether submit to the distinction which they have themselves suggested; 2, they try to enlarge it by making use of the idea of statutes mixed, but without agreement and without success; 3, they rigorously accept it and in some way or other classify all laws, but at the expense of certain essential rules.

"Second, the reality of laws constitutes the general rule, the personality exists only as an exception.

[1] Merlin, Répertoire, s. v. Statuts.

[2] Vareilles-Sommières, i, 11.

[3] Lainé, ii, 5.

" Third, the reality of laws is based on the feudal sovereignty of customs, the personality of laws on the idea of justice."

§ 38. **The Beginning of Modern Law: Livermore.** — Early in the 19th century the history of the Conflict of Laws shifts again, this time to the United States of America. The same cause was operating. A recently formed confederation of states, each of which was legally independent, turned the attention of lawyers to the practical solution of the necessarily resulting conflicts. The earliest American author on the subject was Livermore (1786–1833). This author was a learned member of the bar of Louisiana, where he was brought into contact with the thought of French and other continental authors; and his book is a forceful but belated attempt to reinstate the statutory theory of the medieval commentators. His book in fact proves the objections which have been urged against this theory; for he states at length the doctrine of each author, all differing from one another, and Livermore himself differs from all. His book is a painstaking work, but the logic of events has disproved his thesis. His doctrines could not be applied in a country where both commercial and social intercourse between all parts of it are constant and continuous. His book was familiar to Story, but influenced the great commentator only indirectly, namely by calling to his notice the works of the medieval authors. By presenting his large collection of medieval works to the Harvard Law School, where Story used them, Livermore influenced indirectly but profoundly the thought of American lawyers on the subject of the Conflict of Laws. His collection contained 400 volumes, including the 16th, 17th and 18th century writers on the conflict of laws, and formed the basis of the large apparatus which Story's bibliography describes.

The basis of his doctrine is the later eighteenth century thought, as exemplified in the Declaration of Independence; and his work is an interesting study of statutist theories in the light of the new ideas.

" It having been at last conceded, that foreign laws must be in some instances respected, it has been fashionable, in this country and in England, to impute this to the comity of nations; a phrase which is grating to the ear, when it proceeds from a court of justice. Comity between nations is to be exercised by those who administer the supreme power. The duty of judges is to administer justice according to law, and to decide between parties litigant according to their rights. When an action is brought upon a foreign contract, it is not from comity that they receive evidence of the the laws of the country where such contract was made, but in order to ascertain in what manner and to what extent the parties have obligated themselves. Comity implies a right to reject; and the consequence of such rejection would probably be a judgment ordering a party to do that which he had never obligated himself to do. This phrase has not always been harmless in its effects, for I have not unfrequently seen it inspire judges with so great confidence in their own authority, that arrogating to themselves sovereign power, they have disregarded the foreign law, which ought to have governed their decision, because of some fancied inconvenience which might result to the citizens of their state.

" Even with sovereigns it is not so clear that the recognition of foreign laws is merely a matter of comity. They have the power to forbid the admission of the foreign law; but justice would then require that they should forbid the entertaining of any suit upon the foreign contract. The people of an independent nation may, if they please, surround their territory with an impassable wall, and totally exclude all intercourse with other nations. But if a desire to promote their own interest induces them to cultivate an intercourse with other people, they must necessarily adopt such principles as a sense of common utility and of justice will inspire. They cannot pretend to legislate upon the state and condition, the capacity or incapacity, of persons not subject to them. They may refuse to admit such persons to enter their territory; but if they do receive them, they are bound to receive them with that character which has been imprinted on them by the laws of the country to which they are subject."[1]

§ 39. **Story.** — The focal point in the history of the Conflict of Laws is the work of Joseph Story. In his Commentaries on the Conflict of Laws, published in 1834, he brought together the conclusions of the statutists, and placed beside them the principles developed in the English and American cases before his time. His work was issued at a psychological moment. The work of the statutist had ceased. The impulse which gave it life was spent. The

[1] Dissertations, 26–28.

belated attempt of Livermore to revive it had failed. Unless someone appeared with power to assimilate its sound conclusions, it seemed that it was labor lost. On the other hand, the common law, lighting on new experiences in a new world, lately rescued from the dangers of lay administration,[1] was working out characteristic conclusions in entire ignorance of the statutists and all their theories. Story combined the new impulse with the old learning, and became the creator of the modern science, and his book the point of departure of all the modern theories.[2] With some suggestions from the writings of the Dutch school, and with the help of a meager body of decided cases, he wrote the law anew, and in a way which has fixed the ideas of American and English lawyers at least, and on the Continent gave a new impulse to scholarship. "The work of Story was the signal for new works answering to the new needs which were just making themselves seriously felt. There was a sort of renascence of private international law. In the space of fifteen years, numerous publications were issued in different countries. Among the authors who belong to this first period I may cite: — at Naples, Rocco; in England, Burge; in France, Foelix, Massé, Mailher de Chassat, Demangeat; in Germany, Waechter, Schaeffner, Savigny."[3]

§ **40. The Influence of Story on European Thought.** — The earliest French writer after Story, Foelix, began his work as a series of magazine articles in the very year Story's book was published. He adopted the theory of comity from Story, and spoke of it as follows:[4]

"This result, to which our study and thought has led us, has been confirmed and developed in the learned work of Mr. Story, professor of law at Harvard University, Cambridge, and judge of the Supreme Court of the United States of North America. From him we have not hesitated definitively to adopt this doctrine, and we have followed it in the entire course of our work."

In Germany, Schäeffner's first reference in his notes is

[1] Pound, The Place of Judge Story in the Making of American Law: Cambridge, 1914.

[2] Laurent, i, 553; Rolin, i, 101. [3] Lainé, i, viii. [4] Foelix, i, 4.

to Story,[1] and the Commentaries are listed and described in his bibliography. Savigny in his Preface says:[2]

"In this branch of our treatise [i.e., the Conflict of Laws] the opinions of writers, as well as the judgments of tribunals, have hitherto been wildly confused and conflicting. A remarkable picture of this imperfect but hopeful state of things is presented in the excellent work of Story, which is also extremely useful, as a rich collection of materials, for every inquirer."

Rocco however appears to have been ignorant of Story's work at the time of publication of his first edition, and at the time of his second edition (in 1843) to have known it only through a review.

It thus appears that the doctrines of both the modern European schools were largely based on the work of Joseph Story. From him the law flowed on in three streams: the theory of the neo-statutists, the theory of the internationalists, and the common-law doctrine of territorial law recognizing vested rights. These theories will be considered in the next chapter.

§ 41. **Summary of this History.** — As a restatement of the course of history which has been outlined, one cannot do better than quote the masterly summary of Professor Ehrlich.[3]

"If there is any lesson to be drawn from this rapid resumé of the history of Private International Law, it is the fact that every age has had its Private International Law, responsive to the ideas then prevailing upon the nature of a state and the nature of its law. The ancient state, which had its origin in the group formed by members of a single race, and which was always reverting toward this primitive conception, knows only a law of the dominant race; and at most grants to subject people and races a certain little portion of juridical autonomy. Sensibly and insensibly Rome changed into a territorial state, merging in the conquering race the different peoples and races which inhabited its territory; and thus the law of the dominant race acquired in fact, throughout the extent of the state, the force of a territorial law. In their turn the Germanic states of the middle age appear in history as states based on com-

[1] Schäeffner, 3.
[2] Savigny, 44.
[3] Rev. dr. int. pr., iv (1908), 902, 915.

munity of race. They knew no other law than the law of each different race; but they had at once under their eyes the powerful example of the ancient territorial state which provided one law for everyone within its territory, and starting from that example they created jurisdictions in which justice was granted to every inhabitant of the state according to the law of his race. It is the age of personality in law. When the laws of the different races are replaced by local statutes, customs, or particular law, the theory of statutes which seeks to discover rules to resolve conflicts arising from the diversity of local rights makes its appearance. Circumstances of just the same kind have led to the formation of the modern Private International Law. The development of international commerce and the idea of the *comitas gentium* led to a treatment of the foreigner as one entitled to rights, and led to treating him more and more as entitled to private rights which are the same as those of the inhabitants of the country. At the same time there arose the idea of the juridical monopoly of the state, the effort to refer every law to the state whose sovereignty extends over the territory where the law is applied. According to these ideas, when a state declares that a foreign law should be applied to a juridical relation, it does so because this juridical relation was subject to the law of the foreign state. Now, evidently this idea is an idea of the right of nations. It immediately oversteps the limits which the law of nations assigns to the local sovereign of a state. Like every radical innovation, this idea makes its way little by little, always timidly supporting itself on ideas already recognized. It is the theory of statutes which is gradually transformed into these new conceptions. Then come the theories of Savigny, of Wächter, and the Internationalists, who are already moving altogether within this circle of ideas. Today even the determined Nationalists, like Kahn, admit that private international law finds in the law of nations some of its fundamental rules, against which no state can set itself. They admit that in time we shall achieve a codification of private international law, no doubt still incomplete, but the same for all states, and fixed by convention between the states. The Internationalists naturally go still further along this road. Such an evolution should radically lead to an attempt at an integration of private international law on the basis of the law of nations. This is what Zitelmann is undertaking today, and it dominates his work on Private International Law. He carries to their radical conclusion the ideas which the evolution accomplished in our own time has created, and he professes to open the way for a new evolution."

§ 42. Efforts to Unify the Law: International Conferences. — The fact that there are different theories of law held in different states, and therefore differences in the rules of law themselves, much interferes with the benefits which would follow identity in rules of law. For instance, difference in the rules regulating the law which shall apply to marriage would cause the very evil such rules were intended to avoid, and might result in parties being married in one state and single in another.[1] It is therefore not surprising that efforts have been made to avoid such differences; and, since without a higher power than that of mere opinion differences of opinion must obviously continue to exist, these efforts have taken the direction of international meetings in which the power of a majority may be applied to individual dissent.[2]

The first effort of this sort appears to have been made in 1889, when a conference was held at Montevideo between representatives of the independent states of South America. The result of this conference was a series of draft treaties, intended to be signed by the respective parties.[3] It does not appear, however, that these treaties were actually signed by the parties to them.[4]

[1] See, e.g., Ogden *v.* Ogden (1908), P. 46.

[2] On the general subject of the codification of private international law see the following:

De Vries, J.: Codification of private international law. Soc. Sci. Asso., 1875, 180.

Asser, T. M. C.: La codification du droit international privé. Haarlem, 1901.

Olivi, Louis: De la codification du droit international privé. Rev. dr. int. xxvi (1894), 511–529.

Anzilotti, Dionisio: La codificazione del diritto internazionale privato. Florence, 1894.

Paroldo, A.: Saggio di codificazioni del Diritto internazionale. Turin, 1851.

Vicoforte: Di una codificazione convenzionale parziale di diritto internazionale privato. Turin, 1883.

Silvela, M.: Codificacion del derecho internacional privado. Revista general de legislacion, lv (1879), 382–395.

[3] Pillet, 112.

[4] For books and articles on the Congress of Montevideo see the following:

Actas de las sesiones del Congreso sud-americano de Derecho internacional privado. Buenos Aires, 1889. 2 edition, 1894.

Congreso juridico sud-americano. Derecho comercial internacional. Montevideo, 1889.

Several conferences have been held at the Hague, in the years 1893, 1894, 1900 and 1904. All the European nations except Turkey and England were represented and protocols were adopted on several points in dispute.[1]

Tratados sancionados por el Congreso sud-americano de derecho internacional privado installado en Montevideo. Buenos Aires, 1889; pp. 72.

Pradier-Fodéré: Le Congrès de droit international Sud-Américain et les traités de Montevideo. (Rev. dr. intern., xxi (1889), p. 217).

Contuzzi: Il trattato de Montevideo del 1889 e la codificazione del diritto internazionale privato presso gli stati dell' America meridionale. Il Filangieri (1889), 521.

Ramirez, G.: El Derecho commercial internacional en el Congreso jurídico sud-americano. Montevideo, 1889.

Segovio, Lisandro: El derecho internacional privado y el Congreso sud-americano de Montevideo. Buenos Aires, 1889.

---

[1] Despagnet, 39; Pillet, 112. For general discussions of the subject, see the following authorities:

Bentwich, N.: The Anglo-Saxon Powers and the Hague Conventions on private international law. Zeitschrift f. Volkerrecht u. Bundesstaatsrecht, vi (1912), 338.

Kuhn, A. K.: Should Great Britain and the United States be represented at the Hague Conferences on private international law? Report presented to the 28th session of the International Law Association, Madrid, 1–6 October, 1913. Compte rendu, London, 1914, 556; Amer. Jour. Int. Law, vii (1913), 774–780.

Schuster, Ernest: The Hague convention on matters of private international law. Journal of the Society of comparative legislation, iii (1898), 428.

Asser, T. M. C. La codification du droit international privé. Le traité du 14 novembre 1896. (Rev. dr. intern., xxviii (1896), 573.)

Asser, T. M. C.: Projets de convention de La Haye pour le droit international privé. (Rev. dr. internat., xxxiii (1901), p. 437.)

Buzzati, J. C.: Les projets de convention de La Haye pour le droit international privé. (Rev. dr. intern., xxxiii (1901), 269.)

Contuzzi, Francesco Paolo: Commentaire théorique et pratique des conventions de La Haye concernant la codification du droit international privé. Paris, 1905.

Jitta, J.: Accession de la Grande-Bretagne, des États du nord, du centre et du sud de l'Amérique et en general des États non-européens aux traités de La Haye sur le droit international privé. Report presented to the 28th session of the International Law Association, Madrid, 1–6 October, 1913. (Compte rendu, London, 1914.)

Lainé, A.: La Conférence de La Haye relative au droit international privé. (Clunet, xxxii (1905), 797; xxxiii (1906), 5, 278, 618, 976; xxxiv (1907), 897.)

Legrand: La Conférence de droit international privé de La Haye. (Rec. de l'Acad. des sciences morales et politiques, Feb., 1894.)

Renault: Le droit international privé et la Conférence de La Haye. (Ann. de l'école libre des sciences politiques, 1894, p. 310.)

Renault: Les Conventions de La Haye (1896 et 1902) sur le droit international privé. Paris, 1903.

In spite of the great desirability of a unification of law, there are enormous difficulties in the way of securing unity. Among neighboring nations governed by the same general system of law, like the states of South America and the

Ville-Urrutia: La Conférence de droit international privé de La Haye. (Rev. d'hist. dipl. 1894, n. 2.)

Zeballos, E. S.: La codification du droit international privé aux Conférences de La Haye (1903–1904). (Bull. argentin de droit international privé. Buenos Aires, 1906, p. 1.)

La cour permanent d'arbitrage de La Haye et le droit international privè et penal. (R. de dr. int. pr., vi (1910), 705.)

Beichmann: De internationale Konferencer i Haag til Behandling af Spørgsmaal vedrørende den internationale Privatret. (Tidskrift for Retsvidenskab, viii (1895), pt. 1.)

Ancili: Das internationale Privatrecht u. seine organische Fortentwicklung durch die Haager Kongresse. (Archiv. für Wirtschaftsphilosophie, 1909, n. 1.)

Beer: Die Kundigung der Haager Familienrechts-Konvention durch Frankreich. (Deutsche Juristen Zeitung, xix (1914), 713.)

Cahn, W.: Der internationale Kongress für internationales Privatrecht im Haag. (Zeitschr. für internation. Privat- und Strafr., iv (1894), 1.)

Dove: Die vertragsm. Fortbildg. d. intern. Priv. R. durch d. Haager Konv. Berlin, 1909.

Kahn, Frantz. Die Haager Staatenkonferenzen. (Zeitschrift für internationales Privat- und Oeffentlichesrecht, xii (1902), 1, 201, xiii (1903), 229, 385.)

Kaufmann: Die neuen Haager Abkommen über das internationale Privatrecht. (Deutsche Juristen-Zeitung, xiii (1908), 1077–1081.)

Meili, F.: Das internationale Privatrecht und die Staatenkonferenzen im Haag. Zürich 1896. 2d ed. Zürich, 1900.

Niemeyer, Theodor: Die Haager Konferenzen über internationales Privatrecht. (Zeitschr. für das Gesammte Handelsr., xlv (N.S. xx), 157.)

Neumeyer, Karl: Das Haager Abkommen über internationales Privatrecht. (Zeitschr. für internat. Privat- und Strafr. ix (1899), 453.)

Schwartz, J.: Ungarns Anschluss an die Haager Familienrechts Konventionen. (Zeitschrift f. intern. Recht., xxii (1912), 418.)

Contuzzi, Francesco Paolo: Le Conferenze di diritto internazionale privato all' Aja. Naples, 1904; pp. 320.

Corsi, Alessandro: La Convenzione di La Aja por la procedura civile. (Riv. di dir. internaz. e di legislaz. compar., March, 1901, p. 128.)

Pierantoni, Augusto: Il diritto internazionale privato e la conferenza diplomatica all' Aja. 1895.

Pierantoni, Augusto: Il diritto civile e la procedure internazionale codificati nella convenzione dell' Aja. Napoli. 1906.

Bustamante, Ant. S.: La Conferencia de El Haya. (Revista del Foro, Havana, March, 1894.)

Cambothecra, X. S.: International Conference at the Hague (in Greek) (Kosmodike, December, 1898).

Mandelstam: The Hague Conferences on private international law (in Russian). 2 vol. Petrograd.

Martens: La Conférence de La Haye sur la codification du droit international privé: (Journal du ministère de l'instruction publique. Petrograd, September, 1900.)

European states, excluding England and Turkey, the difficulties should be little felt, since the differences are only, so to speak, those of individual theory; yet even there no important result has followed the conferences heretofore held. Much blame has been heaped upon England and America for not joining the Hague conferences; yet the countries governed by the common law, whose variations from accepted European doctrine are based not on individual opinion but upon basic differences in legal systems, are certainly not to blame for the failure of the states of Europe, whose law is based upon the single law of Rome, to reach an agreement among themselves as to the rules regulating the Conflict of Laws. There are in fact almost insuperable obstacles in the way of eventual unity between England and America on the one hand and France and Germany on the other. Take, for instance, the rule governing personal status, which is one of the most fundamental rules of the entire subject. All Europe is agreed upon the law of nationality as the basis of personal rights, and demands the acceptance of this rule by the Common Law states. In the latter, however, there are two rooted objections to the acceptance of this new doctrine. In the first place, Great Britain and the United States, the two nations concerned, have no national law whatever. In Great Britain each different part of the Union, England, Scotland and Ireland, and every separate colony has its own individual law, and the same is true of the different states of the American Union. It is therefore impossible to apply national law to personal rights, since no such law exists. On the other hand, in both the nations concerned immigration is freely permitted, and in the United States millions of immigrants from all portions of the old world have settled and formed a home. The democratic constitutions of these nations, however, make it politically desirable to delay the technical naturalization of these new inhabitants for several years, until they have to some extent assimilated the political ideals on which their constitutions depend. To abandon these subjects to the law of their native countries would be most unjust, to make them citizens of their new countries would be impossible. England and America are therefore constrained by circumstances to retain the law of domicil as the law governing personal status, a law which up to the middle of the last century prevailed in every civilized country.

A full discussion of the work of the four conferences and of the international conventions which have resulted therefrom may be found in a note by M. Edouard Oudin in Clunet.[1] A summary follows.

First Conference, 12–27 September, 1893.

The final protocol referred to four matters: marriage; judicial and extra-judicial acts; commissions rogatory; successions, with a preamble, safeguarding public order. No conventions resulted from this conference.[2]

Second Conference, 25 June–13 July, 1894.

The final protocol referred to six matters: marriage; divorce and separation of body; wardship of minors; civil procedure; bankruptcy; successions, wills, and gifts *causa mortis.*[3]

A convention on civil procedure, as a result of this conference, was formed in 1896,[4] but was superseded by the later convention of 1905. These conventions dealt with several matters: the proof and execution of foreign judgments and other formal acts; commissions rogatory; the *cautio judicatum solvi;* gratuitous assistance to foreign litigants; and arrest.[5]

[1] Clunet xli (1914), 876–882.

[2] The text of the resolutions may be found in Clunet xx (1893), 1276. See upon this conference the following authorities:

Actes de la conférence de La Haye, chargée de réglementer diverses matières de droit international privé. La Haye, 1893.

Conférence de droit international privé tenue à La Haye, 12–27 September, 1893, Documents. (Archives diplomatiques, 1894, 2, part 2, p. 57.)

The Codification of Private International Law [The Conference of 1893, with its Protocol]. Law Jour. xxx (1893), 226, 520.

Asser, T. M. C.: Communication sur la Conférence internationale de La Haye de 1893 pour la codification du droit international privé. (Annuaire de l'Institut de droit international, xiii, p. 369.)

Lainé, A.: La Conférence de La Haye relative au droit international privé. (Clunet, xxi (1894), 5, 236.)

Meili, F.: Der erste europäische Staatenkongress über internationales Privatrecht. (Allgemeine oesterreichische Gerichtszeitung, xlv, 1894.)

[3] The text of the resolutions are in Clunet xxii (1895), 197.

[4] The text of this convention may be found in Clunet xxvi (1899), 626; Bulletin des Conférences de la Haye, The Hague, 1907, p. 9.

[5] Upon the second conference see the following authorities:

Actes de la deuxième conférence de La Haye, chargée de réglementer diverses matières de droit international privé. La Haye, 1894.

Asser, T. M. C.: La codification du droit international privé (2d Conférence de La Haye, du 25 juin au 13 juillet, 1894). (Rev. dr. intern., xxvi (1894), 349.)

Third Conference, 20 May–18 June, 1900.

Four projects were adopted at this conference: for conventions upon marriage, upon divorce and separation of body, and for the wardship of minors; and for the further discussion of the subject of successions.[1] As a result of this conference, three conventions were issued, June 12, 1902, on the subjects of marriage, divorce, and guardianship.[2] These conventions have been successively ratified by the Netherlands, Sweden, Luxembourg, Roumania, Germany, Belgium, Switzerland, Italy, Portugal, and Hungary. Austria, though a party to the conference, never ratified the conventions; and France, having once ratified them, withdrew her ratification and denounced the conventions.

De Herrera: La seconde Conférence de La Haye sur le droit international privé. (Revista contempor., 30 May, 1895.)

Lainé, A.: La Conférence de La Haye relative au droit international privé (2d session). (Clunet, xxvii (1895), 465, 734.)

Cahn, W.: Zweiter internationaler Kongress für internationales Privatrecht im Haag. (Zeitschr. für internat. Privat- und Strafr., v (1895), 1.)

Breukelman: De tweede conferentie voor het Internationaal Privaatrecht. (Themis, fasc. 55, n. 4.)

Upon the Convention of 1896 see the following:

Asser, T. M. C.: La Convention de La Haye du 14 novembre, 1896. Paris, 1901.

Heidecker: Das Haager internationale Uebereinkommen von 1896, betreffend das Civilprozessverfahren. (Zeitschr. für deutsch. civilprozess, xxiii, 164.)

[1] Upon this conference see the following authorities:

Documents relatifs à la troisième Conférence de La Haye pour le droit international privé. 2 vol. The Hague, 1900.

Lainé, A.: La Conférence diplomatique de La Haye relative au droit international privé (3e session, 29 mai–19 juin, 1900). (Clunet, xxxiii (1901), 5, 231.)

Olivi, L.: Le projet néerlandais de programme pour la troisième Conférence de droit international privé. (Rev. dr. intern., xxxii (1900), 136.)

Buzatti, G. C.: Intorno al "projet de programme" della terza conferenza di diritto internazionale privato. Turin, 1899, pp. 40.

[2] For the texts, see Clunet, xxxi (1904), 476; Bulletin des conférences de la Haye, The Hague, 1907, 21–35. On the conventions see:

Buzatti, G. C.: Trattato di diritto internazionale privato secondo le Convenzioni dell' Aja. I.: Introduzione, Il matrimonio secondo la Convenzione dell' Aja de 21 giugno 1902. Milan, 1907.

Buzatti, G. C.: Le droit international privé d'après les Conventions de La Haye (Trad. de. Rey). I. Le Mariage d'après la Convention du 12 juin 1902. Paris, 1911.

Todaro, Della Galia: La Convenzione dell' Aja del 12 giougn 1902. (Rivista di legislazione comparata, 1903, p. 40.)

Oliver, Bienvenido: Los Convenios de El Haya sobre matrimonio, divorca, tutela, succesiones, quiebras y concursos considerados desde el punto de vista de la legislacion española. (Revista de derecho internacional y política externa, i (1905), 107.)

Fourth Conference, 16 May–7 June, 1904.

Five matters were dealt with in the final protocol: civil procedure; the effects of marriage upon property; interdiction; successions and wills; bankruptcy.[1] Three conventions resulted, on civil procedure, the effects of marriage, and interdiction.[2] The first has been ratified by Germany, Austria-Hungary, Belgium, Denmark, Spain, France, Italy, Luxembourg, Norway, Netherlands, Portugal, Roumania, Russia, Sweden and Switzerland. The second was ratified by Germany, Belgium, France, Italy, Netherlands, Portugal, Roumania and Sweden; the third by the same nations, omitting Belgium, and adding Austria-Hungary.

§ 43. Efforts to Unify the Law: Comparative Study. — Before international agreements to unify the law by treaty-codification can be successful, fuller knowledge of current opinions and of the various doctrines actually applied by the courts of the various civilized countries must be acquired. A most important step toward the acquiescence of such knowledge was taken in the founding of Clunet's Journal of Private International Law in 1874. In the pages of this publication one may read theoretical articles on the conflict of laws, as well as practical treatises on the doctrines of each state; and there are contained also selected decisions of courts of all nations upon controverted questions of the conflict of laws. Too great stress cannot be laid upon the contribution of this Journal, not only in furnishing information as to the position of each nation with regard to the science of the subject, but also in hastening the final achievement of unity. In recent years other influential journals have been established, which have in general followed in the same lines and wielded the same influence.[3] Mention should

[1] The following authorities may be consulted:

Baldwin, S. E.: The Hague Conference of 1904 for the advancement of private international law. (Reprinted from Yale Law Journal.) New Haven, 1904.

Missir, P.: La quatrième conférence de droit international privé de La Haye (successions et testaments). (R. de dr. int. pr., ii (1906), 644–658.)

Breukelman: De vierde conferentie voor het international privaatr. (Themis, lxvii, 1.)

[2] For the text of these Conventions see Bulletin des conférences de la Haye. The Hague, 1907, pp. 13–17, 27–29, 36–38. See also Cluzel (G.). La nouvelle Convention de la Haye sur la procedure civile. Paris, 1910.

[3] Other periodicals dealing with the Conflict of Laws which also collect decisions are Zeitschrift für internationales Privat- und Strafrecht, since 1890; Revue de Droit International Privé, since 1905.

also be made of the excellent statement by Professor Weiss [1] of the doctrines prevailing in modern nations.

Another important step toward mutual understanding is the foundation of chairs of Private International Law or of courses in the Conflict of Laws at the Universities. Fifty years ago there was little serious attention given to the study of the subject. A special course in Private International Law in the French universities was created in 1880.[2] Today it is a regular subject of instruction in the faculties of law of both hemispheres.

[1] Weiss, iii, 185 *et seq.*

[2] Lainé, i, xvi.

CHAPTER III

CURRENT DOCTRINE ON THE CONFLICT OF LAWS

§ 51. The three modern systems of thought.
52. The statutory system.
53. The statute real and the statute personal.
54. Modern statement of the statutory theory.
55. Domicil or nationality as the basis of personal rights.
56. Considerations in favor of the doctrine of nationality.
57. Objections to the doctrine.
58. The doctrine of the *renvoi*.
59. The exception of public order.
60. The principle of autonomy of the will.
61. Pillet's theory of the continuity and the generality of law.
62. Pillet's later theories.
63. The international system.
64. The early German school: Wächter, Schäffner, Savigny.
65. The doctrine of von Bar.
66. The doctrine of Zitelmann.
67. The world-law of Jitta.
68. Criticism of the international theories.
69. International legal systems.
70. The territorial system.
71. The theory of comity.
72. The doctrine of Story.
73. The doctrine of vested rights.
74. Dicey.
75. The doctrine of vested rights in France: Vareilles-Sommières.
76. Bustamante.
77. Criticisms of the territorial theories.
78. Answer to the criticisms.

§ 51. The Three Modern Systems of Thought. — The history of doctrine has been traced to the time of Story; who, gathering together the conclusions of the Dutch school and the decisions of common-law courts, stated the modern problems. His own solution has formed the basis of common-law doctrine on the subject. But other systems of reasoning have grown up or persisted, more or less influenced by Story's work, but more or less divergent in results. Every system necessarily contains within itself a large degree of unassailable truth; each system also necessarily accepts a large body of doctrine which is common to all. Every scholar, accepting this common doctrine, works out, as his contribution to the study of the subject, under the influence of that system of reasoning which is most congenial to his mind or which happens to be most familiar to him, some peculiar aspect of the truth. It follows, therefore, that while all writers on the Conflict of Laws may be roughly grouped into a few classes — into three, according to the classification here adopted — these classes necessarily grade into one another, and a scholar may pursue an eclectic course, following the typical views now of one class, now of another.

This being premised, we may examine the three principal systems of thought now current. The first of these systems supposes two independent laws, effective at the same time and place, and subject to a possible choice between them. The second supposes a single set of principles, binding on all nations, by which the need of any choice between two independent laws is prevented. The third asserts that no law can exist as such except the law of the land; but that it is a principle of every civilized law that vested rights shall be protected, and therefore that in each country it is sought to find what rights have arisen anywhere, and to recognize them, applying in all else the law of the land to every question. These systems may for convenience be called respectively statutory, international and territorial.

It will be clear that the first of these systems of thought is a modern expression of the older doctrine of the statutists. The others are new doctrines, derived from modern ideas about rights and the jurisdiction of states. No one has better explained the origin and growth of these new doctrines and their effect upon our subject than Professor Eugen Ehrlich.

"Our modern conception, according to which law is before all an expression of the will of the state, and the judge is an officer of state who is to administer this state law by virtue of the command and in the name of the state, can be found already in embryo with the Romans of the later empire and with the English of the middle ages; but it is only at the end of the middle ages that this conception was developed on the European Continent. This change of conception must evidently react on private international law; for it is now the state alone which should decide what law can be applied within its boundaries. The judge has no longer to ask what law is applicable to each separate case as it arises. An officer of state, he must apply the law which the state orders him to apply. In future, when one speaks of national law, one understands more and more not the law of a people, that is, of a community of men united in race, language, history or degree of civilization, but the law of a state, that is, of a sovereign organization with a fixed territory, containing perhaps several different races or perhaps only a part or a small fraction of a race. In future this state expresses the intention of binding by its law every person and thing found upon its territory; an intention which it is unable to carry out, though it uses every means open to its law.

"On the other hand, Hugo Grotius and his disciples, with their theory of the law of nature and of nations, have not labored in vain. Everywhere at the end of the seventeenth and in the eighteenth centuries the truth is being recognized that states in fixing their law have in certain particulars duties toward mankind. We are saying, in certain connections, *mankind;* a notion which evidently includes foreigners. Thus is born—first in the minds of jurists of the Netherlands — the idea of a *comitas gentium.* The relations between states result for each state in the obligation of giving to a certain extent an opportunity for the application of the law of other states.

"Two influences from that time are opposed to each other in the matter of private international law. One of these is the principle of the complete power of the state over its own territory; . . . the other attaches an especial importance to the *comitas gentium.* No state can apply its own law in a way contrary to the obligation which its international situation imposes upon it and which the law of nations creates for it."[1]

Other classifications of doctrine might equally well be made. In an acute article in a German periodical[2] Dr. Cybichowski divides the opinions which obtain today into four groups.

First group. The theory of this group, he says, is that private international law is an authoritative provision of the national law. "This might be designated as the provision-principle, as another theory is called the collision-principle." Since this theory obviously involves each state having its own provisions, it also includes a fixing of the jurisdiction of each state to apply its own provisions to a juridical relation. Thus Bar is quoted as speaking of the rules

[1] Rev. dr. int. pr., iv (1908), 911, 912.

[2] Zeitschr. für Int. Pr. u. Strafr., xx (1910), 367–398.

of legislative jurisdiction; and Pillet's phrase is cited: "Every question of conflict of laws is a question of conflict of sovereignties." This branch of law, although it concerns private rights, is not in itself private law, and is to be regarded as a branch of public law.

Second group. The doctrine held by the second group is that each state is subject to the *duty* of using a general determined principle for settling the questions; what might be called the theory of obligatory national law. Each state, according to this doctrine, is bound to have a private international law.[1]

Third group. The theory of authors of this group assumes an international doctrine, outside and above the national law, which of its own force governs all juridical relations having any element foreign to the local law. Each citizen is bound, not only by the local law, but by an extra-national law.

Fourth group. Free law. The judge, not being helped by the other theories, uses his judgment. This is not an uncontrolled judgment, however. Thus von Wächter says that the judge must make use of his "Recht" if sense, spirit and tendency of his statute do not lead to the consideration of the foreign "Recht."[2] Bar says: "Private international law does not require, as a condition precedent to its existence, that it should have been constituted, so far as its leading principles or doctrines are concerned, by treaties or by legislation. It exists because it is a necessity, and it is the force of circumstances, the nature of things that makes it so."[3] And compare Jitta's striking phrase,[4] "Positive law (*loi*) is not the source but the product of legal principles (*droit*)."

The doctrine of Cybichowski's second group is, it would seem, a necessary part of that of the first group. Granting that all juridical relations brought before a court are to be determined by the law of that court, that law must apply some rule to them, a rule by which it feels itself bound; and this rule must be based upon the felt requirements of justice. Scholars of the first group, therefore, would, if they dealt with the subject, adhere to the views of the second group. These two groups, then, include all authors who accept the territorial system of thought. The third and fourth groups are internationalist, distinguished only as the fourth accepts an international common law. Again it seems that authors of the third group would accept the doctrines of the fourth. The theories of the statutists are not considered, although it is probably to them that the author meant to apply his term "collision-principle."

[1] Citing Kahn in Jhering's Jahrb. lx, 40.

[2] Archiv für civ. pr. xxiv, 311.

[3] 2d ed. (Gillespie's tr.), x.

[4] Méthode, 42.

§ 52. The Statutory System. — The statutory system of thought has of course had the widest vogue. It started in Italy in the early middle ages, and extended to France and the Netherlands; it influenced Story's cosmopolitan work; it had a rebirth in Italy in the middle of the 19th century, and again spread through France and Germany.

The particular theories to which it has given birth are as various as its extent is wide. From the almost unrestrained personality of law which the Italians urge to the almost unrestrained territoriality of Huber and Story the space is filled by all shades of variation. Given a doctrine that one must find a rule which will give the precedence now to one law, now to another, the variations of choice are infinite.

The possibility of two simultaneously applicable laws is always based, in the last analysis, on the hypothesis of a law obligatory on a person. No one has expressed this underlying spirit better than Vareilles-Sommières.[1]

> "To govern things is merely to govern the conduct of persons with relation to things. The law really governs persons alone, the only things capable of receiving and executing a command. To ask what persons and what things the law governs is therefore to ask what persons it governs, and with reference to what things it governs persons. And since to govern persons with relation to a thing is to govern their conduct in one particular, the two questions may be advantageously consolidated into one: of what persons does a law govern the conduct?"

According to this conception, it is possible that one law will govern a person, while another law governs the territory whereon he stands or the other person with whom he has juridical relations. In such a case, two laws would be active in the same place and at the same time; and some method must be discovered of selecting one of them to prevail. The law that should do this thing might well be called "a science of sacrifices,"[2] "a law in the brambles."[3]

§ 53. The Statute Real and the Statute Personal. — The original meaning of "statute" in the phrases "statute real" and "statute personal" was, as has been seen, a local

[1] V.-S., i, 1. [2] Weiss, iii, 5, quoting Pillet.

[3] Thaller, Des faillités en droit comparé, ii, 273; cited in Vareilles-Sommières, i, v.

statutory provision which derogated from the general imperial law. It was, therefore, by no means to be expected that these categories should between them exhaust the whole law. The main body of law was still imperial; but of the statutes which modified it in certain particulars some applied to persons and some to property.[1] This fact will explain the original doctrine. When the phrases came to be applied to a different condition of affairs, where they were to cover the entire body of law, the meaning was changed, without however abandoning the doctrines which had become current about them. The statute personal now became the personal law in general, the law made by a sovereign for the government of his people; the statute real became the territorial law. The two phrases between them now covered the whole body of law. A few writers, still influenced by the old meaning of statute real, called for a third category of statute mixed, which, however, meant the law of the land applied to acts, not to things; statutes real and statutes mixed covering between them the entire territorial law.

There was obviously ample ground for difference of opinion as to where the personal and where the territorial law applied; and the differences between the numerous writers was in their rules for determining this question. No agreement was ever reached on the point; as Jitta says, the theory of statutes never succeeded in clearing itself of ambiguities.[2] Nor could this be otherwise in the nature of things. For every law has both a territorial and a personal application; and where a conflict arises, it is because one sovereign wishes to apply his own law to a juridical relation arising on his territory, while another wishes to throw around his own subject, who is one of the parties to the relation, the protection of his personal law. Which of the two independent sovereigns should yield is a question not susceptible of a solution upon which all parties would agree. This is the weakest point in the statutory theory.

A glance at the summary of the various theories in Livermore's Dissertations will make this point clear.[3]

§ 54. **Modern Statement of the Statutory Theory.** — No one has succeeded in stating the statutory theory more

[1] Vareilles-Sommières, i, vii. [2] Jitta, 26. [3] *Ante*, § 38.

clearly and forcibly than Professor Weiss. Weiss represents the modern French neo-statutists, a school which has not been greatly influenced by the extreme nationalist doctrines of the Italian and Belgian schools. Weiss's statement of the statutory theory is as follows: [1]

"Law is not in itself either always and only territorial or always and only personal. There are, no doubt, territorial laws, but there are also personal laws. Let us go further: the same law may be and should be at once territorial and personal, according to certain rules.

"What is the true function of law? It is to provide for the interests of those for whom it is made, that is, for the interests of citizens of the state which has given it force. But it ought also to take care that the social organization, which is the best safeguard of individual interests, should not be compromised. It can protect the citizen, its true function, only if it protects at the same time the society of which he is a part, and the state which represents this society. Like sovereignty, of which it is the formulated expression, law exercises necessarily a double empire. On one side it is its duty to issue commands to persons subject to it, in whatever place they may be; so that the tie which unites them to itself shall not be broken. On the other side, it may in the name of the interest of the preservation of local society command foreigners from every nation who by passing the frontier enter within the material sphere of its application. It is within its function to say to them, *intrasti urbem; ambula circa ritum ejus*. . . . Of these two laws, the personal and the local law, which claim to reach a person and whose provisions are perhaps quite different, which shall prevail? It is not easy to say. And the difficulty which arises from the collision of the territorial with the personal law is even increased, if we suppose that the same legal relation involves several individuals with different personal laws; or if the same individual is bound to a number of states by different personal ties, as by belonging to one by nationality, to another by domicil. Admitting in this case the principle that the personal law should have the preference, to which personal law should this preference be given? . . . It is to this situation and to similar situations that one gives the name of Conflict of Laws. There is a conflict when two or more laws are in competition relatively to a single person, to a single thing, to a single act, and a doubt arises as to which law ought to be applied to the exclusion of the others."

[1] Weiss, iii, 3, 4.

§ 55. Domicil or Nationality as the Basis of Personal Rights. — Before examining this theory of personal law in action, it will be well first to examine a question which has recently been brought to the front: shall one's personal law be taken to be the law of his domicil or the law of his nation?

Until a hundred years ago, this question not had been raised at all. Most practical questions had arisen out of a difference of laws within the same nation: the Italian cities within the empire, the French or Dutch provinces, the German or American or Italian states. The laws concerned being internal, the difference between the persons was one of domicil, not of nation. When England was first brought to deal freely with foreigners, and therefore needed a system to avoid conflict, she accepted from Europe the doctrine that domicil governs personal rights; and this doctrine is still held as part of the common law in England and America.

On the continent of Europe, however, a profound change of thought was wrought by the French revolution. The Code Napoléon, following the current of the new thought, swept away provincial lines and laws, and provided one law for France. This legislation, and the new feeling for nationality which caused it, had a profound effect. The first expression of this new feeling by a writer on the Conflict of Laws was by an Italian, Mancini,[1] whose notable address,[2] delivered in 1851, was a characteristic expression of the Italian's aspiration for national unity. It expressed to the full the feeling of nationality which gave rise to the French Codes, a half century earlier, and which finally culminated in the formation of the Italian Kingdom. This great address did not contain any detailed application of its principles to the conflict of laws, but in a paper read before the Institute of International Law, in 1874, Mancini more fully applied his doctrine to the conflict of laws.[3]

A few paragraphs may be quoted from this paper. . . . "Climate, temperature, geographical situation, whether mountainous or

[1] See Catellani, ii, 129; Laurent, i, 630; Meili, i, 120; Weiss, iii, 62.

[2] Della nazionalita come fondamento del diritto delle genti, in his Prelezioni, Naples, 1873.

[3] Clunet, i (1874), 221–239, 285–304; the extract here given is found on p. 293.

maritime, the nature and fertility of the soil, difference of needs and of customs, determine with every people, almost without exception, their legal system. They determine in a greater or less degree the precocity of physical and moral development, the organization of family relations, the prevailing occupations, and the nature of business and commercial relations which usually occur. For these reasons the status and capacity of persons in the private law of the different nations must differ in accordance with this difference in conditions. . . . Just as in the relations of private law within a state, the principle of liberty which protects the legitimate and inviolable autonomy of the individual lays down the limits of the political and legislative power, so in the same way the principle of nationality lays down a similar limit between foreigners and natives. The reason is found in individual and reciprocal autonomy, a legitimate and inviolable autonomy; and just as the law of nationality which belongs to the entire people does not substantially differ from the law of liberty which belongs to the individuals, so it follows that the individual may demand from nations and states, in the name of the principle of foreign nationality, the same respect for his inheritance of private law that he demands from his own state. Such a guarantee is therefore an act of strict justice, and an inviolable duty. This duty results from a higher principle than the mutual courtesy or good feeling of states, or the utility or interest of a nation, although this utility and interest require the rigorous observance of the duty."

Mancini's doctrine became the basis of the Italian school of writers on the conflict of laws.[1] The fundamental principle of this school is that law is applicable primarily to persons, the law of a nation to all the citizens of that nation, wherever they may go; and that any limitation on this general doctrine comes by way of exception, the principal exception comprising "laws of public order," *i.e.*, laws which the sovereign of the territory imposes upon his territory as important for the conduct of government. It is formulated by Weiss as follows:[2]

"When a law deals with a private interest, it always has the object of utility to the person; it can govern only those for whom it has been made; but as to them, it ought on principle to govern them in all places, and in all their juridical

[1] See Catellani, ii, 118, 170; Bar, 63; Meili, i, 121; Rolin, i, 109; Weiss, iii, 61; Vareilles-Sommières, i, 98.

[2] Weiss, iii, 63.

relations, saving the limitations and exceptions which result from the *international public order*, the rule *locus regit actum*, and the autonomy of the will."

The principles of this school have had a great effect throughout Europe. In Italy, Mancini has been followed by Esperson, Fiore, Fusinato, and a number of less generally known authors; in Belgium, Laurent has accepted them with blind enthusiasm; in France, Durand, Surville and Arthuys, Audinet and Weiss have accepted nationality in place of domicil as the basis of personal rights, and the same principle is the basis of Pillet's original theory. Even in Germany the influence of the Italian school has been considerable.[1] In Spain, the Italian school is criticised, yet the conclusions of the important Spanish authors, like Torres-Campos and Bustamante,[2] are profoundly colored by its doctrines.

§ 56. Considerations in Favor of the Doctrine of Nationality. — The new doctrine has much to commend it. It is simple, it is natural, and so far as nationality and race are identical, it protects racial peculiarities. It is a doctrine which, recognizing the legal equality of all nations, offers the strongest possible inducement to international agreement as to the principles of private international law. "The principle of personality is the only one which can result in a realization of what Demangeat calls the dream of a single law uniting all men." [3] And the doctrine seems without question to be the logical conclusion of the statutory theory. It is thus that Laurent sees it:[4]

"If, then, laws of status are personal, it is because they are the product of those thousand and one physical, intellectual, and moral circumstances which make up nationality. They are personal because they are national. They should consequently follow the person everywhere, because he carries his nationality with him. Of national laws, one may say all that the ancient jurists said of statutes personal. They do more than stick to our bones, they circulate in our veins with our blood, for we receive our nationality with the blood which our parents transmit to us . . . The realists think that sovereign power should embrace all persons and things which are within the territory or which make up the country.

[1] Meili, i, 121.
[2] Catellani, ii, 436.
[3] Laurent, i, 39.
[4] Laurent, ii, 632–636.

That is the feudal system which confounds sovereignty with property. The Italian publicists say, as I do, that sovereignty is a mission rather than a power. It has for its object the defense and preservation of society and it should be invested with such powers as would permit it to fulfill its mission. Each nation, says Fiore, is organized politically in such a way as is most conformable to the needs of the people and their degree of civilization. It has the right to determine the conditions necessary to its preservation. Sovereignty, consequently, insures the regular development of individual liberty, and represses the abuse of it. It provides for the administrative, economic and military interests; it protects the rights of those who live upon its territory. . . . This principle fully declares the right of sovereignty. There is, in international laws, as well as in national laws, a sphere where the right of society dominates, and another where the right of the individual dominates. Society is sovereign in its sphere, and the individual in his. . . . When it is a question as to private interests, sovereignty is out of the case and consequently each nation may and ought to permit the foreigner to evoke his personal, that is his national, law. So far from this extension of personal laws compromising national sovereignty, it is a striking preservation of it, for it is as national laws that personal laws receive their application everywhere."

§ 57. **Objections to the Doctrine.** — Interesting and attractive as are the arguments in favor of the adoption of nationality as the determinant of personal rights, there is unfortunately a practical difficulty which makes it impossible for a federated nation like the United States to accept the doctrine. Since each state is a separate legal unit, while all form a single nation, there is no law of the nation which can fix rights. Recognizing this fact, a few authors have suggested that each legal unit should be treated for this purpose as if it were a nation. But it is submitted that this would result in confusion and difficulty out of all proportion to the theoretical gain.

Sir Frederick Pollock has stated the practical objections to the adoption of this theory in Great Britain and America in his accustomed felicitous way:

"Nationality would be very well if each international unit had one, and only one, system of law within its allegiance; and so it seems the natural and sufficient criterion to a French or Italian lawyer (subject to some little difficulties with African and Indo-

Chinese customs). But it is quite unmanageable for a national sovereignty including many laws and jurisdictions, such as ours or that of the United States." [1]

The impossibility of applying the law of the nation to determining the personal status of a citizen of the United States has been stated more at length by Wharton.[2]

"Nationality leaves the question still open in Great Britain and Germany, where there are several territorial jurisprudences established under the same national head. In the United States, this union of sovereign jurisprudences under Federal nationality is established by the most solemn constitutional enactments as well as by the results of the late civil war. Each State of the North American Union has its own distinctive law. . . . If the status of a citizen of the United States, therefore, is to be in litigation abroad, it would be idle to appeal to his nationality. His nationality would determine nothing. His only nationality is that of the United States; and the United States government, while determining his political status, does not determine his personal status. To get at that status we have to inquire in what State he is domiciled. Here, then, we find ourselves in direct opposition to the new Italian school. The function of Italy, as reconstructed, is to fit a territory to a compact and homogeneous nation. Ours has been to adapt a nation composed of various elements to a territory containing almost every variety of soil, of climate, of traditions, of capacities for cultivation. Nationality, therefore, in Italy means uniformity of jurisprudence; and to know what is the personal law of an Italian, we have simply to inquire what is the jurisprudence of Italy. But nationality in the United States determines, with the single exception of bankruptcy, only political status; and to ascertain what is the personal status of a citizen of the United States, we have to inquire in what State he is domiciled."

A more special difficulty in adopting the new doctrine is felt in the United States, where naturalization is, for political reasons, only granted after several years' residence. To treat a man who had settled down in a new country, accepted its ways of thought and action, and identified himself with its affairs, according to the laws of some distant nationality of birth, now quite alien to him, would be unjust.

Not understanding these difficulties, certain European

[1] Law Quart. Rev. xxxi (1915), 106. See also J. Westlake in Soc. Sci. Asso. 1880, 141.

[2] So. Law Rev. N. S., vi (1880), 680, 700.

jurists have blamed England and the United States as feudal, illiberal and unprogressive because they have not followed many European states in substituting nationality for domicil as the basis of personal rights. It is submitted that these countries are not open to criticism on such grounds. Until some way can be found of substituting state for nation, and taking care of the man waiting naturalization, the United States, at least, must continue to govern personal status by the law of the domicil.

§ 58. **The Doctrine of the *Renvoi*.** — Wherever the statutory theory is accepted, and the laws of the two states concerned differ as to whether the law of the nation or the law of the domicil shall be applied, a troublesome doubt appears. Where the law of the forum provides that a juridical event shall be governed by a certain foreign law, and that foreign law in turn remits (*renvoie*) it to the law of the forum to determine by its law, the situation arises which has been termed the *renvoi*; and this situation has proved puzzling to courts and authors.[1] Suppose, for instance, that a for-

[1] The doctrine of the *renvoi* has given rise to a multitude of articles. The following may be consulted:

English:

Abbot, Edwin H.: Is the *renvoi* a part of the common law? Law Q. Rev. xxiv (1908), 133.

Baty, Th.: Note in Law Mag. and Rev. (1899), 100.

Bodington, Oliver E.: A breach in the doctrine of *renvoi*. Law Times, cxx, 237.

Brown, W. Jethro: *In re* Johnson, Law Q. Rev. xxv (1909), 145.

Lorenzen, Ernest G.: The *renvoi* theory and the application of foreign law, Columbia L. Rev., x (1910), 190, 327; an exhaustive and admirable article, to which the reader who wishes to follow further the doctrines of European jurists may be referred.

French:

Asser, M. T. C.: La question du renvoi devant la troisième conférence du droit international privé. Rev. dr. int. (1900), 316.

Quelques observations concernant la théorie ou le système du renvoi. Clunet, xxxii (1905), 40.

Audinet, E.: Notes, Sirey, 1899, 2, 105; 1908, 2, 257.

Bartin, E.: Les conflits entre dispositions législatives de droit international privé. Rev. dr. int. (1898), 129, 272.

Beirao, F. A. da Veiga: La théorie du renvoi devant les tribunaux portugais. Clunet, xxxv (1908), 367.

Buzzati et Lainé: Des conflits entre les dispositions législatives de droit international privé. Avant-rapport à l'Institut de droit international. Annuaire de l'Institut, xvi, 47, xvii, 14.

eigner domiciled in France dies, leaving a will; by the law of his country testamentary capacity is determined by the

---

Colin, A.: Note in Dalloz, 1907, 2, 1.

Dios Trias: De la théorie du renvoi devant les Tribunaux espagnols. Clunet, xxviii (1901), 905.

Fiore, Pasquale: Du conflit entre les dispositions législatives du droit international privé. Clunet, xxviii (1901), 424, 681.

Keidel, J.: De la théorie du renvoi en droit international privé, selon le nouveau Code civil allemand. Clunet, xxviii (1901), 82.

Labbé, J. E.: Du conflit entre la loi nationale du juge saisi et une loi étrangère relativement à la détermination de la loi applicable à la cause. Clunet, xii (1885), 5.

Lainé, A.: De l'application des lois étrangères en France et en Belgique. Clunet, xxiii (1896), 241, 481.

La théorie du renvoi en droit international privé. Rev. dr. int. pr., ii (1906), 605; iii (1907), 43, 313, 661; iv (1908), 720; v (1909), 12; reprinted, Paris, 1909.

Ligeoix: La théorie du renvoi et la nature juridique des règles de droit international privé. Clunet, xxx (1903), 481; xxxi, 551.

La question du renvoi en droit international privé. Périgueux, 1902.

Mazas: De la combination entre la théorie du renvoi et celle de l'autonomie de la volonté à propos du régime matrimonial. Clunet, xxxiv (1907), 603.

Pic, P.: De l'état et de la capacité des étrangères dans les pays de capitulation, et notamment en Tunisie. Théorie du renvoi. (Dalloz, 99, 2, 410.)

Potu, E.: La question du renvoi de droit international privé. Paris, 1913.

Sewell, J. T. B.: Du renvoi d'après la jurisprudence anglaise en matière de succession mobilière. Rev. dr. int. pr., iii (1907), 507.

Surville, F.: La question du renvoi dans les litiges internationaux. Rev. crit., 1899, 215.

Wagner, Albert: Note, Dalloz, 1910, 2, 145.

Westlake: Note sur les conflits entre les dispositions legislatives de droit international privé. Annuaire de l'Institut de droit international, xviii, 35.

German:

Bar: Die Rückverweisung im internationalen Privatrecht. Zeitschr. für internat. Privat- und Strafr., viii (1898), 177.

Buzzati, J. C.: Nochmals die Rückverweisung im internationalen Privatrecht. Zeitschr. für internat. Privat- und Strafr., viii (1898), 44.

Die Frage der Rückverweisung vor dem Institut de droit international. Zeitschr. für internat. Privat- und Strafr. xi (1901), 3.

Kahn, Franz: Der Grundsatz der Rückverweisung im deutschen bürgerlichen Gesetzbuch und auf dem Haager Kongress für internationales Privatrecht. Jherings Jahrbücher, xxiv (1896), 366.

Klein: Die Rück- und Weiterverweisung im internationalen Privatrecht. Arch. f. bürg. Recht, xxvii (1906), 252.

Italian:

Buzzati, J. C.: Des conflits entre les dispositions législatives de droit international privé. Rivista di diritto internazionale e di legislazione comparata, i (1), p. 49.

La questione del rinvio davanti all' institutio di diritto internazionale. Rivista di diritto internazionale e di legislazione comparata, 1901, 2.

El Rinvio: Rivista del foro, June and July, 1899, 181.

law of his domicil, by the law of France such capacity is determined by the law of his own country. France sends the question to the law of his country; that law remits it to the law of France, his domicil; and so the question is absorbed into an apparently endless circle.

Three courses are open to the law of the forum:

1. To refuse the *renvoi*, remit the case in turn to the foreign law, and thus engage in a perpetual deadlock.

2. To accept the *renvoi* and decide the question in accordance with the terms of its own law, on the ground that the attempt to settle it in accordance with the foreign law has failed: "an expedient resorted to in order to reach a solution." [1]

3. To disregard the *renvoi* and decide the question in accordance with the terms of the foreign law, on the ground that the foreign substantive law alone concerns the question, and there is no submission to the foreign doctrines as to the conflict of laws.

The second course has its supporters; but on the whole the partisans of the third course prevail.[2]

"The science of private international law has as its object to designate directly the very law which is to regulate a juridical relation, and it should not restrain itself to referring to the laws in force in a state for the solution of conflicts of international law.

"When the science teaches us, for example, that the status of

---

Cavaglierei: La teoria del rinvio in qualche sua speciale manifestazione. Il Filangieri, xxx (1905), no. 5; reprinted, Milan, 1905.

Fiore, Pasquale: Dei conflitti tra le disposizioni legislative di diritto internazionale privato. Giurisprudenza italiana, lii (1900), 129–158; reprinted, Turin, 1900.

Lué, G. B.: L'applicabilità della legge di rinvio nel diritto internazionale privato. Il Filangieri, xxiii, 721.

For discussions in treatises, see: Bate, Notes on the doctrine of renvoi, London, 1904; Dicey, 715–723; Westlake, 5th ed., 25–42; Pillet, 155–166; Vareilles-Sommières, ii, 96–98; Weiss, iii, 77–81; Niemeyer, Methodik, 15, 17; Niemeyer, Kodifikation, 80–86; Zitelmann, i, 238–248; Anzilotti, La questione del rinvio, etc., in Studi, 193; Buzzati, Theoria del Rinvio nel diritto internazionale, Milan, 1898.

---

[1] Lorenzen in Col. Law Rev., x, 199.

[2] A list of jurists who have expressed an opinion on the subject (many of them only in the discussions of the Institute of International Law), on one side or the other, will be found in the article already referred to, by Professor Lorenzen, Col. Law Rev., x, 194 *n*.

an individual is governed by his national law, it is the national law regulating the status that is meant, and not a disposition of the national law which might declare another law, for example, that of the domicil of the individual, applicable to this status.

"The science, in declaring applicable the national law, or the law of the situation of the property, or any other law, has been guided by considerations derived from the nature of the legal relationship in question. It is, therefore, the law itself indicated by it that must be applied, and not another law to which it refers and which could not have been considered by the science."[1]

We may be the less troubled about the finer points of this discussion because the territorial theory of the conflict of laws, which is accepted by the American courts, has no room for any doctrine of *renvoi.* If an American court, having according to the territorial theory to apply its own law to existing rights, finds that a right has, by its law, arisen under another law, it has only to learn the terms of that law and the nature of the right which it created; if, on the other hand, it is a question of a new right, created by the law of the forum, but the latter law in creating the right acts in accordance with the provisions of some foreign law, as for instance the law of a foreign domicil, again it has only to learn the terms of that particular foreign law and apply it. In no case is the court concerned with the views of any foreign court on a question of the conflict of laws.

§ 59. **The Exception of Public Order.** — As the theory of comity is put forward to limit the principle of absolute territoriality, so the advocates of the modern Italo-French theories limit the principle of absolute personality of law by two exceptions: that of "public order" and that of "autonomy of the will."

The principle of "public order" is universally accepted, not only by the modern statutists but also by the international school.[2] It is, in brief, that any regulation of the

[1] Asser in Clunet, xxxii (1905), 40; the last two paragraphs were translated by Lorenzen, Columbia Law Review, x (1910), 196.

[2] For the exception of public order, see:

French:

Bartin, E.: Les dispositions d'ordre public, la théorie de la fraude à la loi, et l'idée de communauté internationale. Rev. dr. int., vii (1897), 385, 613.

Boissarie: De la notion de l'ordre public en droit international privé. Paris, 1888.

territorial sovereign for the good government of his territory must be obeyed by a foreigner within the territory, no matter what his personal law may be. Agreement on what laws are of public order is very difficult to attain, and the principle is therefore vague and ambiguous. Like all the theories of the statutists, it bears the marks of having been worked out in the closet instead of in the courts.[1]

This difficulty and uncertainty of application seems to be sufficient argument against the adoption of this theory; but there is an even stronger theoretical argument against it. To say that the territorial sovereign may at his will make and enforce rules of public order against a foreign person is really to admit the supremacy of the territorial law, since he has only to regard a law as important to him to have

---

Despagnet, F.: L'ordre public en droit international privé. Clunet, xvi (1889), 5, 207.

Fedozzi, P.: Quelques considérations sur l'idée d'ordre public international. Clunet, xxiv (1897), 69, 495.

Fiore, Pasquale: De la limitation de l'autorité des lois étrangères et de la determination des lois d'ordre public. Clunet, xxxv (1908), 351.

De l'ordre public en droit international privé. Instit. dr. int., Paris, 1910.

Moutier, M.: Du conflit des lois étrangères avec les lois d'ordre public françaises. Paris, 1892.

Naquet: Note, Sirey, 1892, 2, 201.

Pillet, A.: De l'ordre public en droit international privé. Grenoble, 1890.

Vareilles-Sommières. Des lois d'ordre public et de la dérogation aux lois. Paris, 1899.

German:

Fiore, Pasquale: Ueber die Begrenzung der Autoritat ausländischer Gesetze und die Bestimmung der Gesetze der öffentlichen Rechtsordnung. Zeitschrift f. Völkerrecht u. Bundestaatsrecht, iii (1908), 1.

Kahn, Franz: Abhandlungen aus dem internationalem Privatrecht: I. Die Lehre vom *ordre public.* Jhering's Jahrbücher, xxxix (1898), 1; Jena, 1898 (brochure).

Klein: Abhandlungen aus dem internationalem Privatrecht: III. Die Lehre vom *ordre public.* Arch. f. bürg. Recht, xxix (1906), 311.

Italian:

Rapisardi-Mirabelli, A.: L'ordine pubblico nel diritto internazionale; saggio critico. Catane, 1908.

Spanish:

Bustamante, Antonio, S. de: El orden publico. Estudio de derecho internacional privado. Havana, 1893.

---

[1] See the article of Kahn, above cited, which is full of wit and satire directed at the uncertainty of the doctrine. Its use as a sort of formula to conceal difficulties in the application of the theory of statutes will be illustrated in the extracts from Pillet's works, *post,* § 61.

it universally respected within his territory. The doctrine of the supremacy of personal law, limited by the doctrine of public order, becomes identical with the doctrine of the supremacy of territorial law, limited by the doctrine of comity: the territorial sovereign permits the application of the personal law whenever he thinks it worth while, that is, whenever it is not of the first consequence to him to have his territorial law obeyed. The doctrine of public order is in reality the negation of the theory of the statutists.

§ 60. **The Principle of Autonomy of the Will.** — Dumoulin suggested, and many modern authorities have accepted, the doctrine that in cases where human action is not constrained by law such action is to be governed by free will; and the law, thus consecrating the freedom of the will, gives legal effect to the expression of it. This is the so-called doctrine of "autonomy of the will."[1] According to this doctrine, contracts, sales, wills and other voluntary juridical acts are governed by the law which the actor has in mind; but Dumoulin's most celebrated application of it to the law of marital property is questionable.[2] It is founded, says Aubry, on an idea which is formulated in Article 1134 of the Civil Code, that agreements take the place of law to the parties.[3] In other words, the law of contracts permits one to create in every particular his own right; he may choose how to create it, as well as what to create.[4] The principle, however, is limited by rules of public order. As an example, Aubry cites the provision that a married woman may not make a contract; which is a law of public order, and therefore a married woman cannot by choosing some other law by which to be governed make herself capable of contracting.[5]

In its application to contracts, this doctrine has been adopted by the English courts, and will later be criticised when the English cases are considered. It is enough here to point out that it is the function of law to determine the

[1] For the literature of the subject see Weiss, iii, 112; Olive, Louis: Étude sur la théorie de l'autonomie en droit international privé. Paris, 1899. Trouiller, Maurice: Du rôle du consentement dans les actes juridiques. Valencia, 1894.

[2] Aubry in Clunet, xxiii, 465.

[3] *Ibid.*, 468.

[4] *Ibid.*, 469.

[5] *Ibid.*, 470.

rule which governs a transaction, and to allow the parties to choose that rule is to grant them legislative functions.

§ 61. **Pillet's Theory of the Continuity and the Generality of Law.** — Two modern French writers, fundamentally different in every respect — training, mode of thought, character of mind — have put forward remarkable original theories which cannot be passed over without particular notice. One of these theories will be considered in a later section; the other will here be examined.

Professor Antoine Pillet, then of Grenoble and now of Paris, in a series of articles in Clunet's Journal of Private International Law, beginning in 1894, put forward the idea of two sorts of law, applicable the one to persons, the other to territory.

A full understanding of the theory requires copious citation, which follows.[1]

"Whenever the question is raised as to the international nature of a law, one of two answers must be given; the law may be either territorial or extraterritorial. It may be territorial, and then every one in the country is submitted to its jurisdiction without distinction between natives and foreigners domiciled or not domiciled, but, upon the other hand, on leaving the country, each ceases to owe it obedience; or it may be extraterritorial, and the contrary effect produced; where upon once being applied to a person (by virtue of his nationality or his domicil, opinions differ) the law follows him everywhere. . . .

"Law should combine, and always does combine, certain characteristics which are indispensable to its effect, qualities without which it would have no reason for existence. . . . We shall notice here but two, the only important qualities from an international point of view, but of the utmost importance: continuity and generality of application. When we say that law is by its nature continuous, we mean that its authority should be uninterrupted; from the day of its promulgation to the day of its repeal the law must always be heard and obeyed. . . . It is just as necessary that every law should be general in application to its subjects. . . . Order is necessary to every State, and order exists in the domain of law only in so far as the law is applied without distinction to every person within the limits of the State. . . .

[1] Clunet, xxi (1894), 417, 711, xxii (1895), 241, 500, 929, xxiii (1896), 5. The extracts are from the first two articles.

"From an international point of view, continuity necessarily implies extraterritoriality; generality of application, territoriality. . . . For a law to be truly continuous, it must apply under all circumstances to the person subject to it, it must follow him abroad when he leaves his country, and it must rule all his affairs there as well as in his own. . . . To take the common example of a law of capacity: suppose it ceases to apply to a person when he leaves his own country, or that it only remains inapplicable to such of the person's property as is situated in a foreign country, and it will be clear that the law misses its object because it misses continuity of effect. . . . One can see that if, in the case of the same person, a period of complete incapacity is followed by a period of limited capacity, all the results that the legislator might attain by the rules he established will be forever compromised by the breach of continuity which will be produced in the application of the rule. In the same way generality is inseparable from territoriality. . . . That order which it is the object of the law to establish would not exist, unless all matters within the control of the society which is ruled by the law were equally subject to its provisions. . . .

"Now let us see what would happen if each State in administering justice should carry the consequences of this situation to its logical conclusion. . . . No State would then suffer the application of any foreign law in its territory. Trusting in the generality of its own law, and the territoriality which logically flows from it, the State would assert its authority in all foreign interests which asked aid of its justice. But on the other hand, by a deduction drawn from the character of continuity and extraterritoriality, equally belonging to it, it would apply its own law also to the interests of its own subjects in foreign lands. One must conclude that the harmony which should exist between the laws of various countries can be obtained only through a sacrifice. . . .

"The solution of this question cannot depend in every case on the will or the fancy of the one who, as jurisconsult, or as judge, has it to solve. In other words, the territoriality or the extraterritoriality of laws cannot be abandoned to arbitrary will, or as we say, in terms at once fitter and more classic, to the comity of nations. . . . We must discover some law of harmony, choose indifferently or for simple reasons of equity, either the territoriality of laws or their extraterritoriality; find the principle of harmony which will destroy as little as possible the useful effect of the law, or in other words leave intact as great part as possible of the authority of law. . . . Let us suppose a conflict on the age of majority, in our country twenty-one years, but by the foreign personal law of the party twenty-five years. The French judge has before him two solutions, two means of putting an end to conflict and establishing harmony: to apply the local law by virtue of its territoriality, or the personal law of the foreigner by nature of its extraterritoriality. Each of the solutions has its advantages and disadvantages. The first is more favorable to the public order and credit; if it is adopted, every one within the territority will be of age at twenty-one years, and one will never have to suspect hidden facts which may lead to the application of a foreign law. On the other hand, it will have the disadvantage that the foreigner in question will suddenly come of age upon crossing the boundary of the country. The other solution would have neither this disadvantage not the corresponding advantage. Can one suppose that a judge, if not bound by any provision of positive law, could hesitate between the two? The experience of the past answers the question clearly. Hesitation is impossible, because, of the two solutions, the first in return for a slight advantage involves a disadvantage which almost totally destroys the utility of such a law. What is the use of prolonging minority until a given age, if the minor may by a journey free himself from the incapacity? Such a solution reduces almost to naught the authority of the law on this point, whilst the other solution maintains the chief and essential features of its authority, and sacrifices only a territorial effect of little importance in this connection. . . . The great school of "statutaries" thought that the international effect of laws should depend on their object; meaning by this ambiguous word, object, the person or thing which is directly and immediately affected by the law. We thus reach the essential distinction between the two classes, — real laws which were territorial, and personal laws recognized as extraterritorial, — so completely that the two expressions were synonymous. . . . The extraterritorial application of laws relative to the person did not cease to cause them doubt and even remorse. They accepted it, but usually in spite of themselves; as is sufficiently proved by the eagerness with which they recurred to territoriality whenever on the slightest pretext they deemed themselves authorized to do so. In fine, the distinction made by this school, even supposing it applicable to the facts (which the invention of "statutes mixed" shows to be doubtful) had no principle behind it; this error was its greatest, but it was irremediable. . . .

"One cannot deny that the essential feature of law is its social object. If, in fact, one analyzes the idea of law in any one of its applications, one necessarily reaches this first conclusion, that law is always the means employed by the legislator to reach a determined social object. . . . The object of a law is not the immediate effect it has in view : that is the very content of the law, the means employed by the legislator to reach the object, not the object itself. . . . The social object to be attained is the *raison d'être* of the law, gives it its distinctive characteristics, assigns it its period ; is it not logical, therefore, to conjecture that its international effect should be measured by its social object? Such is in fact the rule we propose. We know that laws are by nature at once territorial and extraterritorial, that they may in international relations preserve but one of these characters ; we think that in each case the choice of character should be determined by considering the social object of the law. We shall declare territorial all laws the object of which could not be attained if in each country they did not apply as well to foreigners as to citizens ; extraterritorial all laws the object of which requires that they should follow everywhere the person who comes under the force of their provisions. In every case, then, we shall consult the social object of the law under examination ; that will be the only key to the problem of conflicts, the rule by which we shall resolve whether a law should be regarded as territorial or extraterritorial. . . .

" Like the needs which it is their purpose to satisfy, laws can have one only of two objects : to protect the private interests of individuals, or to secure the conditions of existence and the functional operations of the body politic. That is their social object, the result to which they tend ; a result which concerns the legislator only by reason of the influence it exercises on the condition of society. To the first category will belong laws which have for their end to place the individual in the position most favorable for his development and preservation ; such are laws of the family, which have for end to establish in the persons concerned a unity of interests and responsibilities conforming to their natural affinities ; in the same way, laws which have for end to advise, to guide those who cannot look out for themselves ; finally, those which will have the good result of saving one from his own devices. To the same category belong laws destined to assure to every one the fruits of his toil. The second class of laws is made up of those which have for their end to determine the general conditions of society ; one will generally recognize them easily by the circumstance that within the borders of a country they interest all persons equally, whatever their condition, because the interest of each one in having them observed is the same as the interest all have in the maintenance of the political body based upon them. . . .

"Laws for individual protection should be extraterritorial. This is in fact implicitly included in the very idea of protection. For protection to be efficacious it must be complete, or, to return to familiar terms, continuous. It should be continuous in time and space; suffer no interruption, for one moment of interruption always compromises, and may suffice to ruin the effect of long continued protection. It must be continuous in space, by which we understand that the person should be protected everywhere; and if, as often happens, he owns goods in several countries, thus subjected in fact to several different sovereignties, the law which protects him should extend to all his interests in spite of differences in the laws which complicate matters. All protection is armor, which does not fulfill its office unless it is without flaw. . . .

"Laws for the security of society include all provisions deemed by the legislature necessary to the existence of the State, and to the performance of its various functions. It is of the first importance that within a country the wills of all without exception, including both natives and foreigners, should yield obedience to laws for the security of society. These laws are imposed on citizens only because they are absolutely requisite for the interest of society; those sacrifices of interest required of citizens may all the more be required of foreigners, mere guests. . . .

"Does a law have in view individual interests or the interests of society? Supposing it to be applied, is it the individual to whom it is applied who will be benefited, or is it society as a whole? . . . One may ask (which amounts to the same thing) whether an individual or the body politic would suffer loss by its repeal or non-enforcement. . . .

"A third method may be usefully employed in the most embarrassing cases. When a law has been made for the purpose of the security of society, all citizens profit equally every time it is applied; if it has been made for the protection of individuals, those benefit by it directly who enjoy the rights it creates, and the common good is only an indirect and minor consequence of the good of those individuals. Let us consider together two doctrines, the right and the lack of right, respectively, to establish paternity. They seem equally to concern the State and individuals. The law which authorizes the establishment of paternity may seem to be a law for the security of society, for it facilitates the natural classification of individuals; but it is easy to see that society derives advantage from its provisions only as a result of the fortunate effect which its application has upon the condition of the parties. To the legitimate child it is a matter of entire indifference. On the other hand, the law which forbids it has evidently been passed not out of favor to the seducer, but by reason of a quite legitimate fear of the scandal which such suits cause. No one can claim an individual interest in the application of this law, but all the members of society have an equal interest in its being observed; the interest is entirely political, and the rule should be regarded as territorial."

Professor Pillet's theory is ingenious, interesting and specious; but we seem not to reach firmer ground if, accepting it, we try to determine the application of law by deciding whether in establishing it the legislator was regarding it more important that the law should be universal or that it should be continuous. In the first place, the meaning given to the word *continuous* seems hardly sound. The continuity which a law needs in order to attain its end is a subjective, not an objective, continuity; it is important that there be no break in its existence, rather than that it be applied continuously to a particular person. True continuity of law — that which is necessary to prevent the failure or forfeiture of acquired rights — demands territoriality, in order that this continuity may be enforced.

But, without further laboring this objection, a more fatal objection to Pillet's theory as a practical working principle is, that it offers no certain or simple method of distinguishing the two classes of laws. The very example he gives of a law which must be continuous disproves the possibility of the distinction he seeks to make. His suggestion that everyone would agree that the law of majority *must*, in order to attain its ends, be applied continuously is met, first, by the fact that no common-law court has so held, and the opposite has been often decided; secondly, by the fact that however unanimously the French courts accept the rule in theory, in fact they frequently refuse to follow it.

The theory in question, therefore, is too uncertain in its application for acceptance as a working theory. "Truth in law, like beauty in architecture, is simple, clear, restful; characteristics which M. Pillet's doctrine does not possess." [1]

[1] Vareilles-Sommières, i, 165.

" M. Pillet is right in saying that there is only one public order, but his definition of public order is pure fantasy, and his theory that laws of status and capacity are not of public order is the height of paradox." [1]

§ 62. **Pillet's Later Theories.** — In a later work [2] Professor Pillet modified to a certain extent, or at least amplified, the statement of his theory. The statutists, as he says, are seeking a universal rule for the settlement of conflicts, which is not easily distinguishable from a rule of international law: a " general and truly international form " of solution, but still " not international law, but national systems of solutions of international questions," [3] as to which " it is of public interest to sovereigns to see that its principles are carried out, so as to protect its subjects." [4] This common system for the solution of conflicts is not the international system, which prevents all conflicts by postulating doctrines of international law, binding on every nation, and by its own force creating international rights and duties.[5]

Pillet seems, however, to go beyond the statutists in the direction of an internationally binding law. He emphasizes the existence as a matter of fact of an association of civilized nations, bound together by social and commercial ties; and while he does not admit that there is a binding law of this association which transcends the separate laws of each state,[6] he cannot conceive of an international society living without an international law, unless it lives in disorder and anarchy.[7] He appears to conclude that there was at one time an agreement upon identical principles in the different civilized countries, which have with time become diversified by legislation.[8]

§ 63. **The International System.** — Sharply contrasted in some respects with the statutory theory, though not altogether distinct, is the doctrine that there is a body of

[1] Vareilles-Sommières, i, 104 *n.* See Pillet's theory expounded at length and criticised by this author, i, 154–183.

[2] Principes de droit international privé (1903).

[3] Pillet, 91. [4] Pillet, 70.

[5] In the sense in which the word "international" is here used, it does not mean "concerned with the rights of nations as persons," but merely "having relation to the affairs of more than one nation."

[6] Pillet, 8, 55. [7] Pillet, 95 *n.* [8] Pillet, 97, 100; and see 64 *et s.*

international principles for solving all legal questions which arise where more than one nation is concerned. It differs from the statutory theory in that it supposes no separate laws contending for the mastery, but a single system, which by its own force inhibits all laws not in harmony with itself. Pillet suggested that at one time there may have been such a single international system; but in his opinion the tendency is rather toward diversity, through legislation, than toward unity. Lainé, however, finds a distinct tendency in private international law toward a unity which it will sometime attain.[1] But the true internationalist goes further. He holds that private international law is an existing customary law, growing out of a gradually accepted custom. "It can be demonstrated that there is to a certain extent a real *communis consensus* of civilized states, a true law of custom." [2]

Laurent, to be sure, accepting the Austinian notion of law, argues that this cannot be law at all, because it lacks all sanction; the customary law of a country, having a sanction, is tacit *law*, but this is merely tacit *agreement*.[3] "The law of nations," he adds, "is as yet only history, on its way to become law." [4] But the internationalists brush this objection aside.

"Of course," says Bar,[5] "every state has, in the abstract, the power of denying effect within its own territory to such a law of custom. But up to that limit the general law of custom, if it can really be shown to be such, will be recognized in the individual state. We cannot admit the objection, therefore, that there can be no such thing as a general law of custom, with reference to the rules of private law, for the whole of the civilized world. The boundary of the state has this significance merely, that it can deny effect to such universal propositions of customary law, a denial which, as a rule, will draw down upon itself and its citizens considerable disadvantages." Lainé points out[6] that the will of each state to admit this law is constrained by reasons of justice and interest, while Catellani suggests[7] that the will of each state is limited by "that association of states which, like all collective bodies, necessarily subordinates or limits each of the single bodies that compose it."

1 Lainé, i, 44. 2 Bar, 5, § 4. 3 Laurent, i, 12. 4 Laurent, i, 67.
5 Bar, 6, § 4. 6 Lainé, i, 3. 7 Catellani, i, 10.

§ 64. The Early German School: Wächter, Schäffner, Savigny. — The doctrine of an internationally binding doctrine has been developed by the German jurists. Soon after the publication of Story's treatise, the German lawyers began more seriously to turn their attention to the subject.[1] The author who accomplished the transition from the older law to the peculiar doctrines of the German school was Charles George Wächter (1797–1880), professor at Tübingen and at Leipzig.[2] According to his doctrine, the territorial law must always be applied by a court; if the territorial law provides that a juridical relation be governed by a foreign law, then and only then will that law be applied.[3]

William Schäffner (1815–) followed with a doctrine which contained the germ of a theory of vested rights.[4] According to this theory, every juridical relation is to be determined as a matter of right by the law of the place in which it came into existence.[5] This theory has been not unfairly criticised as artificial and crude.

The ideas of these two authors influenced to a certain extent the doctrine of a great lawyer who next wrote upon the subject in Germany. Friedrich Carl von Savigny (1779–1861), professor at Marburg, Landshut, and Berlin, included an examination of the doctrine of the Conflict of Laws in his System des heutigen Romanische Rechtes.[6] Savigny's doctrine is thus summarized by Laurent.[7] The territoriality of laws is a secondary question; one must see first of all what is the nature of the juridical fact which the judge has to pass upon and then find the law which ought to be applied to this fact, in order to solve the difficulty. This law will be applied without distinction of whether it is native or foreign. As Savigny himself states the question, it is "to ascertain for every legal relation that law to which, in its proper relation, it belongs or is subject,"[8] except that "laws of a strictly imperative nature, clothed with a public interest, are always enforced by their own courts; and

[1] For the German School in general see, Bustamante, 459; Catellani, ii, 1; Weiss, iii, 50.

[2] Catellani, ii, 49; Weiss, iii, 51.

[3] Weiss, iii, 52; Meili, i, 116.

[4] Meili, i, 115; Weiss, iii, 53.

[5] Bar, 49.

[6] For Savigny, see Catellani, ii, 92; Laurent, i, 608; Meili, i, 117.

[7] Laurent, i, 608.

[8] Savigny, 70.

peculiar legal institutions of a foreign state, not recognized by the law of the forum, are given no effect." [1]

"The strict right of sovereignty might certainly, among other things, go so far as to require all judges of the land to decide all the cases that come before them solely according to the national law. . . . Such a rule, however, is not to be found in the legislation of any known state. . . . The standpoint to which this consideration leads us, is that of an international common law of nations having intercourse with one another. . . . This sufferance must not be regarded as the result of mere generosity or arbitrary will, which would imply that it was also uncertain and temporary. We must rather recognize in it a proper and progressive development of law." [2]

The proper law is ascertained by a universal, that is, an international, principle of law, which may be discovered by the exercise of reason. This, as Vareilles-Sommières says,[3] is a recrudescence of the ideas of the early Italian statutists; and he adds that the so-called doctrine of Savigny is not a doctrine, but simply a method, and a method which, "logically applied, reconstitutes in every part the theory of statutes."

Savigny was the first to state, in a form in which it has been widely accepted, the theory of an international origin of the doctrines of the conflict of laws. As Bar truly says,[4] "He was the first to take up with full consciousness his starting point in the idea of an international community of law which restricts all territorial laws, and defines their competency, and in thinking, not of a conflict of legal systems, but of a harmonious combination of all."

Savigny's influence on the development of the subject has been profound; and a long list might be made of the authors who have more or less absolutely accepted his doctrine.[5]

§ 65. **The Doctrine of von Bar.**— Ludwig von Bar took up Savigny's theory of an international law and developed it

[1] Savigny, 78. [2] Savigny, 69, 70.

[3] Vareilles-Sommières, i, 143. [4] Bar, 56.

[5] Weiss enumerates the following (iii, 54 *n*): *German:* Walter, Gerber, Windscheid, Mommsen, Bar. *Austrian:* Vesque de Puttlingen. *Dutch* and *Belgian:* Asser and Rivier, Rolin. *Spanish:* Torres Campos. *Italian:* Brusa. *Russian:* de Martens. *Swiss:* Brocher. *French*: Lainé, Despagnet. *English* and *American:* Phillimore, Westlake, Beach-Lawrence, Wharton, Minor.

into a consistent body of doctrine, starting with the allegation that private international law is "an independent department of law . . . not merely a part of the domestic law of each state."[1] While not prepared to deny that in a sense the doctrines which he among the first called private international law are part of "the juridical principles of each particular state,"[2] he denied to the state arbitrary power in settling these doctrines.

"Rules of private international law," he says,[3] "cannot possibly be dependent merely upon the arbitrary determination of particular states. The state cannot assert the competency of its own legal system in absolute independence of other states, and in the face of their sovereign rights, which are of as much weight as its own. Such a claim will most assuredly be met by certain limitations belonging to the law of nations."

"To pay regard to foreign rules of law to a certain extent is the legal duty of every State, and is not a matter of mere caprice and goodwill — the duty of every State, that is, which wishes to maintain the commercial relations of civilized peoples. If now and again the word *comitas* is still used for the considerations on which the application of foreign rules of law ought to depend, that is rather a difference of expression than of real meaning.

"Private international law, then, as it is to be inferred from what has been already said, is not a product merely of the sovereign legal system of each particular State, but is a result of the nature of the subject itself, claiming recognition as in a sense necessary, a result of the requirements of commerce, and of the reciprocal recognition of their legal systems by the different States. No doubt each individual State may to a certain extent permit itself to deviate from the rules of international law, and these deviations, however perverse they may be, are for the time positive law for that State, which can be carried out so far as the sphere of its power in fact extends. But capricious deviations of this kind generally bring great disadvantages in their train, even for the State which allows itself to practise them. They are not truly law, any more than the deviations from the law of nations in its technical sense, *i.e.*, public international law, which a State may allow itself to practise, are law, although it may see that these deviations are carried out, so far as its own power extends, by its officials and official machinery against private persons.

[1] Bar, 2, § 2. [2] Alb, L. J., xii, 232. [3] Bar, 2, § 2.

"The material principle of private international law, as we have figured it, requires no further sanction from special statutes or international treaties, because the nature of the subject, by its inherent reasonableness as a principle, will obtain recognition and prevail by its own strength. But that principle may no doubt be modified in many points by the law of custom and special treaties."[1]

§ 66. The Doctrine of Zitelmann. — Ernst Zitelmann of Leipzig is the latest and most advanced author of the international school; and his doctrine will repay a careful study.

Such a study has fortunately been made by one of the ablest of his contemporaries, Professor Eugen Ehrlich of Czernowitz; and since his analysis is far truer and clearer than that of any foreign scholar could be, it is here reproduced.[2]

"The attempt of Zitelmann goes beyond everything that the Internationalists have hazarded before him. Starting from the principles of the Law of Nations, which all recognize, he attempts to build up a system of private international law absolutely complete, resolving with certainty every question that can arise. According to Zitelmann, the principles furnished by the law of nations do not merely, as the other Internationalists have it, provide the limits within which the legislation and jurisprudence of the states may move. These principles, in his eyes, make up Private International Law itself; and they decide directly, according to law, how different litigated questions should be solved. These principles constitute an integral portion of the law of nations, and therefore individuals cannot evoke them any more than any other rule of the law of nations; for the law of nations confers rights only on states and imposes obligations only on states. The legislature of a state, which the judge of a state must obey, may certainly pass laws which are contrary to private international law, though founded on the law of nations; but it is quite clear that in so doing they cannot deprive that law of its own power. The law in that case has the same validity as before; but this validity exists only from the point of view of international law. The only result of this contradiction would be, that beside a private international law based on the law of nations, and superior to states (which, like every rule of the law of nations, binds states

[1] Bar, 77, § 32.

[2] Revue de droit int. privé, iv (1908), 902, 917; translated from the original in *Deutsche Rundschau* for March, 1906.

only), there would be also a private international law peculiar to the state in question, which would bind the judge of that state. The supra-state private international law contains fundamental principles, upon which the different states ought to base their own intra-state international law in order to put it in conformity with the law of nations. So far as the judge is concerned, the only value of the supra-state law is to furnish rules to which the judge may refer whenever, on a particular point, his own intra-state private international law furnishes him with no solution; for one may assume in such a case that the state itself has willed on this point to conform to the general rules of the law of nations. This supra-state law may again be applied when the parties, without allowing the court to intervene between them, are ready themselves to govern their situation by taking advantage of juridical principles. One may suppose in that case that they have willed to decide according to the principles of the law of nations the questions of private international law which might arise between them.

"The private international law in force in each state is therefore composed: first, of statutes passed by the state itself, and concerned with private international law; second, of the rules of the supra-state private international law which bind the parties and the judge in default of statute. Zitelmann calls the body of the two groups rules of application destined to determine the law which should be applied. The first he calls 'rules of conflict,' and the second 'rules of subsidiary application.'

"All authority in a state derives its source, according to the law of nations, either from personal sovereignty or from territorial sovereignty. When a state assumes to apply its own law to a particular litigation, it must necessarily base its action either on the fact that the person sued is submitted to its authority because he is a member of the state, or on the fact that the object of suit is situated in the territory over which he has jurisdiction. On these two fundamental rules of the law of nations, Zitelmann constructs his entire private international law. One might certainly argue that since the law of nations recognizes a fundamental rule, all the consequences of this rule should also be admitted even if the law of nations does not recognize them. But Zitelmann does not teach such a doctrine. He says only 'since the consequences of a rule of law should have juridical force equal to that of the rule itself, unless this force is specially taken from it by the effect of a contrary rule, in the same way the principle deduced from the admitted rule may properly claim the same validity as a principle of the law of nations.'

"It follows that when a state wishes that its law be applied to a certain relation, the state cannot by virtue of the law of nations justify this desire except by evoking its personal or territorial sovereignty. By virtue of the personal sovereignty, the state exercises its jurisdiction over its members. By virtue of territorial sovereignty it exercises jurisdiction over all things movable or immovable which are found on its territory. When an individual sets in motion his right over another, this right can be guaranteed only by the state of which this last person was a part, and to the sovereignty of which he is submitted. When the right is claimed over a thing, the solution should be furnished by the law of the state in the territory of which the thing is found. In the law of civilized people rights belonging to individuals over persons have their only source in family rights or rights of contract. Rights over things have their source in real rights. Therefore, a family right should be governed by the statute personal of the person submitted to the right, a contract right by the statute personal of the debtor, and a real right by the statute real of the situation of the thing. For all other rights one would apply the law of the state in which the acts are done which are alleged to have created the right, or in which the acts were committed which were forbidden by the law, that is, the territorial statute.

"Therefore, the law of that state should always be applied, in the sphere of whose sovereignty the effect of the right created is to take place. If this effect should concern a person, it would be the statute personal; if it should concern a thing, it would be the statute real. If several effects flow from a single situation, the statute will be determined for each effect according to the nature of that effect. If several situations act together in producing a single effect, they are all to be judged according to the statute of this effect. To several situations with a single effect one should apply one single statute; to a single situation with several effects one would apply several statutes.

"The conception of law which serves as a basis for all the work of Zitelmann is very remarkable. That Zitelmann sees in a state the source of the objective law is a very natural thing in a modern Internationalist. For him, as for all of them, conflicts between the laws of different states are the only ones with which private international law occupies itself. But Zitelmann draws from this idea the most extreme conclusions. He sees in the state the source of every subjective right. When a person has a right, he always gets it in the last analysis by reason of a concession of the state or of a recognition of this right by the state. Zitelmann knows very well that this conception is contrary to history; subjective rights are older than the state and even today there may exist in Europe individual subjective rights which in their origin go back to a period before the existence of states. But to construct the private international law of today it is necessary to utilize only the concepts which are today alive, or which at least are in course of formation, upon the nature of the state and of law; and the ideas which today are more or less current on these questions have found a strong expression in Zitelmann's theory. From this point of view Zitelmann's work marks, in a way, the actual present condition of evolution.

"One may say as much for the other fundamental idea of Zitelmann's work, his Internationalism. In the face of the nationalist tendency in private international law, the internationalist tendency presents itself to us as more modern, and more advanced. When Nationalists claim that every judge decides first of all in conformity with his own law, they really leave to chance, which determines what judge has to decide the question, the task of deciding the law which is to be applied. The Internationalists, on the contrary, ask what the law is which, according to purely international reasons, ought to govern such and such a legal relation. But like all novel ideas, the internationalist idea has to win a difficult fight before entrenching itself deeply in the mind. Today, everybody, perhaps, is in a way nationalist, not even excepting the Internationalists. The latter cannot escape the current notion that the judge has the preeminent duty of applying the law of the state which appointed him. The law of his own state is to him the normal and natural law; the foreign law is a law which may be taken into consideration in exceptional cases, and in very peculiar circumstances. In fact, the difference between Nationalists and Internationalists today is not as profound as it seems.

"Now from this point of view Zitelmann marks the extreme point at which the evolution of ideas has arrived. In no other system of private international law have the national law and the foreign law, taken altogether, been placed upon a footing of equality. Zitelmann's system presents us a theory free from every trace of nationalism and entirely international. In this it is completely rationalistic, and in its inmost essence, and in the goal which the author pursues without wavering, it is absolutely antihistoric; for nationalism always constitutes the historical element of the law. Zitelmann sets before us one ideal alone, an ideal which we must accept if, with a rigorous logic, we deduce the consequences and the conclusion from the initial proposition.

"The exponents of private international law have always at this point met one particular difficulty: there is not yet any international juridical language. The particular juridical tendencies of each of the several national laws are so different that it is scarcely possible to express them by making use of the approved terms of a foreign law. Each law has its own terminology and its group of particular conceptions. Representatives of the nationalist tendency have often presented this difficulty as an argument. Suppose, for example, that the rule of application of a state decides that a transaction by a foreigner incapable of contracting by himself shall be valid, if it is authorized by the authority which a guardian exercises over the foreigner; what is going to happen if the law which is to be applied by virtue of this rule takes the words "incapacity to contract," "authority of guardian," "authorization," in a sense quite different from the law which orders the application. The Nationalists then reach the conclusion that the national law of the judge should in this case also settle the question. This solution is simple, but it is not always possible to be applied. Anyone who has had to do with foreign documents knows how difficult it often is to say whether a certain document, executed abroad, is a specialty with regard to the national law; whether the juridical consequences that follow it are governed by the law of things or by the law of obligations. Since the foreign law upon these points may have quite other conceptions than the law of the forum, it may be very difficult to arrive at a clear solution in making use of the provisions of the latter law. The difficulty is even greater for the internationalists, who absolutely lack the assistance of the principle indicated above. If private international law is to include not rules of law of such and such a particular state, but rules governing the laws of all states, these must not be understood and interpreted by the aid of terminology and conceptions of any particular state law."

§ 67. **The World-Law of Jitta.**— Professor Joseph Jitta, of the University of Amsterdam, has propounded a theory which seems an altogether original extension of the German doctrine of international principles. The principles for the solution of conflicts of laws are, in his opinion, not so much international as ultranational. He bases them not on any law of nations, but on a law of humanity. There is an eternal conflict, he says, between humanity and territorial claims.

The object of private international law is to put private law into harmony with life. The complex relations of humanity are innumerable, and, as in case of private law, cannot be brought within the narrow bounds of a code or a treaty. His object is to make sure that the law applied to these international relations is the best proper law. This cannot be accomplished by leaving the settlement of legal principles to the nations. The legislator must be humanity; society itself must fix the principles of private law applicable to international relations.

This has been rightly called a new *Jus Gentium;* [1] but it is a *jus gentium* properly so called, a law of all people, not a law fixed by a single dominant state and called by a seductive name.

"The law," he says,[2] "arises out of the lack of harmony between the juridical life of man and the positive law of each state. Life creates daily, between all members of the human family, relations which require a juridical sanction, whilst positive law is developed with reference only to a single group of men." He continues: [3] "Our science is based on the corporateness of the human race, which is derived from the social nature of man, a gift of the Creator; it has as its object the development of the positive private law of this body, so as to assure the individual his full legal rights, in every sphere of human relations. There being no such political organization now, we are forced to begin with the present law of existing states; but the end in view is the reign of law in the world-state. This is not a mere dream; the theory deals with actual facts today, but they are dealt with in view of the desired end.

"Each state has duties to fulfil, not only towards the national sovereign, but also toward the world-federation of individuals." The object of the law is to submit to rules of law the relations between individuals, and not, as other authors would have it, to regulate private relations between states, or between a state and an individual, or rather between the different national laws. Thus the search is for general rules which shall determine with certainty the application of one or another law to the national controversy, instead of deciding what should be the law governing the particular relation in question, which is the object of Jitta's search.

To his theory there are two branches: one, in each state, the individual method, that is, the working out of the principles of

[1] Juridical Review, xx, 109. [2] Jitta, Méthode, 1. [3] Méth., 96 *et s.*

world-law through their adoption in any particular state; the other the universal method, the working out of principles into law created by the collective body of states. As to the individual method he says: [1] "The legislator of each state should apply to every juridical relation, considered under all the forms in which it presents itself in the actual condition of mankind, the principle which fits its nature, that is, the purpose which it fills in the world-federation of men." As to the universal method, the "juridical rules intended to receive their application throughout mankind," [2] he says [3] that "states as a body have the common duty of insuring the application of private law to all mankind by formulating positive and universal juridical rules, based on a common belief of states with relation to the social end of juridical relations."

Jitta's theory, when worked out in "the individual method," is almost indistinguished from Savigny's. It is his universal method which is original and striking. He has expressed it in a few words: [4] as there is a common law of each nation, so there is a common law of humanity, of which national laws are a source. The theory is not without support from other thinkers. Thus Fusinato somewhere says that if one once goes beyond the region of purely positive law, no distinction can any longer be made between the interests and the laws of society; and several authors have laid stress on a quality of modern law, that is, respect for the human being.[5] Mérignhac [6] asserts that "each man is a citizen of a particular country; at the same time, he is a citizen of the world." But those very authors refuse to postulate a general law of humanity which could transcend national law. It would be "too vague, too narrow, too embryonic" [7] to be vouched against the political law of an organized nation.

And indeed the most unanswerable criticism of his theory seems to be found in the nature of law itself. However jurists may disagree as to the nature or genesis of law, all agree that it is a creature of a politically organized society. Humanity, not organized into a single political societie, or nation, cannot possess a law in this sense, the sense in which the word must always be used by lawyers.

[1] Jitta, Méth., 196. [2] Méth., 221. [3] Méth., 238.
[4] Méth., 42. [5] Laghi, i, 155 *et s.*; Lainé, i, 20; Pillet, 55 *n.*
[6] Traité de droit public international, i, 6.
[7] Pillet, 55.

Yet while the ideas of humanity cannot be laws, they may and must be the source of law. Thus Pillet, after denying the name of law to the tenets of humanity, adds that they "protect human life, liberty and honor," [1] that is, that they accomplish the ends of political law; and Jitta himself [2] finds the existence of a legislative force in the requirements of human society: "How explain the authority given, in certain cases, to foreign law or to the judgments of a foreign court? Should one say that the state allows this authority by comity, or for its own interest, or that it fulfils a juridical duty; and in the latter case, upon what is this duty based?"

§ 68. **Criticism of the International Theories.** — The theory of internationality has many things to commend it. It would bring about identity of rule throughout the world, and this identity is greatly to be desired. It would furnish a basis for the protection of rights much more firm than that offered by either of the other theories. And since it would be a law principally made by jurists it would be a philosophic and reasonable science in every part. Dr. Franz Kahn, who does not accept the theory, admits [3] that it has rendered a greater service than the opposite theory.

It is not altogether surprising that this theory should have been authoritatively put forward by Savigny, who had thoroughly studied the development of European law from the Roman law, or that it should find numerous adherents among the scholars of Europe. The existence of a method of legal thought common to the law of several states, and the acceptance of the system of Civil law which transcends national lines and forms the basis of national laws, justify a conception that such a law has an international force. The received name, private international law, by suggesting an analogy to the law of nations, adds force to the conception.

And yet even more cogent arguments disprove the theory. A truly international law must have two characteristics: a well-defined body of rules, and a universal acceptance of these rules by civilized nations. Both these characteristics are lacking in the Private International Law of Savigny and Bar.

[1] Pillet, 55. [2] Méthode, 4. [3] Kahn in Jherings Jahrbücher, xl, 18.

First, there is no such definite body of rules on which nations can agree. It has already been seen how many contesting and contradictory theories have been put forward by the statutists: and the same contradiction is found in the internationalists. Wächter would apply the *lex fori;* Eichhorn and Goschen the *lex domicilii;* Schäffner the *lex loci;* [1] while Savigny and Bar are in agreement neither with these nor with each other. If a common international doctrine is to be found by the aid of the jurists, its discovery, or at least its general acceptance even among scholars, is yet to come.

Second, civilized nations have not agreed to receive a single system. It may be possible, through European conventions, to bring unity out of the contending doctrines, but only for the law of such countries as have received the Civil law. In the countries of the common law the acceptance of this agreed system is not merely improbable but impossible. As has been seen, the political situation is such, and is likely to remain such, in the countries governed by the common law, as to make inapplicable to them many of the most firmly held doctrines of European law.

A system of law which is neither clearly defined nor universally accepted cannot fairly be called international.

§ **69. International Legal Systems.** — While, however, no single system of international rules can be found to govern international juristic relations, it is of course true that two systems of law divide between them the nations of the civilized world, and that no national law can escape the dominion of the principles of one or the other system. Certain ideas as to the nature and jurisdiction of law and the characteristics of juridical rights and relations are common to the laws of all European nations, and form part of those laws. In a restricted sense those principles may be called international, though only in the same sense that the "civil law," so-called, is international. In the same way, certain principles are held by our common law, and are therefore received into the positive law of every common-law country from this common source, and are held by these positive laws in substantially identical terms. If, therefore, we confine our-

[1] Jitta, Méth., 111.

selves to general systems of legal thought of which positive laws are merely the application, we shall find not one but two private international laws, dividing the civilized world between them.

This fundamental distinction is clearly described by Lainé:

"The English common law differs fundamentally in two respects from the law of the European states. It has no trace of Roman law. The Roman domination, of short duration in Britain, left no trace; and the study of Roman law has had no sensible influence upon the private law. On the other hand the feudal [territorial] law has penetrated throughout the civil law, and even today gives it a quite individual character among the laws of Europe. In the second place, England having always possessed, from the time of the Norman conquest, with a few exceptions, territorial unity in its law, and having carried its law into Wales and Ireland, has known no conflict of laws and customs. It has therefore no anciently formed rules fit to serve as the basis for its private international law."[1]

These considerations really reconcile the philosophies of the German and the common-law writers. That system of law may in a fair sense be called international which is accepted as the basis of its law by several independent countries, although in each legal unit its own law, based to be sure on the common system, lies within the jurisdiction of its own legislative will. The rules adopted in each state are its own affair, not forced upon it by any legal constraint; and yet those rules are most likely to be identical with those of the general system on which its laws are based. Truly one may say, with Dr. Franz Kahn, that our subject is "a national law with an international method."[2]

§ 70. **The Territorial System.**—For a long time certain authors have refused to accept either of the prevailing European theories, and have insisted on the exclusive power within the territory of the national law. Grotius, one of the earliest dissenters from the doctrine of the statute personal, insisted that a foreigner contracting with a citizen would be subject to the local law, because he who contracts in any place becomes a temporary subject to the laws of that place.[3]

[1] Lainé, i, 37. [2] Kahn in Jherings Jahrbücher, xl, 18.

[3] Grotius, War and Peace, lib. 2, c. 11, § 5.

Despagnet, in our own time, says:[1] "The law, which is only the manifestation of the sovereign power of the state, should be absolutely without rival within the territory where it is passed; this goes so far that on principle (excepting limitations later considered) one is to understand that it excludes from this territory the application of any foreign law, for any reason whatever." Dr. Franz Kahn says categorically,[2] "Private international law is national law," and again, "The conflict of positive laws is no conflict from the standpoint of the local judge."[3] He adds, that if the courts of two countries differ as to the rules to apply in case of a conflict of laws "they are both right, each right according to the law of its own country."[4] And Bard puts the same idea neatly: "The solution of private litigation and the infliction of punishments do not depend upon international agreement, but exclusively on the law of the court in which suit is pending; even though the judge should take into account the provisions of a foreign law. In doing so he does not obey that law, but his own."[5]

The English and American judges have most consistently followed this theory. Thus Turner, V. C., in Caldwell *v.* Van Vlissengen[6] says: "I take the rule to be universal, that foreigners are in all cases subject to the laws of the country in which they may happen to be; and if in any case, when they are out of their own country, their rights are regulated and governed by their own laws, I take it to be not by force of those laws themselves, but by the law of the country in which they may be adopting those laws as part of their own law for the purpose of determining such rights." And this doctrine has been followed by the writers on the common law. Thus Story says:[7] "In regard to foreigners resident in a country, although some jurists deny the right of a nation generally to legislate over them, it would seem clear, upon general principles of international law, that such a right does exist; and the extent to which it should be exercised is a matter purely of municipal arrangement and policy." And the

[1] Despagnet, 19.

[2] Ueber Inhalt, Natur und Methode des int. Privatrechts, in Jherings Jahrbücher, xl, 87.

[3] Gesetzeskollisionen, in Jherings Jahrbücher, xxx, 54.

[4] *Ibid.*, 55. [5] Bard, Précis, v. [6] 9 Hare, 415. [7] Story, § 541.

Canadian Lafleur takes the same attitude:[1] "When the foreign law is allowed to control the case, it is because rights have been acquired under that law, and it would be an injustice to the parties to have those rights subjected to the test of another law." [2]

§ 71. **The Theory of Comity.**— It is obvious that while the territorial law has the right to make such rules as it pleases for the solution of the conflict of laws, the exercise of this right without consideration of the laws of other countries or of the rights created under these laws would be unjust. In order to avoid this injustice, the Dutch writers, followed by Story and Foelix, put forward the theory of Comity. According to this theory, the territorial law alone has controlling force, but in some cases, out of comity or enlightened self-interest, the territorial sovereign allows the personal law to prevail.[3] This, it will be seen, is only the reason for a *sovereign's* adopting a certain rule of law; the *courts* do not exercise comity, and are as much bound by the rule adopted by the legislative power as by any other portion of the law. "It is not the comity of the courts, but the comity of the nation, which is administered and ascertained in the same way, and guided by the same reasoning, by which all other principles of the municipal law are ascertained and guided." [4] "The duty of judges is to administer justice according to law, and to decide between parties according to their rights." [5]

The doctrine of comity has been very severely criticised by jurists and by courts.[6] Despagnet suggests that it withdraws reason and makes the law a series of varying positive rules.[7] Livermore says:[8] "The phrase has not always been harmless in its effects, for I have not infrequently seen it inspire judges with so great confidence in their own authority, that arrogating to themselves sovereign power,

[1] Lafleur, 12.

[2] See also A. V. Dicey, Private international law as a branch of the law of England, Law Q. Rev., vi, 1.

[3] Laurent, i, 69, 573; Pillet, 49 *n*, 52; Rolin, i, 100; Story, §§ 33, 38.

[4] Story, § 38, quoted and applied by Taney, C. J., in Bank of Augusta *v.* Earle, 13 Pet. 519, 589.

[5] Livermore, Dissert., 26.

[6] Bar, 26, 57; Schäffner, 130.

[7] Despagnet, 25.

[8] Diss., 27.

they have disregarded the foreign law, which ought to have governed their decision, because of some fancied inconvenience which might result to the citizens of their state. Even with sovereigns it is not so clear that the recognition of foreign laws is merely a matter of comity. They have the power to forbid the admission of the foreign law; but justice would then require that they should forbid the entertaining of any suit upon the foreign contract." Lord Wensleydale in Farton *v.* Livingstone[1] makes this trenchant criticism. "If we examine more nearly how the principle of *comitas gentium* was carried out, we see with amazement that it was in truth nowhere properly applied, or at least that in most cases an appeal was made to something quite different from comity. How could any reasonable results be attained with an idea so infinitely vague and unlegal? In fact, one cannot even approximate to a correct decision of the simplest case of private international law upon this principle. Where is the beginning or the end of comity? How can questions *of law* be solved according to views of policy, which are the most shifting and uncertain things in the world?"

Perhaps a criticism of a slightly different sort might also be made. The doctrine seems really to mean only that in certain cases the sovereign is not prevented by any principle of international law, but only by his own choice, from establishing any rule he pleases for the conflict of laws. In other words, it is an enabling principle rather than one which in any particular case would determine the actual rule of law. And thus we are again forced to conclude that it is impotent to determine when personal law displaces territorial law.[2]

§ 72. **The Doctrine of Story.** — Story quoted liberally from Boullenois, Huber, the Voets, and other European authors, but while his language is occasionally moulded by their phraseology, he is the first to develop and consistently hold the doctrine of the complete territorial jurisdiction of law. His doctrine may best be stated in his own words.

"Every nation possesses an exclusive sovereignty and jurisdiction within its own territority. The direct consequence of this

[1] 3 Macq., 497, 548. [2] Jitta, 104.

rule is, that the laws of every State affect, and bind directly, all property, whether real or personal, within its territory; and all persons who are resident within it, whether natural born subjects or aliens; and also all contracts made, and acts done within it. A State may, therefore, regulate the manner and circumstances under which property, whether real or personal or in action, within it shall be held, transmitted, bequeathed, or transferred, or enforced; the condition, capacity, and state of all persons within it; the validity of contracts, and other acts, done within it; the resulting rights and duties growing out of these contracts and acts; and the remedies, and modes of administering justice in all cases calling for the interposition of its tribunals to protect, vindicate, and secure the wholesome agency of its own laws within its own domains.[1]

"No State or nation can, by its laws, directly affect or bind property out of its own territory, or persons not resident therein, whether they are natural born subjects or others. This is a natural consequence of the first proposition; for it would be wholly incompatible with the equality and exclusiveness of the sovereignty of any nation that other nations should be at liberty to regulate either persons or things within its own territory.[2]

"Every nation has a right to bind its own subjects by its own laws in every other place"; [3] but "the obligatory force of such laws cannot extend beyond its own territories. And if such laws are incompatible with the laws of the country where they reside, or interfere with the duties which they owe to the country where they reside, they will be disregarded by the latter. Whatever may be the obligatory force of such laws upon such persons, if they should return to their native country, they can have none in other nations where they reside. They may give rise to personal relations between the sovereign and subjects, to be enforced in his own domains; but they do not rightfully extend to other nations. *Clauduntur territorio.* Nor, indeed, is there, strictly speaking, any difference in this respect whether such laws concern the persons or the property of native subjects. A State has just as much intrinsic right, and no more, to give to its own laws an extraterritorial force, as to the property of its subjects situated abroad, as it has in relation to the persons of its subjects domiciled abroad. That is, as sovereign laws, they have no obligation or power over either. When, therefore, we speak of the right of a State to bind its own native subjects everywhere, we speak only of its own claim and exercise of sovereignty over them, and not of its right to compel or require obedience to such laws on the part of other nations. On

[1] Story, § 18. [2] Story, § 20. [3] § 21.

the contrary, every nation has an exclusive right to regulate persons and things within its own territory according to its own sovereign will and polity.[1]

"From these two maxims or propositions there flows a third, and that is, that whatever force and obligation the laws of one country have in another, depends solely upon the laws and municipal regulations of the latter; that is to say, upon its own proper jurisprudence and polity, and upon its own express or tacit consent."[2]

"The true foundation on which the administration of international law must rest is, that the rules which are to govern are those which arise from mutual interest and utility, from a sense of the inconveniences which would result from a contrary doctrine, and from a sort of moral necessity to do justice in order that justice may be done to us in return."[3]

§ 73. The Doctrine of Vested Rights. — Instead of the Dutch theory of comity, the common law has worked out indigenously a theory of vested rights, which serves the same purpose, that is, the desire to reach a just result, and is not subject to the objections which can be urged against the doctrine of comity.

As early as the time of Story the courts were already saying that an act or obligation valid by the laws of the place where made was valid everywhere;[4] and that a foreign judgment by a court of competent jurisdiction was conclusive of the right it decided.[5] The fullest statement of this new doctrine was by Sir William Scott in Dalrymple *v.* Dalrymple:[6] "The cause being entertained in an English court it must be adjudicated according to the principles of English law applicable to such a case. But the only principle applicable to such a case by the law of England is that the validity of Miss Gordon's marriage rights must be tried by reference to the law of the country where, if they exist at all, they had their origin." Story accepted and developed this theory,[7] which from his time has been the accepted theory in the English and American courts.

This doctrine may be stated and explained as follows.

[1] § 22. [2] § 23. [3] § 35.

[4] Potter *v.* Brown, 5 East, 124; Blanchard *v.* Russell, 13 Mass. 1.

[5] Croudson *v.* Leonard, 4 Cranch 434.

[6] 2 Hagg. Consis. 54: 2 Beale Cas. 41. [7] Story, § 451.

Although the law to be applied to the solution of the Conflict of Laws is the territorial law, this does not mean the law by which such rights as those brought in question would be created within the territory. As Westlake says,[1] "The will which imposes a national law within territorial limits does not necessarily decree the application of that law to all the cases there arising, when great inconvenience would result from so doing." The national law which is applied to the solution of conflicts is that portion of the national law which deals with the solution of conflicts. If by the national law the validity of a contract depends upon the law of the place where the contract was made, then that law is applied for determining the validity of a contract made abroad, not because the foreign law has any force in the nation, nor because of any constraint exercised by an international principle, but because the national law determines the question of the validity of a contract by the *lex loci contractus*. If it were really a case of conflicting laws, and the foreign law prevailed in the case in question, the decision would be handed over bodily to the foreign law. By the national doctrine, the national law provides for a decision according to certain provisions of the foreign law; in the case considered, according to the foreign contract law. The provisions of this law having been proved as a fact, the question is solved by the national law, the foreign factor in the solution — *i.e.*, the foreign contract law — being present as mere fact, one of the facts upon which the decision is to be based.

To explain the territorial theory in other terms, all that has happened outside the territory, including the foreign laws which have in some way or other become involved in the problem, is regarded merely as fact to be considered by the national law in arriving at its decision, and to be given such weight in determining the decision as the national law may choose to give it.

The author summarized this theory in 1902 as follows:[2]

"The topic called 'Conflict of Laws,' deals with the recognition and enforcement of foreign created rights. In the legal sense, all rights must be created by some law. A right is artificial,

[1] Westlake, 21.

[2] Beale, Summary of the Conflict of Laws (in Cases, Vol. iii), §§ 1–5.

not a mere natural fact; no legal right exists by nature. A right is a political, not a social thing; no legal right can be created by the mere will of parties. Law being a general rule to govern future transactions, its method of creating rights is to provide that upon the happening of a certain event a right shall accrue. The law annexes to the event a certain consequence, namely, the creation of a legal right. The creation of a right is therefore conditioned upon the happening of an event. Events which the law acts upon may be of two sorts; acts of human beings, and so-called "acts of God," that is, events in which no human being has a share. Rights generally follow acts of men; though sometimes a right is created as a result solely of an act of God (as lapse of time: accretion). When a right has been created by law, this right itself becomes a fact; and its existence may be a factor in an event which the same or some other law makes the condition of a new right. In other words, a right may be changed by the law that created it, or by any other law having power over it. If no law having power to do so has changed a right, the existing right should everywhere be recognized; since to do so is merely to recognize the existence of a fact."

"A right having been created by the appropriate law, the recognition of its existence should follow everywhere. Thus an act valid where done cannot be called in question anywhere."[1]

§ **74. Dicey.** — The foremost representative of this doctrine today, among common-law writers, is Professor Dicey. It could be expressed no more forcibly and succinctly than he has expressed it.

"The nature of a right acquired under the law of any civilized country must be determined in accordance with the law under which the right is acquired."[2]

"The object for which courts exist is to give redress for the infringement of rights. No court intends to confer upon a plaintiff new rights, except in so far as new rights may be necessary to compensate for, or possibly to guard against, the infringement of an existing right. The basis of a plaintiff's claim is that, at the moment of his coming into court, he possesses some right, *e. g.*, a right to the payment of £20, which has been violated; the bringing of an action implies, in short, the existence of a right of action. When, therefore, A applies to an English court to enforce a right acquired in France, he must in general show that, at the moment

[1] *Ibid.*, § 47. [2] Dicey, 58.

of bringing his action, he possesses a right which is actually acquired under French law, and which he could enforce against the defendant if he sued the defendant in a French court. A complains, for example, of the non-payment of a debt contracted by X in Paris, or seeks damages for an assault committed on him by X in Paris. To bring himself within the principle we are considering, he must show that his right to payment or to damages is actually acquired. He must show that the debt is due under French law, or that the assault is an offence punishable by French tribunals. English law does not, speaking generally, apply to transactions occurring out of England; hence the foundation of A's claim is that he wishes to enforce rights actually obtained in France, and he will, as a rule, fail to make out his case unless he can show that the grievance of which he complains is recognized as such by French law, or, in other words, unless he can show a right to redress recognized by the law of France.

"Whether such a right actually exists, *i.e.*, whether A has an 'acquired right,' is a matter of fact depending upon the law of France and upon the circumstances of the case."[1]

§ 75. The Doctrine of Vested Rights in France: Vareilles-Sommières. — In France the Count de Vareilles-Sommières, Professor at Lille, has, with great originality and force, put forward and supported the doctrine of vested rights, or, as he calls it, of the non-retroactivity of laws. This theory, while it has become the accepted theory in countries governed by the common law, has been given scant attention on the European continent. Even in his pages it is not systematically developed; it is stated almost in passing, and by way of criticism of other theories; yet it is stated forcibly and clearly.

The fundamental truth "is the principle of the reality or more clearly the territoriality of laws, that is to say, the principle by virtue of which every act done on the territory of a state is legitimately governed by the laws of that state: and consequently (subject to exception) receives a force from them which should be recognized and respected in the entire world."[2] "The interest of the state requires as its principle unity of government for all the inhabitants of the territory."[3] "To inhabit a territory is to submit to its sovereignty."[4]

[1] Dicey, 26. [2] Vareilles-Sommières, i, vi. [3] V. S., i, 114.
[4] V. S., i, 112, quoting from Rousseau's Contrat social.

"The principal cause of the grave defects in modern systems of private international law," he says,[1] "is that in discussing the question whether a foreigner's acts should be governed by the local or the foreign law, they do not distinguish between acts done by the foreigner in his own country and acts done by him in the state where the problem arises. . . . No one says nor sees that there is an exact and decisive reason for not applying the local law to acts done outside the territory by foreigners, which does not exist when their acts are within the territory; and that reason is the principle of the non-retroactivity of laws." "It is not only with regard to the state on whose territory acts are done that these acts are governed by the law of that state; it is the same with regard to all other states. Acts which are done on the territory of a state in conformity with its laws ought on principle to be regular and in force in the eyes of the entire world. Acts accomplished on the territory of a state contrary to its laws are null everywhere."[2] Thus the French law, he says, should not be applied where its application would refuse recognition to a foreigner's right acquired in the past, or take away a right for the future by reason of a past act which was accomplished according to the law which applied to it, though we may now criticise the conditions of its validity.[3]

§ 76. **Bustamante.**—One of the most interesting theories based on the doctrine of vested rights is that of Professor Bustamante of the University of Havana. Starting from the proposition that international law limits the jurisdiction, he reaches the logical conclusion that within its jurisdiction a law may create rights which are of world-wide validity.

"The simultaneous existence of sovereignties," he says,[4] "makes it necessary to fix limits in space for their respective legislative jurisdictions. There can exist on the face of the earth no juridical relation without some law, jurisprudence, custom, precedent or principle applicable to it. Since humanity is divided into nations and they are fundamentally equal in the exercise of legislative power, there must exist some principle, precedent, custom, jurisprudence or law, of universal and absolute application to all things and persons. To assert the coexistence of nations is to assert the coexistence of laws, and to suppose coexistent laws is to suppose them limited in application. That the power of the world may not be wasted in strife, science must assign to each its

[1] V. S., i, 183. [2] V. S., i, 19. [3] V. S., i, 31. [4] Bustamante, 37.

sphere of action; and it is fighting with reality to deny the name international to a law which proposes to keep the peace between the laws of different states."

"By legislative jurisdiction is meant not only the power of the positive law to submit to its sway certain groups of juridical relations, but also the power of the state to legislate with respect to them. In other words, we are to deal with a double problem: to fix for the legislator the sphere in which to move, and for the law the limits of its obligatory effect. Some authors take the opposite view, limiting this topic to the study of the territorial application of the law of a given country. I affirm that the legislative power, the origin and fountain of all law, instead of responding to caprice and arbitrary power, must confine itself within determined bounds, out of which it cannot go. In short, when a code transcends the limits of its laws in space, it can do no more than accept a system of private international law, to which its courts must submit, in which men of science may condemn or applaud with absolute freedom.

"Legislative jurisdiction, thus explained, has two classes of limits. Law appears by successive steps within a single nation, but simultaneously throughout the world, divided as it is into many states which in legislative power are equal. In other words, law is born in time and lives in space."

§ 77. **Criticisms of the Territorial Theories.** — Authors who accept the statutory or the international doctrines have criticised the territorial doctrine as narrow, unjust, and unsocial. Laurent has voiced these criticisms in the most extreme form. "England and the United States," he says,[1] "are still governed by a customary law which is rooted in feudality, an essentially territorial law; the anglo-american judges recognize no law but that of their own country, which amounts almost to denying a private international law." And again:[2] "when one passes from the Italian Code to the common law of England and America, one might think he was leaving the 19th century to return to the middle ages. An English writer (Phillimore) admits that there is a complete opposition between the general law of the European continent and the law which governs England and the United States. Whatever be the diversities in the laws and doctrines of the continent, one finds, at least in principle,

[1] Laurent, i, 15. [2] Laurent, i, 35.

that there are personal laws there which govern status and capacity, laws inherent in the person which follow it everywhere. England admits only territorial laws. Phillimore is right in deploring this fundamental disagreement; how shall we hope to succeed in bringing in the reign of law in the private relations of peoples when a powerful nation isolates itself in its sovereignty and refuses to recognize any other law than its own?"

The Belgian jurist, who appears to deny the name *law* to public international law,[1] and whose national law denies access to its courts and even the enjoyment of civil rights to a foreigner, reproaches the common law with being medieval; though the common law accepts as law the doctrines of the law of nations, and extends to the foreigner the right of access to its courts and substantially all other civil rights. Whether the system of private international law, which, as he says, is ill-defined and disputed in almost every rule, and practically incapable of statutory amendment, is superior to a system of national law which guards vested rights at every point, is well-settled in almost every particular, and is capable of easy legislative definition in the few disputed points, will doubtless always remain a matter of opinion; but persons versed in the common law will probably continue to regard an ignorance and provincialism which may properly be called medieval as not confined to either side of the English channel.

Another objection frequently expressed is that the acceptance of the territorial theory means the jeopardizing of rights acquired abroad.[2] This is of course a possibility; one, however, which, as has been seen, the honest advocates of either theory admit. Given a sovereign determined to commit the injustice of refusing effect to foreign rights, the power to ignore them is present. But a sufficient answer to the objection lies in the necessary acceptance, in any civilized law, of the doctrine of vested rights. The objection appears in fact to rest on a confusion due to peculiarities of vocabulary. As will be seen, the same word serves in most European countries to signify both *law* and *a right*. A translation into a European language of the statement in English that foreign *laws* are not recognized as such might

[1] Laurent, i, 14. [2] Weiss, iii, 9.

naturally be misunderstood as a statement that foreign *rights* are not recognized.

§ 78. **Answer to the Criticisms.**—It is recognized as fully by the common law as by the early statutists that to solve all questions by the *lex loci* would be unreasonable and unjust; and the assertion of the nationalist doctrine does not involve this injustice. For it is part of the doctrine, as will be more fully set forth hereafter, that a right vested under a foreign law will be recognized and (unless forbidden by public policy) enforced. If the national law is a civilized law this will of course be done; and if it is not, the principles of a supposed private international law would not constrain its actions. The binding force of the dictates of justice is not created, and cannot be created, by extra-national constraint. No civilized law, national or international, could be oblivious to the just requirements of recognizing the legally accomplished fact. All civilized countries have the common ideal of justice. In the working out of details for accomplishing justice, they necessarily differ; in particular, the two general systems which between them divide the allegiance of the civilized world, differ in many points; but no one, not a blind partisan of one of them, can say that an alleged "international" private law, framed by those versed in one of the systems, will more certainly accomplish justice than the national laws of countries which accept the other.

The only question, it is obvious, is really this: by what law shall it be determined whether the law of a certain country had the legal power to create an alleged right, since if the right was created all civilized nations should recognize the fact. Certain jurists say it should be determined by an alleged international law, upon the terms of which hardly two of them can agree. Other jurists say that this question should be determined by the law of the country in whose courts it arises.

As an actual fact it will of course be determined in accordance with the law of the forum; since it will be determined by each court in accordance with that court's understanding of the law, no matter by what name the court calls it. Why not recognize and admit the truth?

Whatever may be the not unnatural errors in interpreting the common law by those not bred to it (errors to which the author admits his own liability in attempting to summarize and criticise the European civil law) it is clear that in applying their own law the states governed by the common law are neither ignorant nor neglectful of foreign laws, and that so far from denying they are most insistent in preserving the rights of foreigners.

BOOK II

PRELIMINARY CONSIDERATION OF JURISPRUDENCE

CHAPTER IV

LAW AND JURISDICTION

§ 100. Nature of the discussion.

TOPIC 1. SOVEREIGNTY AND JURISDICTION

101. Law as a function of sovereignty.
102. The extent of sovereign power.
103. Jurisdiction under international law.
104. Territorial jurisdiction.
105. Extent of territorial power.
106. Extra-territorial rights.
107. Legislative jurisdiction.
108. Adoption of foreign law.
109. Divided sovereignty.
110. Legal units.
111. What determines the legal unit.
112. Legal units in the United States.
112a. Is there a federal common law?

TOPIC 2. THE NATURE OF LAW

113. Necessity for determining the nature of law.
114. Definition of law.
115. Statute law.
116. Judicial law.
117. Principle or doctrine.
118. The difference between law and fact.
119. Foreign law as a fact.
120. How far knowledge of law extends.

TOPIC 3. THE SOURCE AND GROWTH OF MODERN LAW

121. Legal systems.
122. The principal modern legal systems.
123. Other legal systems.
124. Acceptance of a legal system.
125. The part played by judicial decisions.
126. The causes of change in the unwritten law.
127. The part played by equity.

Topic 4. The Characteristics and Function of Law
128. The social character of law.
129. The generality of law.
130. The universality of law.
131. The continuity of law.
132. The purpose and method of law.
133. Social interests.
134. Private interests of person.
135. Interests of property.
136. Interests of will and act.
137. Vested rights.
138. The legal protection of interests.

§ 100. **Nature of the Discussion.** — It has been seen that certain doctrines, ordinarily dealt with in works upon jurisprudence, must necessarily be studied before the principles of the Conflict of Laws can be mastered. It is the purpose of this Book to state and, to a certain extent, discuss these doctrines. Since, however, this is a mere preliminary study, and not the principal subject of this treatise, no attempt at an exhaustive treatment of the subject, or a consideration of the doctrines of others, will be made; and such citation of authority as is made will be illustrative merely. Legal rights might be analyzed in almost as many ways as there are analysts. The analysis here offered is not presented as supported by better authority or more convincing reasons than that of other writers; but as one that has been found a satisfactory basis for the study of the Conflict of Laws.

Topic 1. Sovereignty and Jurisdiction

§ 101. **Law as a Function of Sovereignty.** — Law has to do with the action of society organized into a state; it can only exist because of state action. Yet on the other hand the state itself, in the modern sense, rests upon law; it is law which secures its existence, determines its constitution, defines its functions, empowers its acts. Law is at once the source and the expression of sovereignty. Law creates the state and the state creates law by a common and mutual impulse; the two are born at an instant, are inseparable through life, and must die together.

But the law which coexists with the state is public law; and public law is one branch only, and for our purposes not the important branch of law. The law which creates and controls the relations of private individuals is private law, and private law presents no paradox of cause or consequence. It cannot exist without the will or at least the acquiescence of a political sovereign. It is needless to explain that this sovereign may be of any kind, from the loose popular association of primitive folk to the most complexly organized modern monarchy or republic. Somewhere in any political society must be found a ruling power, be it the folk, the oligarchy, or the king; and in that power the law-making function inheres. There is no law, then, without a sovereign; and the fundamental inquiry in any study of the application of law must be, what sovereign created the law in question.

§ **102. The Extent of Sovereign Power.** — It will at once appear that this question really involves the settlement of another; in order to decide which sovereign created a law or a legal right, we must first determine the extent of a sovereign's power to create law. Whatever be his profession of power, whatever the terms of his law, if he attempts to act beyond his power his attempt is merely null. No one can do what he has no power to do, whether he be an individual or a sovereign. Before the rise of international relations each sovereign did as he pleased within the limits of his physical power. His own will was his law and there was no other will to check it. In all ancient civilizations this was the case. There was nothing to restrain the strong arm of Egyptian or Persian, of Goth or Hun. And this was necessarily the case; for power physically supreme can be restrained only by law, and the existence of a restraining law requires some sort of organization with wider sovereignty than that of the restrained. Primitive law has behind it the force of opinion of the community, which becomes a legal force as soon as it has greater power than the individual will; the opinion of the community is sovereignty, which through its various transmutations continues supreme until a greater than sovereign power restrains it.

Until this greater power arose, the power of the sovereign was checked by physical limits only. So far, therefore, as his physical power extended, the sovereign could create law; but the law so created had no effect beyond the boundaries of his physical power. The inconsistent laws of another sovereign had equally unrestrained force within the physical boundaries of his power.

§ 103. **Jurisdiction under International Law.** — Sovereign power, then, could be subjected to no restraining force except that of another political association more powerful than itself. Such association came into existence for the first time when a group of nations acquired the consciousness of common interests and common principles of action; in short, when the first imperfect rules of international law came into being. It is only by international law, backed by the force of opinion of civilized nations, that the actual power of a sovereign can be restrained within the limits of legal jurisdiction. Yet, as will be seen, the desire of a sovereign to find himself included in the number of civilized nations is so great as to constrain his acceptance of the principles of international law, and among them the rules governing international jurisdiction. Once the general body of international law has been accepted as part of the law governing a nation, it is impossible, as will be seen, for that nation of its own will to alter any principle of international law or withdraw its adhesion to a portion of international law, at least so far as its relations to other states are concerned.

Among the most important of the principles of international law are those which define the jurisdiction of the sovereigns respectively. These principles are of course limitations on the power of the sovereigns, but they are limitations which no one sovereign has a right to dispute while he remains within the number of civilized states; and if he acts contrary to the principles of international jurisdiction his act is without legal force. Every sovereign, therefore, has a right to disregard, as contrary to law and null, any act of another sovereign which transcends his international jurisdiction.

It will thus be seen that every question of jurisdiction raises primarily a question of law. Whether a certain sovereign act has transcended the jurisdiction of the sovereign actor must always present itself as a question of law to the government of another state. But since the basis of all jurisdiction is power, which is merely limited, not done away altogether, by the action of international law, it will be clear that a thing within the power of a sovereign is *prima facie* within his jurisdiction, and it will lie on the person or state denying jurisdiction to produce a principle of law which limits the right to exercise the existing power.

§ **104. Territorial Jurisdiction.** — In the modern world, sovereigns who are parties to international law are regarded as possessed of a territory of which the boundaries are definitely limited. No body of persons who lack such limited territory can claim the position of a sovereign nation. Through this territory the sovereignty extends and outside it the sovereign's territorial power ceases.

The greater part of the land surface of the earth is thus delimited among states. The high seas remain free from occupation by any sovereign power. Over the high seas, therefore, there can be no territorial jurisdiction extended. Within the boundaries of states there are roving tribes who form no part of the nation within whose territory they exist and have no standing among the sovereign states of international law. Such are the tribes of Indians in the United States and Canada. At various periods in the past, bodies of men with this tribal organization have been common and powerful, and the law of their time was forced to take account of them. Such a condition existed at the time of the breaking up of the Roman Empire, when the barbarian tribes, as the conquerors of the territorial sovereigns, necessarily found a place and a legal jurisdiction. As has just been pointed out, this condition of affairs has entirely come to an end, and all sovereignty is now territorial; though the older condition has left its mark on the law of Europe.

§ **105. Extent of Territorial Power.**— The territorial power of a sovereign extends throughout the land surface of his territory; but the extent of the land does not always measure the limit of territory. Where one state borders upon another on land, there is of course a definite boundary line which is the limit of power of the respective sovereigns. But where the territory of a sovereign borders on the sea, the case is different.

It has been pointed out that the high seas are not subject to territorial occupation; but on the other hand the sovereign of land bordering on the sea is entitled to a certain jurisdiction over the border sea, at least for the purpose of protection. The distance over which this jurisdiction extends was anciently fixed at three miles, as the assumed maximum range of a projectile. Since modern projectiles can be fired over a much greater distance, it has been argued that the territorial jurisdiction of the sovereign bordering on the sea extends further into the ocean than three miles. This, however, has been denied, and it is still an unsettled question. Within the limit of jurisdiction on the sea, whether for three miles or ten, the territorial sovereign has certain rights of policing and fishing, and he appears also to have full territorial rights in the land beneath the sea. It is certain, however, that below high water mark the sea is a highway of nations and the sovereign has no right in ordinary times to prevent the passage of peaceful private vessels through the sea even within the limit of his territorial authority.

Within bays and harbors the case is a more difficult one. It seems to be agreed that his territorial jurisdiction extends throughout a bay or harbor where two points of land at the entrance are within six miles of one another, and the same thing would of course be true of an inner bay or harbor within the point where the opposite shores approach one another nearer than six miles. But greater jurisdiction has been claimed than this. Deep bays and gulfs which lie entirely within the general shore line of a country, but are wider at the mouth than six miles, have been claimed as territorial waters. Such are Delaware Bay in the United States, Conception Bay in Newfoundland, and the Bay of Fundy in Canada. The claim is an unsettled one, but a sensible view appears to be that waters are territorial whenever they lie geographically within the land surface.

Whatever may be the rule for determining territorial waters, it is certain that the rights of the territorial sovereign within these territorial waters are substantially the same as his rights within the land territory, and that a vessel entering a harbor of this sort is as clearly within the territorial jurisdiction of the sovereign as if it were passing through his territory on a railroad train.

§ **106. Extra-Territorial Rights.** — Such being the extent of the territory of sovereigns, it will be convenient to consider what exceptional jurisdiction a sovereign is permitted by international law to exercise within the territory of another sovereign. With one kind of extra-territorial jurisdiction, which raises no question of the conflict of laws, we shall not concern ourselves. This is the jurisdiction which a sovereign exercises over his ambassadors and over his war vessels, and to a less degree over his private property, while they are within the territory of a foreign sovereign. The class of extra-territorial jurisdiction with which we are concerned is the jurisdiction which a sovereign exercises over his subjects and the vessels which fly his flag wherever on earth they may be.

A sovereign may always rightfully oblige his subject, on his allegiance, to obey a command or rule laid upon him. This jurisdiction is in no sense exclusive of the territorial jurisdiction of the sovereign of the territory where the subject in question happens to be. A private foreigner is always within the territorial jurisdiction of the sovereign in whose borders he is. But his own sovereign exercises additional rightful jurisdiction over him, a jurisdiction which is called personal. It will be noticed that personal jurisdiction is based only on law, while territorial jurisdiction is based both upon power and upon law. The latter is the stronger, and personal jurisdiction must always yield to it. It would therefore seem clear that the exercise of personal jurisdiction by a sovereign must be confined to negative commands. An affirmative command cannot rightly be given. To order one's subject abroad to do something would cause him at once to act under the foreign law of the territorial jurisdiction, and subject his act to the independent commands of both sovereigns. This would hamper the ordinary affairs of life, and tend to bring the two sovereigns into conflict. Such conflicts it is the object of international law to avoid, and it is clear therefore that the principles of international law will neither create nor permit them. In other words, international law gives no power to a sovereign to issue positive commands to his subject abroad; personal jurisdiction is limited, so long as the subject stays in the territory of a foreign sovereign, to the forbidding of acts. Furthermore, since the territorial sovereign may command the doing of acts and since his command must prevail, and since international law by its very nature cannot create a conflict of rights, even the commands issued by the personal sovereign to refrain from acting must be limited to such commands as are consistent with the subject's duty to the sovereign of the territory in which he resides. Such commands are usually in fact limited to criminal statutes placing a penalty upon the commission of acts, therein declared criminal, wherever those acts may be done; and the commands have always this limitation, that any justification for an act given by the sovereign of the territory in which the act is done will necessarily be a valid justification for violating the personal command.

Over vessels which bear the sovereign's flag the jurisdiction is somewhat more complex. Such a vessel has been called a floating portion of the sovereign's territory. This is not a happy or a true phrase. In no sense is the jurisdiction over a vessel territorial. A vessel does, however, constitute a community of itself, subject to government by law, and while it is on the high seas, as has been seen, there is no territorial law to govern it. Under these circumstances it is governed by "the law of the flag." The case is slightly different from that of the individual over whom, when abroad, jurisdiction is purely personal; for the law that prevails on the vessel is a complete law, sufficient to govern all actions done upon it, and not in competition with the law of any other sovereign. If one bear in mind the quality of continuity which must be inherent in all law, it will be clear that some law must prevail on the vessel at all times and that in the absence of some power changing that law it will continue throughout the entire history of the vessel to be the same. The law, therefore, which in the absence of some change prevails at a given time on a vessel, must be the law which she brought with her upon her first leaving land. This must have been the law of the flag, unless indeed she was not only built in, but started on her first merchant voyage from a foreign country. For this exceptional case the law makes no provision, but lays down the general proposition that the law of the flag is at all times the law governing the vessel.

When, however, a merchant vessel enters a foreign port, she is subject to a double jurisdiction. The jurisdiction of the sovereign of the flag still continues, but beside it and in certain cases superseding it is the jurisdiction of the territorial sovereign. Since, however, the vessel is in port only temporarily, and since it cannot enter into the ordinary affairs of life ashore, international law permits the continued jurisdiction of the sovereign of the flag in all respects where the direct and necessary interests of the territorial sovereign do not prevent it. This is usually expressed by saying that the jurisdiction of the territorial sovereign prevails only in so far as is required by considerations of public order.

§ 107. **Legislative Jurisdiction.** — The extent of territorial power of a sovereign being thus fixed, the jurisdiction of the sovereign to make law cannot be open to serious doubt. Throughout his territories he is the supreme legislative power, and the law of no other sovereign can be effective. This seems self-evident. Since legislation is a function of sovereignty, and since the sovereignty within the territory is and must be exclusively lodged in the territorial sovereign, he alone must be the lawgiver.

Axiomatic as this seems, it is nevertheless strenuously denied by a school of European jurists, who assert some natural or international right in a sovereign to affect by his own law the rights and the acts of his subjects abroad, even though these subjects be at the time within the territory of another sovereign. This doctrine, however, carries with it its own disproof. For it is universally admitted by the same jurists that the subject is controlled in all things by the local "laws of public order" or police laws; and it is also agreed that the territorial sovereign may make any law he pleases a law of public order. Which laws shall come within that description rests in his own will. It follows that his own legislative will is supreme over every person as well as thing within his territory; and that if a foreigner exercises his own personal law there it is because such is the legislative will of the territorial sovereign, and not at all because such is the will of his personal sovereign.

§ 108. **Adoption of Foreign Law.** — It is clear, however, that by the will of the territorial sovereign a foreigner may exercise his own personal law; in other words, a sovereign may adopt a single provision or a whole system of foreign law for application to the relations of particular persons or classes of persons. Several instances of this sort may be enumerated.

The institution, in the near and the far Orient, of consular courts for administering justice to and between foreigners, and in accordance with their own law, is perhaps the most striking instance of the adoption of foreign law.[1] The consular court administers, it is true, the law of its own nation; but not as such law, nor is it in truth sitting as a national court.[2] It is in reality a court of the nation within whose territory it is sitting; and it administers a different law, to wit, the law of its own nation, only by the legislative will, express or tacit, of the territorial sovereign.

There are other examples of the same general nature. Thus, in British India, the Hindu and the Mohammedan laws are permitted to govern the rights and the acts of persons of those creeds; not because Mohammed and Manu still possess legislative power, but because England, the territorial sovereign, so wills it. Similarly when the Ottoman sovereign permits his Christian subjects to be judged as to matrimonial affairs by their Church courts, in accordance with the Canon Law, this is done not as bringing the Canon Law into competition with the law of the territorial sovereign, but as making the Canon Law *pro hac vice* Ottoman law.[3]

An example in our own law is the doctrine that goods are transmitted at death according to the law of the domicil of the deceased foreign owner. This doctrine does not suppose the domiciliary law to apply to the goods as law. The territorial sovereign is still the lawgiver. But the territorial sovereign, for reasons deemed good by him, chooses to dispose of the goods in accordance with the provisions of a foreign law, adopted by him for this purpose as part of his own law.

§ 109. **Divided Sovereignty.** — Thus far sovereignty has been regarded as a simple fact, a single power lodged somewhere in the body politic, legislating by a single will. Modern forms of government have however developed a more complex

[1] Papayanni *v.* Russian Steam Nav. Co., 2 Moo. P. C. N. S. 161, 1 Beale, 87; *In re* Ross, 140 U. S. 453, 1 Beale, 89; Fichera *v.* De Strens, 16 Clunet, 141, 1 Beale, 89 (Belgian Consular Ct. in Egypt).

[2] Thus the Constitution, though part of the law of the land, does not prevail in the Consular court. *In re* Ross, *supra;* Fichera *v.* De Strens, *supra.*

[3] Farag *v.* Mardrous, 19 Juris. des Trib. de la Réforme, 231, 1 Beale, 85.

form of sovereignty. The most striking and important instance of this is that of the United States of America.

In this country the United States and the separate States are law-making sovereigns; and in each state the statutory law has a double source. Acts of Congress and acts of the State legislature are equally potent within the territory of the state. If no rules existed to govern the exercise of this double power, the result would be inconsistent provisions on the same subject, and consequent anarchy. But the same power which created the double sovereignty — the Constitution of the United States — made provision for its exercise. Certain topics of law are by that Constitution placed entirely within the legislative power of the United States; certain other topics are left to the states until Congress chooses to act, and are then within the legislative power of the United States; while, in the absence of any constitutional provision, legislative power over the remaining topics of law is left to the states.

§ 110. **Legal Units.** — While the law-making power is an attribute of sovereignty, it does not follow that the law is identical throughout the bounds of a single sovereign's territory. Thus in the United States there is one law of New York, another law of Louisiana, and another law of Alaska. Though the sovereign may make law as he will, it does not follow that he will have it the same in all parts of his territory. A difference may arise in two ways. As new territory is added to old, or as two countries are combined under a single sovereign, the laws of the formerly separate units continue distinct unless the sovereign by his law-making will assimilates one to the other; which he seldom does. In the second place, when new law is to be made, the sovereign frequently legislates for part only of his territories; either because he has created separate legislative bodies in the separate units of his dominions, or because a single legislative body acting throughout his dominions creates a new law for a portion only of his territory.

It must be obvious, in view of what has been said, that the extent of territory through which a given law prevails can never be in the ordinary sense a question of law. Whether the territory be domestic or foreign territory, the extent of its boundaries must be accepted as a political fact. The civilized portion of the earth is divided up into certain units of territory in each of which a particular law proper to that territory alone prevails, and we may call the territory a legal unit.

§ 111. **What determines the Legal Unit.** — It has been seen that the existence of separate legal units within the dominions of a single sovereign is a fact, the result of historical accidents: division or annexation of territory, conquest and colonization, federation and decentralization, all affect the extent of territory within which a single law prevails.

When new territory is annexed to a sovereign's domains, this new territory may retain its ancient law, thus giving rise to a new legal unit, or it may become merged with the territory of the new sovereign, forming with it a single unit. This does not necessarily depend upon the size and importance of the annexed territory. Thus when Hawaii was annexed to the United States it remained a separate legal unit; but when Wales was gradually conquered by England it became a part of the legal unit, England. Cession of small portions of territory by a rectification of boundary between contiguous states furnishes a common instance of merger of new territory into the old unit.[1]

Division of territory between two independent sovereigns results necessarily in the creation of a new legal unit, unless the territory so divided is merged into the domain of one or both sovereigns; since the laws of the two parts must necessarily diverge under the new sovereigns. Thus upon the separation of West Virginia from Virginia and upon the division of the Territory of Dakota into two states, new legal units were necessarily created.

It has been said that the size of the territory in question does not necessarily determine whether or not it shall remain a separate legal unit. Usually, of course, a small portion of territory will be merged in the state to which it is joined. One striking instance, however, constituted a unique case. The District of Columbia was formed by the cession of a few square miles of territory by the state of Maryland, and the same amount by the state of Virginia. Though these portions of territory were small, they were not annexed to a larger

[1] Chappell *v.* Jardine, 51 Conn. 64, 1 Beale, 77.

existing territory; there was no existing body of law into which the law of the ceded territories could merge; so long therefore as the District was so constituted, although its territory was small, it consisted of two entirely distinct legal units. The portion of the District south of the Potomac was soon retroceded to Virginia, and its law became merged again in that of Virginia.[1]

To repeat what has already been said at length, no rule can determine what portion of territory shall become a legal unit; the determination of this is an historical accident.

§ **112. Legal Units in the United States.** — From what has already been stated, it is clear that there cannot be two independent laws within a territory, even though that territory be subject to the legislative jurisdiction of two independent sovereigns. The law of the territory, resulting from the legislative action of both sovereigns, is a single law. The law of a single legal unit must be one law, the one and undivided law of that territory.

The case of the United States offers a peculiar illustration of this principle. The smallest legal unit, it is clear, is the state; for the law of each state prevails throughout its territory, while no other state or portion of any state has law in all respects identical. But the law of a state comprehends not merely the common law and the statutes of the state, but also the constitution and treaties of the United States and the Acts of Congress. These are, to be sure, identical elements of the laws of all the states; but this does not mean that there is a legal unit extending throughout the United States. This should surprise us no more than the fact that the general system of the common law is a common element in the law of most of our states. If we could find a larger unit than the single state we must find a single law of that unit prevailing throughout its territory. Such a single law, passing state lines, does not exist. If we take two contiguous states of the union we find that their laws have certain large common elements, but that they also differ from one another in many particulars. They are, therefore, separate legal units. It is perfectly correct to say, as the Pennsylvania court has said, that the law of each of the states consists

[1] Tyner *v.* U. S., 23 D. C. App. 324, 361.

of the constitution, treaties and statutes of the United States, the constitution and statutes of the particular state and the common law of that state.[1]

§ **112 a. Is there a Federal Common Law?** — Under the peculiar organization of our federal courts a question has arisen which tests the fundamental conceptions of law. In each of our states there are two sets of courts, with concurrent jurisdiction over ordinary civil actions, the resort to one or the other being determined merely by the citizenship of the parties at the time of bringing suit. The question of law is the same, whether suit is brought in the federal or in the state courts; and, as has been seen, each court is administering *as law* the law of the only legal unit in which they have judicial power, that is, the state. Since the two sets of courts are entirely independent, neither can be absolutely bound by the action of the other. The Supreme Court of the United States, in Swift *v.* Tyson,[2] held that on ordinary questions of unwritten law, not involving statutes of the state or special doctrines concerning the title to property, the federal courts were at liberty to follow their own idea of the common law of the state, and should not feel bound by prior decisions of the state court which were in opposition to the opinion prevailing throughout the country as to the "general commercial law." This decision, unfortunate in that it unsettled the minds of lawyers as to the law and thus made it difficult to advise clients, was nevertheless quite within the right of the court; the federal court in the state was given by the Constitution of the United States as full power to declare the law as the state court. The law thus declared was of course the law of the state, but the way in which it was decided, the weight given by the court to the decisions of courts, and especially of federal courts, in other states, led lawyers to apply the name of "federal common law" to the doctrine.

Meanwhile, a new controversy arose which gave a new and more restricted meaning to the phrase. Soon after the passage of the Interstate Commerce Act a suit was brought in the Federal court for the Northern District of Illinois by a shipper, to recover the excess of freight exacted by a railroad, before the passage of the Act, on an interstate shipment, on the ground that the rate charged was illegally high. In this case, Swift *v.* Philadelphia & Reading Railroad Company, 58 Federal Reporter, 858, Judge Grosscup, in

[1] Mitchell, J., in Forepaugh *v.* Delaware L. & W. R. R., 128 Pa. 217, Beale, 136.

[2] 16 Pet. 1, Beale, 95. For a collection of the later authorities on this doctrine, see 5 L. R. A. 508. See post § 125.

the Circuit Court, held that since the regulation of interstate commerce had been committed to Congress by the Constitution of the United States, the separate states could no longer by their own law, common or statutory, regulate commerce; and there was therefore no existent principle of law, before the Interstate Commerce Act, requiring carriers to limit their charges to reasonable rates on interstate commerce.

A few months later Judge Shiras, in the Northern District of Iowa, dealt with a similar situation in the case of Murray *v.* Chicago and Northwestern Railway Company, 62 Federal Reporter, 24. He reached the opposite conclusion, holding that a principle of the common law existed in Iowa before the Act which required interstate carriers to charge no more than reasonable rates. He argued that "the final disruption of all political ties between the colonies and the mother country did not terminate the existence of the common law in the colonies"; that "the adoption of the Constitution did not deprive the people of the several colonies of the protection and advantages of the common law"; that "the principles and modes of procedure of the three systems of law, equity, and admiralty, in force previous to the adoption of the Constitution, remained in force after its adoption, save as to such modifications as were created by the provisions of the Constitution"; and therefore that "in the absence of Congressional regulation of interstate commerce, the courts called upon to decide cases arising out of interstate commerce must apply the principles of the common law." He added that "if the law of the particular State does not govern [the carrier's] relation, and prescribe the rights and duties which it implies, then there is and can be no law that does until Congress expressly supplies it, or is held by implication to supply it." In the course of his opinion he used language which might be taken to suppose the existence of a common law created by, or at least referable to the United States, rather than to the States; but his conclusion as a whole seems to have been that the common law of Iowa covered the case.

In a subsequent proceeding in the Swift case, reported in 64 Federal Reporter, 59, Judge Grosscup again took up the question. He first summarized his formal opinion in the following paragraph.

"The right to recover from common carriers for unreasonable exactions must be found in some positive law of the land, applicable to the case in hand. Such a prohibition is in fact found in the common law; but it is not applicable to the case in hand, unless there be a common law of the United States, as a distinct sovereignty, because the regulation of the rates upon which the suit is dependent is within the scope of interstate commerce, and an exclusively national affair, in which the need of uniformity is imperative. There is no common law of the United States, as a distinct sovereignty; and there being no pronouncement of Congress upon this subject, either expressly or impliedly, outside of the Interstate Commerce Act, and this action not having been brought under the Interstate Commerce Act, there is no law, either of the United States or the State, applicable to the case in hand, and there can therefore be no recovery."

The only link in this summary, he said, that had met with serious objections, was the one which affirmed the non-existence of a United States common law. He thereupon proceeded to combat this theory of a separate federal common law, which he did with great learning and ability. "No one," he said, "doubts the existence of some law of the land everywhere. No plain or valley, no nook or corner, to which the dominion of man has extended itself, is without some law of the land. Indeed, law is the breath of dominion." He then laid down the proposition that, "the state has not the power to prescribe rules within the fields exclusively belonging to the nation. From each of these two fields, the nation and the state, as the case may be, is excluded as a law giver. Now, this must apply as well to the system of law to which the sovereign succeeds as to that which it immediately creates; to the common or civil law as well as to that which comes from its own legislative or judicial will. In other words, the state or nation, having no power to give law in the fields exclusively belonging to the other, logically can have succeeded to no law applicable to such fields. Neither can a common law or a civil law within fields to which it can extend no law at all." He continued with the assertion that "there cannot be separate systems of law over the same subject matter and the same territory, emanating from separate sources of authority. If the nation already has a system, and such system is within its field of power, the state cannot invade that field to change or modify it." He then came to the conclusion that since the constitution and congress had adopted no system of common law in this matter which was within the exclusive federal jurisdiction, there could be no common law bearing upon the matter.

Meanwhile a war of pamphlets had been excited by the decisions. Editorials in several law journals,[1] which immediately followed the decisions, mistook the point, confusing the "common law of the United States" with which the cases were dealing with that so-

[1] University Law Review, 236; 27 American Law Review, 614; 28 Chicago Legal News, 38, reprinting an editorial from the New York Law Journal, 1895, p. 1462.

called common law of the federal courts, established by the case of Swift *v.* Tyson, which, as has been seen, was nothing more than the creed of the federal courts that in applying the ordinary unwritten law of their various jurisdictions, they should apply it as they understood it, without being absolutely bound by the decisions of the State courts. An interesting and valuable article, giving the same meaning to the phrase, and thus missing the entire point of the judicial controversy which inspired it, may be found in 52 Albany Law Journal, 247, by William Hepburn Russell.

A much sounder and more scholarly discussion was that of Professor Blewett Lee in 2 Northwestern Law Review, 200. Professor Lee accepted the doctrine of a federal common law, both in ordinary cases of commercial law and in the special cases under discussion. He said (on p. 213): "The laws of the States are in force in the United States courts only because the United States in its sovereignty by statute or by comity has made those laws its own, and in those courts they are laws by virtue of the sovereignty of the United States, not of the sovereignty of the individual state which enacted them." This reasoning seems to invert the facts. It is the States which by the Constitution allowed the United States courts to administer their law in their territory. Surely if A, resident in New York, made a promissory note to the order of B, the law of New York governed the obligation; and if B indorsed to C, a native of New Jersey, who sued A in the federal court the same law must continue to govern A's obligation. "For fear of misapprehension," continued Professor Lee, "let it be remembered that no contention is made that the Supreme Court has purported to administer a national common law — the point is that they have in fact, not in all, but in a large class of cases, administered one. Perhaps they have never admitted they were doing so. From Swift *v.* Tyson down most of the decisions could be explained on the theory that the court was administering the law of a state, but simply differed with the state courts as to what it was. This theory is ably put by Mr. Justice Matthews in Smith *v.* Alabama, 124 U. S. 465, 478. But in the face of the well-known fact that the common law differs in all the states, it taxes our credulity when the court finds it to be the same on nearly every important question in each State, unless there be one common law, the same in them all. Moreover in many cases there is no State common law. Unquestionably there is a common law in force in the Territories, and what common law can it be if not the common law of the United States?" The answer is obvious: in each Territory its own law, which continues the same after the admission of the Territory to Statehood.

The immediate controversy was closed by the decision of the Supreme Court in Western Union Telegraph Company *v.* Call Publishing Company, 181 United States Reports, 92, 1 Beale, 127. The court (Mr. Justice Brewer delivering the opinion) held that "the principles of the common law are operative upon all interstate commercial transactions except so far as they are modified by congressional enactment"; "not, it is true, of a body of law distinct from the common law enforced in the States, but as containing the general rules and principles by which all transactions are controlled, except so far as those rules and principles are set aside by express statute." The opinion of Judge Shiras in the Murray case was approved, not as establishing (what had been understood by several lawyers) that there is a separate federal common law, but that there is a general common-law system of legal reasoning (see *post,* §§ 117, 121) by which the federal courts will be guided in declaring the law of the States.

From what has been previously said, it must be clear that the solution of the question presents no difficulty. The United States, as we have seen, constitutes no legal unit as distinct from the separate States and territories; in each of the latter legal units its own law prevails and no other. If the phrase "federal common law" is taken to mean that there is a particular common law, extending throughout the territory of the United States, being the common law as administered in the federal courts, or the unwritten law over which Congress has legislative power, *i.e.*, power to *change* it (all the power which by the Constitution was conferred upon the United States or any of its departments), and that this law is distinct from the law of the states, this meaning is untrue. All the territory of the United States is exhausted by its division among smaller legal units; all the law that exists in each of these units is the one all-pervading law of its territory; there is no room left for the United States to be a legal unit or to have a particular law of its own. If on the other hand the phrase means to describe that portion of the particular common law of a state over which Congress has legislative power the expression is correct, but has no legal significance. As will be seen in the discussion of the continuity of law (post, §131), law is not changed by a change of legislative power, such as took place, with regard to interstate commerce, upon the adoption by each state of the Constitution of the United States; the old law as it existed before such adoption continued in existence until changed by Congress. The so-called federal common law, therefore, before any Congressional change is absolutely identical with the common law of the State.

TOPIC 2. THE NATURE OF LAW

§ 113. Necessity for Determining the Nature of Law. — Whatever meaning and scope be given to our subject, it necessarily involves, as its fundamental requirement, an accurate knowledge of the meaning of law. If we are to find a solution for a conflict of two independent laws, we must first study the nature of those laws, their method of action, the extent of their power; if we predicate an international rule, we must learn the meaning of such an international rule, and discover how it comes to control matters within the apparent jurisdiction of a single sovereign; and if we are to investigate only a particular law, it is equally necessary to know its nature and the scope of its action.

Writers on the various branches of the common law have seldom thought it necessary to define the term *law*, though it is of course a fundamental conception in every legal work. Blackstone does, to be sure, define law as "a rule of civil conduct prescribed by the supreme power in a state, commanding what is right and prohibiting what is wrong,"[1] and explains in a helpful way the meaning of his terms. But if we desire further light on the meaning of law we must turn, not to treatises on the conflict of laws, or on other branches of the law, but to writers on jurisprudence and the theory of law.

§ 114. Definition of Law. — Law is the body of general principles and of particular rules in accordance with which civil rights are created and regulated and wrongs prevented or redressed.

No more exact definition, it is believed, can be framed. For the whole body of law consists of several parts, as will be seen, each part having the same effect with regard to rights and wrongs, but differing in origin and nature. For ordinary purposes, the parts of the law may be enumerated as: (1), formulated provisions of the legislature; (2), the special rules of law applied by the courts; (3), the general body of principles accepted as the fundamental principles of jurisprudence. The definitions which have been suggested have usually been especially applicable to one of these parts only.

[1] 1 Bl. Com. 44.

§ **115. Statute Law.** — The writers of the analytical school of jurisprudence, emphasizing the positive character of law as an expression of sovereign will, have proposed definitions which fit one portion of the law only; that is, the rules made by the legislative body.

"Law, or the law, taken indefinitely, is an abstract or collective term, which, when it means anything, can mean neither more nor less than the sum total of a number of individual laws taken together."[1] "A rule laid down for the guidance of an intelligent being by an intelligent being having power over him."[2] "The speech of him who by right commands somewhat to be done or omitted."[3] "A general rule of external human action enforced by a sovereign political authority."[4]

These definitions appear to ignore the principal element of law, the so-called "unwritten law." So important is this portion of the law, and so widespread is the distinction, that in other languages than English different terms are used to distinguish the two. The positive law formulated and fixed by a legislative body is called *lex, loi, Gesetz;* the general unwritten law is called *ius, droit, Recht.*

The definitions of the analytic school are properly applicable only to *lex.* Austin, realizing this defect, fitted the facts to his theory by assuming a tacit command by the sovereign to his judges to express the rules of law which they lay down in their decisions; thus assimilating judicial to statute law.

A second objection to these definitions, even extended (by a fiction) to cover the unwritten law, is that they all ignore that quality of the law which is absolutely characteristic: that it tends to form a single homogeneous philosophical system. Any definition of law which treats each part of it as an isolated thing, instead of as part of an embodied system, misses its nature altogether.

A third objection to these definitions is that they do not accord with the usage of those who best know the law. This objection has been so well phrased by Mr. Salmond that nothing further is necessary than to quote his words.[5]

[1] Bentham, Works, I, 148.

[2] Austin, I, 88.

[3] Hobbes, Works, II, 49.

[4] Holland, Jurisprudence, 11th ed., p. 42.

[5] Salmond, Jurisprudence, 4th ed., p. 10.

"Most English writers have, in defining law, defined it in the concrete, instead of in the abstract sense. They have attempted to answer the question: 'What is a law?', while the true enquiry is: 'What is law?' The central idea of juridical theory is not *lex* but *jus*, not *Gesetz* but *Recht*. To this inverted and unnatural method of procedure there are two objections. In the first place, it involves a useless and embarrassing conflict with legal usage. In the mouths of lawyers the concrete significance is quite unusual. They speak habitually of law, of the law, of rules of law, of legal principles, but rarely of a law or of the laws. When they have occasion to express the concrete idea, they avoid the vague generic expression, and speak of some particular species of law—a statute, act of parliament, by-law, or rule of court. In the second place, this consideration of laws instead of law tends almost necessarily to the conclusion that statute law is the type of all law and the form to which all of it is reducible in the last analysis. It misleads inquirers by sending them to the legislature to discover the true nature and origin of law, instead of to the courts of justice. It is consequently responsible for much that is inadequate and untrue in the juridical theory of English writers."

The distinction has been neatly and concisely stated by Professor Pound:[1] "Not merely laws, expressions of the popular will for the time being, but law, an expression of reason applied to the relations of man with man and of man with the state."

§ **116. Judicial Law.**—Writers of the historical school emphasize that sort of law which has grown up as a result of the decisions of the courts, "broadening down from precedent to precedent," and while they may deny that it has been made by the courts, they insist upon its character as the rule upon which courts proceed. Thus Thayer defines law as "a rule or standard which it is the duty of a judicial tribunal to apply and enforce."[2] Salmond's is even more concise: "The creed of the courts of justice";[3] "The body of principles recognized and applied by the state in the

[1] The judicial office in the United States, Worcester, 1914, p. 18.

[2] Thayer, *Preliminary Treatise on Evidence.*

[3] Salmond, Jurisprudence, 4th ed., 13.

administration of justice."[1] Professor Gray emphasizes still further the requirement of enforcement by the courts: "The law," he says, "is composed of the rules which the courts lay down for the determination of legal rights and duties."[2]

A serious difficulty with most of these definitions is that they confuse cause and result. Courts are sworn to enforce the law, not to make it; and though it is strenuously contended that they do in fact make the law, it must be admitted at least that they make it before they enforce it.[3] As Sir Frederic Pollock well says, law is enforced by the state because it is law: it is not law merely because the state enforces it.[4] These definitions, therefore, define merely by stating one general characteristic of law. And, as will be seen, even this is not always a characteristic.

§ **117. Principle or Doctrine.** — The authors whose opinions have been examined neglect, or at least too little emphasize, the one most important feature of law: that it is not a mere collection of arbitrary rules, but a body of scientific principle. That part of the law which in other languages is known as *ius*, *Recht*, *droit*, is a branch of practical philosophy; by which, through the use of reason and experience, legal generalizations may be made. Purity of doctrine may be lost through wrong decisions of courts, thus warping legal principle by bad precedent; but wrong decisions are after all uncommon, and the law is not seriously affected by them. The application of general principles may be inhibited by legislation: but the amount of legislation which affects ordinary private law is relatively small, and doctrine is not greatly changed by statute. Much the largest and most important part of the law, therefore, is this body of principle, or as it is almost invariably called by European writers, *doctrine*. The changes in principle made by legislation and by wrong decisions constitute the greater part of the peculiar local law of any jurisdiction, as distinguished from the general doctrine of the prevailing legal system.

Law, therefore, is made in part by the legislature; in part it

[1] *Ibid.*, 9.

[2] Gray, *The Nature and Sources of the Law*, § 191.

[3] Professor Thayer's definition is not open to this criticism.

[4] Pollock, *First Book of Jurisprudence*, 27.

rests upon precedent; and in great part it consists in a homogeneous, scientific, and all-embracing body of principle; and a correct definition of law in general must apply to all these varieties of law. Sir Frederic Pollock has met this necessity in a definition which may be succinctly stated as the sum of the rules binding members of the state as such.[1]

If this definition can be criticised, it is in the statement that the rules of law bind individuals. Parties are bound, not by the law, but by obligations created by the law. To confuse the law and the legal obligation is like confusing the law and the decision. "All law is concerned with the acquisition or the preservation or the restriction of rights."[2] If for the idea of rules binding a party we substitute the idea of law creating the obligation, we arrive in substance at the definition first proposed.

§ 118. **The Difference Between Law and Fact.** — In the last analysis the law under which we live is as much a fact of our lives as the officers who administer that law. Any differentiation, therefore, between law and fact cannot rest upon any real or logical difference between them. The body of principles which we call law does not differ in kind from the body of principles which we call ethics. It is only to the lawyer that law and fact offer themselves as opposing categories, and this distinction in the lawyer's mind reduces itself to a distinction between what he ought to know as a lawyer and the facts of which a lawyer has no peculiar knowledge. To the learned lawyer, and especially to the really learned judge, law is a part of himself, a part of his actual thought and existence. The thought of my nearest friend is to me a fact, while my own is something more than that, it is my experience and my life. In this way his law presents itself to one who is really learned in it. Such a man solving a legal problem presented to him does not say, such and such a solution seems reasonable or reaches a practical result: he says, it is law. To a learned judge, argument of counsel is not instruction. It does not purport or attempt to tell him what he does not already know. Argument recalls, stimulates, or corrects in a judge his own line of thought. A sound judge

[1] Pollock, *First Book of Jurisprudence*, 7.
[2] Ulpian in Dig. 1, 3, 41.

in deciding a case does not consciously exercise his will to reach a new interpretation or a new development of law. He merely follows out his own line of thought as a lawyer and registers the conclusion to which he is led as a lawyer by this line of thought. Law, to a lawyer, is a part of his own mind; and it is only thus that it differs from fact.

§ 119. **Foreign Law as a Fact.** — It follows from these considerations that the law of another state must always present itself to a lawyer, and especially to a judge on the bench, as a fact. To be sure, if the foreign law is based on the same system as his own the judge will, as a lawyer, be familiar with that general system, but the system will have been changed in the foreign state, not only by legislation but also by changes in the unwritten law; and in its actual condition therefore he will not know it as law, but only as a fact, of the nature of which he must be informed. The foreign law must be proved to him as a fact.[1]

The New York Court of Appeals has unfortunately overlooked these considerations, and has asserted its right to find as law the law of another common-law state.[2]

The fallacy of this reasoning is easily recognized. As to the common law in the broadest sense, the system of doctrine common to English-speaking nations, it is of course correct. But in the sense in which the common law was to be found by the court, that is, the unwritten law of the particular state, the statement is entirely and obviously false. So far from its being true, the particular common law of New York and the particular common law of Tennessee must necessarily be different, unless the two states form a single legal unit, which we know not to be the case.

§ 120. **How far Knowledge of Law Extends.** — In a simple legal unit like England the extent of the court's knowledge is easily determined. An English court knows no law

[1] Kline *v.* Baker, 99 Mass. 253.

[2] Faulkner *v.* Hart, 82 N. Y. 413; St. Nicholas Bank *v.* State Bank, 128 N. Y. 26, 1 Beale, 142.

The basis of this view as expressed by Mr. Justice Earl in St. Nicholas Bank *v.* State Bank is that "There is no common law peculiar to Tennessee. But the common law there is the same as that which prevails here and elsewhere, and the judicial expositions of the common law there do not bind the courts here."

except that of England. Where, however, a court has appellate jurisdiction from several states or colonies having different law, its knowledge must extend so far as to embrace all laws prevailing in the places from which appeals may be taken to it. Thus the Judicial Committee of the Privy Council of Great Britain must know as law the laws of all the British colonies. The result of this principle in our own country is a complex one. The Supreme Court of the United States must know as law the law of each state, territory and colony of the United States, since it is a court of appeal from each of them in cases brought in the federal courts. Since that is true, it seems to be accepted as a corollary that every federal judge, and it would seem to follow, every member of the federal bar in any state, must know as law all these laws.[1] Curious results follow from this doctrine. Thus all federal courts know as law the Spanish law up to the independence of Mexico, and the Mexican law previous to the Texas Revolution, since that is part of the law of Texas and known to the Supreme Court as such.[2] These problems will be considered at length in a later chapter.

Topic 3. The Source and Growth of Modern Law

§ 121. **Legal Systems.** — The distinction between the two kinds of unwritten law — the law formulated by the courts, and based upon their decisions, and the general body of legal principles known to lawyers — has already been examined. As it happens, the modern world possesses two such bodies of principle, or legal systems, one or the other of which is the basis of the law of each civilized state. The greater part of the continent of Europe has derived its legal principles from Rome; while England and the United States, together with most of the English colonies, are governed by principles of law which arose on English soil, and are known as "the Common Law."

It has been seen that each legal unit has a particular law of its own, peculiar to it, which is known as its "common law." There is a common law of New York, and a quite

[1] Story, J., in Owings *v.* Hull, 9 Pet. 607.

[2] Bradley, J., in United States *v.* Perot, 98 U. S. 428.

distinct common law of Tennessee or of England; and this fact has already been emphasized. In what sense, then, can this general common law, this system which is accepted by all so-called common-law jurisdictions but is the particular and peculiar law of none, be called law?

Most writers, indeed, deny it the name. Both the analytic school, which bases law upon sovereign will, and the historical school, which bases it upon precedent, refuse to recognize as truly law this philosophical system which has neither basis. Yet the universal usage of lawyers sanctions the use of the word as applied to a body of principles which forms the doctrinal basis of a number of particular unwritten laws. The unqualified phrase "the common law" is in as good use as the qualified phrase "the common law of England" or "the common law of New York." That there is an unwritten law in the true sense common to most of the English speaking countries is recognized by every lawyer. The common law of England is not the common law of New York or of Virginia; yet the Common Law is the basis of study in every law school in America which professes to be more than a mere trade-school for local artisans, and is the foundation of the principles discussed in every legal treatise of more than local authority. To say that the Common Law in this broader sense is not truly law would logically lead to the abolition of every law school of more than local importance and the transfer of its students to the faculty of philosophy. No lawyer would deny that such general bodies of principle exist and are capable of scientific development; which is in accordance, in the case of each, with its own peculiar constitution. If the universal usage of experts is to fix the meaning of their terms, these systems must be allowed the name of law, though no sovereign directs their development, and no court has lent its sanction to many of their principles.

§ 122. **The Principal Modern Legal Systems.** — The two systems of law which between them divide the modern western world have had a quite different origin, as Professor Pound has pointed out.[1] The Roman law, having run its course as a narrow city law and reached the period of maturity, was

[1] *A Feudal Principle in Modern Law;* International Journal of Ethics, xxv, 13.

broadened and fashioned into a systematic body of doctrine, at a time when the barbarians were established within the empire and the conception of tribal law was therefore familiar. It was then subjected to comment by the brilliant lawyers of the middle ages, who were familiar with a system under which each city and each province had its peculiar statutes and customs while at the same time they formed integral parts of the empire; the text thus interpreted was received in all the countries of continental Europe, and is now the fundamental system of law prevailing in those countries. At its first reception it was therefore a complete and systematic law.

In England, on the other hand, a law common to the realm was imposed in the twelfth century, developed in court at the outset by judges whose experience was in the old Germanic folk-courts, developed from its archaic beginnings in complete isolation from contact with other systems of law; and it had its first experience as a system governing more than one legal unit when it was extended by colonization into America. The modern Roman law of the continent, therefore, ordinarily called the Civil Law, reached its maturity before it became the law of any now existing state. The law of England and English-speaking America, on the other hand, has developed through eight centuries and has not yet reached such maturity as to have been systematically and authoritatively stated.

The course of growth of the civil law has been from diversity toward unity. At the time of its reception in Europe it became the underlying law of every portion of the continent.[1] Until the beginning of the nineteenth century the countries of Europe were subdivided into small provinces, the law of which differed to some extent even though the basis of all those laws was the modern Roman law. Beginning, however, with the French codes there was a constant tendency during the nineteenth century to unify the law of each country. The provincial laws of France disappeared in 1803; and since that time local laws have been altogether or to a considerable extent abolished in Holland, Belgium, Italy, Switzerland, Russia, Spain and the German empire. The unification in each

[1] It is of course not contended that this reception was at one time in all parts of Europe.

of these states was the result of a complete system of codes; this codification being rendered possible by the fact that their fundamental law was already a mature, systematic body of doctrine. This law has also been extended by a single act of codification to the French, Dutch, Danish, Spanish and German colonies.

The common law has had a very different history, a history which had profound effect on the development of its doctrine of conflict of laws. One of the great colonizing peoples of the later middle ages was England; English colonies have been planted in all parts of the world, and the course of English colonization has been the settlement of colonists of English descent, at least in her colonies in the temperate zone, as not merely the dominant but the predominant stock. In the United States and Canada, in Australia and South Africa the English race occupied the land and fixed the speech, the law and the habits of thought of the whole body of inhabitants. It will be seen that law is continuous so long as organized society exists. English colonists went to these colonies as politically organized bodies of men. Except, therefore, in so far as they themselves changed their law by legislation, the English law under which they had been bred remained their law under their new skies.

"When our ancestors first settled this country, they came here as English subjects; they settled on the land as English territory, constituting part of the realm of England, and of course governed by its laws; they accepted charters from the English government, conferring both political powers and civil privileges; and they never ceased to acknowledge themselves English subjects, and never ceased to claim the rights and privileges of English subjects, till the Revolution. It is not therefore, perhaps, so accurate to say that they established the laws of England here, as to say that they were subject to the laws of England. When they left one portion of its territory, they were alike subject, on their transit and when they arrived at another portion of the English territory."[1]

But these colonies, though united in their dependence on England, were entirely independent of one another; and, following the conception of freedom which had been fostered by the common law, each of them began by legislation of

[1] Shaw, J., in Com. v. Chapman, 13 Met. 68, 1 Beale, 72.

some sort to fit their law to its new surroundings. These changes of law were only in part made by the legislatures which the English government granted to its colonies. They were made also in considerable measure by such tacit changes in the unwritten law as were necessary to fit it to frontier conditions. By these processes each colony acquired a law of its own, containing in it individual peculiarities resting some on statute, some on judicial authority; while all their laws had in common a system of fundamental principles or body of doctrine which we have come to call the Common Law. The progress of the common law, therefore, has been from unity to diversity, and it is only within the last generation that there has been any decided effort to secure unity. The condition of the United States, then, with respect to its law is the same as that of Europe in the eighteenth century; and questions of the conflict of laws commonly present themselves to American lawyers as questions arising out of the conflict of local laws in different divisions of the same nation. We have, it is true, the usual number of questions arising out of conflicts with foreign laws, but we have in addition a much larger body of litigation concerning conflicts of laws within the nation. No American lawyer has suggested any important distinction between conflicts of national law and conflicts of local state law.

§ 123. **Other Legal Systems.** — In addition to these two general systems of law which divide the western world between them there are other systems of even broader influence.

As intercourse between nations grew, many customs came to be observed, boundaries of jurisdiction were established, various rights of neutrals were admitted, until at last an enlightened scholar discovered general principles underlying established observances and described the laws of peace and war. The general principles so laid down by Grotius were developed by jurists, by diplomats, by courts of arbitration, and by treaties until there has come to be an accepted body of International Law by which all nations profess to be governed.

The principles which have governed traffic on the seas may be traced to a time back of the Christian era, and have been developed and spread by the growing commerce of maritime nations. Thus developed, Admiralty forms a system of law of which the general principles are recognized in every modern nation.

In a similar way the international commerce of merchants developed a body of practice accepted by the merchants of civilized countries and applied in commercial courts. This system of law, the so-called Law Merchant, also is in its general principles accepted and recognized throughout the civilized world.

Another similar body of principles has frequently claimed the name of law — the so-called "natural law" of the seventeenth and eighteenth centuries. This is a body of principles of justice which are supposed to underly all law and to be necessary elements in every civilized legal system. Such principles are: the duty of a subject to obey his sovereign; the duty to respect the rights of others; the rights and obligations inherent in an expression of the will; the responsibility for a caused act; and the "natural rights" to life, liberty, and the pursuit of happiness. In these principles justice finds its ideal; and it may be granted that they play a large part in modern law, and that rational deductions from them must influence the development of every law. But after all, they are only the material for law, like the laws of business or of society. They differ from principles of political law in that they lack the political element. They are addressed to the individual conscience rather than to magistrates and jurists. If we regard natural law as the expression of ideal justice, we may fairly admit that all laws tend toward it; but no principle of natural law can be regarded as law, even in the broader sense in which the common law and the civil law are such, until it is established as a principle of some actually living and working system of positive law.

That natural law as apprehended by a people and its actual civil law may become one and indistinguishable by the acceptance of a religious system as the basis of political obligation may be seen by such examples as the Chinese law, based on the philosophy of Confucius, the Hindu law, based on the Vedic religion, and Mohammedan law, based on the precepts of the Koran; but it is only by this acceptance as positive law that it becomes law at all.

On the other hand, there are still known and studied systems of law, once law in the true sense, but now dead: the laws of Hammurabi and Moses, the laws of the Medes and Persians, the laws of ancient Greece or ancient Scandinavia, laws only in the eyes of history. They are in no sense a body of principles received as the basis of social obligation, though they were once just that.

§ **124. Acceptance of a Legal System.** — What then differentiates a system of law truly so called but used in the broader sense from law in an improper sense: law that has been, or that never was: law that is dead or that is not yet living? What creates law as a real living system? It is clearly the reception of that system as the basis of law. If it is accepted in one jurisdiction only it becomes the positive law of that jurisdiction; if in more, a legal system. There was no *system* of Roman law, as distinguished from the particular law of Rome, at least until two emperors divided the allegiance of the Roman world; and no "civil law" in the proper sense until it was received in the middle ages in the Empire, in France and in Spain as the systematic basis of their individual laws. The common law (as distinguished from the particular law of England) came into existence when it became the common systematic basis of the law of the colonies. International law became law when its principles were accepted by the civilized nations of Europe as a part of their municipal laws. Maritime law came to exist as a system when all the maritime nations of Europe received its principles as establishing the laws applied in their courts of admiralty. These legal systems, then, live as law because they have been received as law in several existing states.

But though in these cases the same legal system — the same *law* — is received in several states, it is necessarily distinct from the law of each of these states, since such laws are not the same; and in each state therefore the local law may, and practically must, vary to some extent from the accepted general system. The common law is received in Massachusetts as the basis of its law; but the positive law of Massachusetts, by mistake or design, is gradually differentiated from it: "So shakes the needle and so stands the pole," as stands the general system of the common law to the unwritten law of a particular state. The common law is one law; the law of Massachusetts, even her unwritten law, is another. To confuse the two is easy, since one is based upon the other, and this accounts for the fact that the difference is often not realized. Indeed there is an easily recognizable tendency in the judicial law of each American state to approach again the common law, and reach unity not by legislation but by means of judicial decisions, correcting former erroneous decisions and bringing the unwritten law of the state into harmony with that of other states.

While the general system exists apart from positive law, the application of its principles is the work of a tribunal which, being human, may err; and the common law, or international law, being mistakenly applied, the positive law of the state becomes different from the basic system. We may then say, if we please, that the common law of New York, or the international law of the United States, differs from that of other states. But it must be obvious that neither by legislative nor by judicial legislation can the basic system of law be changed.[1] But of course the reception of a particular system of law may be intentionally withdrawn, as for instance when in Texas the common law was substituted for the civil law as the basis of its law. This fact is of especial interest in connection with international law. This law is received by all civilized sovereigns because its reception and substantial observance is a condition of admission to the "family of nations," and nations, like individuals, desire to be in good society. But while the general reception of law will for that reason not be cancelled by a state, its reception with regard to a single other state may be withdrawn, and as a result its conduct toward that state restrained by no legal limitation. This condition is war. But while hostile nations have no rights and obligations as to one another, they continue to possess all the rights which international law gives them against neutral nations, and they cannot escape their obligations toward neutral nations; hence the law of neutrality. Such being the legal nature of war, it will continue just so long as nations permit one nation to throw off the obliga-

[1] That such a system of law does change is obvious, and cannot be denied. The method of such change will be indicated *infra*, § 126.

tions of international law as to another nation without forfeiting its place in the family of nations; and it will continue no longer than such partial repudiation of law is permitted. But while a nation may withdraw its acceptance of a system of law, and among others its acceptance of the system of international law, yet the general withdrawal of its acceptance of that system would put it outside the pale of civilized states. No nation, therefore, is likely so to withdraw its acceptance of the principles of international law. Without so doing a nation has no right by reason of erroneous decisions of courts or by reason of peculiar legislation to alter those principles to its own advantage, even though it is professing to alter its own law only. The importance of this observation will be seen in examining the question of international jurisdiction. The legal bounds of a nation's power are fixed by the accepted law of nations. If they are so fixed, no nation claiming to belong to the family of civilized states can by any means extend or alter the legal exercise of its own powers to the prejudice of other states. While, therefore, the question of legal jurisdiction is a question to be determined by the law treated as a whole, it cannot properly be settled either by legislation or by decision, but must be left for settlement to the body of doctrine which the particular state in question has accepted in accepting the general principles of international law.

§ 125. **The Part Played by Judicial Decisions.** — Very different views have been expressed as to the part played in the making or change of law by the decisions of courts. The persuasive power of a decision differs greatly in different countries. It is the highest of all in Spain, because in Spain the decision, in order to be valid as such, must be approved and promulgated by the minister of justice, and when so approved it has the force of statute.[1] Almost as conclusive is the effect given to a decision of the highest court, the House of Lords, in England, where in theory the decision must stand as law itself unchangeable except by legislation, although in fact many decisions of the House of Lords have been so distinguished and narrowed by explanations as to be practically overruled.

[1] A recent change in the law may make it necessary to qualify this statement in some particulars, but in principle it remains true.

The decision of one of the lower courts in England is in theory equally binding upon the same court; and yet there have been many cases where the decision of a court has been disregarded by a court of coordinate jurisdiction; and there are even cases in England where an inferior court disregarded the decision of a superior court. In this country the mere fact of multiplication of courts in the different states and the general recognition of an underlying system of law common to all states have caused in practice far less conclusive force to be allowed to the decisions of courts than is the case in England. The court of a particular state receives as persuasive authority the decisions of courts in other states; and not every court distinguishes sharply between its own decisions and those of other states. As a result we in the United States have almost reached the condition of affairs which prevails in France, Germany and Italy; where rules of law are accepted as fixed by precedent only when there is a great and practically unanimous body of decision behind them. A proposition supported by a single decision stands a fair chance of being overruled if the court can be convinced of its unsoundness.

In France, Austria and Italy, and in the European states generally, the decisions of courts are theoretically regarded as not affecting the law at all; or at least as establishing a proposition of law only when supported by a considerable body of jurisprudence. The method of reporting decisions in several of these countries adds plausibility to this theory, by omitting from the printed report all mention of the decisions which had been cited to and by the court in argument. The real fact as to the use made of decisions is not accurately represented by the form of the report; for the report usually contains only the judgment and not the reasoning upon which the judgment proceeds, or at most the reasoning is briefly indicated. When occasionally the reasons of the court are reported in full they are found to be based in large measure on previous decisions. The mere fact that decisions are reported in vast numbers in the European states, and are eagerly purchased by lawyers, indicates their practical value in the determination of the law.

It is the prevailing fashion among thinking lawyers, learned in the common law, to assert that under guise of discovering legal propositions the judges of common-law courts make the law which they purport to find. This view has, perhaps, been expressed most clearly and forcibly by Professor Gray.[1] There are various reasons, however, for declining to accept this doctrine even where it is confined to the common law; and as we have seen, the force of precedent differs in degree only and not in kind in the common law and in the civil law courts. Among the reasons for discarding the view that the decision of a court in and of itself makes law are the following.

First, the function of changing the law has never been committed by the sovereign to the judge, and consciously to make a change in the law would be a usurpation on the part of the judge. This usurpation the judges strenuously deny, and have claimed that in no case were they exercising the power of changing the substantive law. If then they make law they do it unconsciously, by inadvertence, and contrary to their legal duty and their official oath.

Second, if the judge makes the law he declares, then the law did not exist at the commission of the alleged wrong with which he is dealing in the litigation. In that case, if he decides that a right existed he is creating the right, subsequently to the doing of the act, and the defendant is held for a wrong which was not a wrong at the time he did it. This is contrary to all conceptions of justice.

Third, states are constantly overruling their own decisions. A striking instance of this was the course of decision in Michigan on the question of exemplary damages. For several years the court held alternately that exemplary damages could, and that they could not be recovered, each decision being apparently made on the faith of the last published decision, while a later unpublished decision the other way was overlooked.[2] If we assume that each decision made the law, we have the singular result that the law was changed

[1] Gray, Nature and Sources of Law, §§ 191, 229–231. "It has been sometimes said that the Law is composed of two parts, — legislative law and judge-made law, but, in truth, all the Law is judge-made law. The shape in which a statute is imposed on the community as a guide for conduct is that statute as interpreted by the courts." *Ibid.*, § 276.

[2] See 1 Sedg. Dam. § 358, note 61.

in Michigan backwards and forwards a dozen times within a few years.

Fourth, several cases are known of courts having coordinate jurisdiction to declare the law of a particular state and without a common superior. For instance, for several years after the independence of the state of Georgia, there were two supreme courts, one sitting in the Eastern and the other in the Western half of the state, each declaring the law of the whole state; for there was only one law of Georgia, that state being one and not two legal units. If, as must have happened, in a term of years, contradictory decisions were rendered, it would be impossible to find any existing law of Georgia made by the courts. Even today this condition prevails in every state of the Union; for the courts of a state and the federal courts sitting in the state have coordinate jurisdiction to declare the law, and there is no superior court of appeal. The result is, in many cases, a difference of opinion between the state court and the federal court sitting in the state as to the law of the state. This condition is quite incompatible with the court declaring the law.[1]

§ **126. The Causes of Change in the Unwritten Law.**— The problem in this country is made more difficult because it is supposed to be bound up with the question of whether the common law changes. It is assumed by most authorities that if the judges did not make, but discovered the law, then in the absence of legislation the law must remain what it has always been, and therefore, by a process of backward projection, it is argued that unless the courts changed the law the law must have been the same in 1200 that it is today. This line of reasoning, which has seemed convincing to many persons, is quite obviously a mere begging of the question. It is certain that the common law changes; not merely the common law of a particular jurisdiction, but the common-law system in general. This must be true, or the science of law, differing from all other sciences, would be unprogressive. The law of today must of course be better than that of seven centuries ago, more in accordance with the general principles of justice, more in accordance with the needs of the present age, more humane, more flexible and more complex. There

[1] See Swift *v.* Tyson, 16 Pet. 1, 1 Beale, 95.

are many sources of this change of law, of which, it is true, the decisions of the courts are one and in many ways the most important. The law of a given time must be taken to be the body of principles which is accepted by the legal profession, whatever that profession may be; and it will be agreed that the judges have a preponderating share in fixing the opinion of the profession. They are, however, not the sole element in forming this opinion. Legal thinkers who are not judges have at all times played a considerable part. The teachers of law today have an increasing influence, and one which is comparable in degree with the part played by the judges, in the development of the law; and their power to mould professional opinion is likely to increase in the future more rapidly than that of the judges. The expressed opinions of writers on the law also is powerful in the moulding of professional opinion, and the argument of practicing lawyers is of great persuasive effect in determining the course of decision. In all these ways, then, professional opinion is being influenced, and thus the nature of the unwritten law is being changed.

The same causes lead to change of the unwritten law in Europe. In England the opinion of the court has a much greater effect and that of teachers of law much less than in this country. In France and Germany the reverse is true. The teachers and writers influence the development of the law to a greater extent than the judges. But the differences in all these countries are merely in degree. It is generally true that the unwritten law changes with the change of the professional opinion about it, and that the decisions of the courts play sometimes a preponderant, always an important, part in the development of this professional opinion.

§ **127. The Part played by Equity.** — The development of law by means of equity has given rise to much discussion and to considerable difficulty. Equity may mean one of two things: — either the modification of rights by reason of other conflicting rights, or the administration by a separate tribunal, or at least as a separate judicial act, of a distinct system of law dealing with rights in a different way from the legal way.

In the first meaning of the word, equity is of course a universal fact, present, necessarily, in all law; for all civilized law, at least, must have some method of satisfying conflicting rights by reaching a reconciliatory result in a particular case. In this sense of the term equity is simply one of the principles of law, working in a regular way beside the other principles; and there is no separate body of doctrine involved. In the second sense, which is the sense in which the word is used in the common law, we meet with a difficulty. If equity as a separate body of doctrine forms its own principles and regulates rights in its own way, it is perfectly possible to have a legal right in A which conflicts with an equitable right in B, and with no possible solution of the conflict. This has seemed to be the case in the common-law system, where the exercise of legal rights is enjoined in equity on the ground that the equitable rights are opposed to the legal rights; and yet if the enjoined party violates the injunction, he may enforce his legal right in a court of law. If this seeming condition is a true one, we are at once presented with an insurmountable difficulty in dealing with foreign law; for if the person possessed of the legal right appears in a foreign state demanding the recognition and enforcement of his right and the person having the equitable right appears and demands the same thing, a dilemma is presented to the foreign court which it has no means of solving.

It is submitted that the commonly received explanation of the distinction between law and equity in common-law jurisdictions is inaccurate. It is true that in each of those jurisdictions the theory upon which courts proceed is the theory of separate and independent systems of right. The court of law regards the equitable right as subordinate to the legal right, while the court of equity takes the opposite view. The view of the court of law has this apparent support, that the party who is willing to ignore the equitable decree and take his punishment therefor, may enforce his legal right in the teeth of the counter-right in equity. It is clear, however, that there cannot be two separate and distinct laws prevailing in the same place at the same time; and therefore in fact, whatever may be the theory of the courts, one of the conflicting rights must be valid and the other invalid. It is submitted that the true explanation of the difficulty is that the equitable right is the prevailing one, that the legal right represents a prior condition of the law, before the unwritten law was changed by the acceptance on the part of the profession of the equitable doctrines as law; that the profession has so accepted equity as a part of the law within the last four centuries, and that as a result a court investigating the law of a foreign state should take the equity doctrine as determining rights there created. Such authority as there is on the point is to this effect, and this opinion is fortified by the fact that where, as in many states, law and equity are fused, the resulting body of doctrine includes the doctrines formerly administered in the court of equity. The part of equity, therefore, in the development of the common-law system is that of the progressive element, continually modifying ancient doctrine which has become outgrown and obstructive of justice.

Topic 4. The Characteristics and Function of Law

§ 128. **The Social Character of Law.** — It is obvious that law must have certain general characteristics which distinguish it from other things of a similar nature. Thus, law is distinguished both from the principles of natural science and from the rules of ethics in that it is a social or political rule. The use of the words to describe the orderly sequence of natural events is foreign to the lawyers' use. We speak of natural law, the law of gravitation, Mendel's law; but however correct this use may be, it is not one which concerns lawyers. To them the only law is that of politically organized society. That law in general conforms to natural requirements is of course true. No civilized society would fail to protect human agreements or secure the sanctity of the person. To this extent, there are no doubt rules of natural law, so-called, which somewhat constrain the action of the law-giver. They are, notwithstanding, quite consistent with his absolute free will, and the result of his legislation contains no element which can be said to be natural law rather than law made by sovereign power. In the same way the rules of ethics greatly influence the action of the law-giver; no civilized state could maintain a system of law which was generally agreed to be immoral. Yet, on the other hand, it is not a function of law to sustain ethical requirements. Law does not and cannot purport to make and keep men good; a law which should attempt to do so would break down in the effort. This was tried by the Massachusetts Bay colony, to a slight extent; but the attempt was soon found to be beyond the power of social law, and the maintenance of a moral standard was relegated to the church, where it belongs. Law has a social, not a religious object. Such immoral acts as are also anti-social it should restrain; but the restraint is in the interest of society, not directly in the interest of morality. A law that should promote immorality would be a bad law; but a law that failed to promote morality would not necessarily be bad. Law, in short, is unmoral; it must not be immoral.

That right and wrong are subject to rules capable of discovery by thought and experience few persons would deny; and that these rules bear some analogy to true law is clear. Fashionable society also has its rules fixed by usage and courtesy, and these rules also are discoverable by thought and experience. In the mind of an inexact or loose-thinking lawyer a confusion may arise between these rules and principles of law properly so-called. Such confusion was shown by Lord Coleridge, C. J., in the case of Regina *v.* Instan,[1] where he said: "Every legal duty is founded on a moral obligation." But, as has been seen, this is an error. Law as the lawyer knows it is absolutely distinct from any rule of conduct based on a moral ground no matter how strong.

§ 129. **The Generality of Law.**—Another essential characteristic of law is its generality; since justice requires equality of treatment for all persons, and this means generality. It is, as has been seen, a body of general principles, not a collection of special commands. A set of rules for the action of a particular person would lack this character of generality. Thus, the decision and judgment of a court, determining a particular controversy and laying an order upon one party to it, lacks this element and can in no sense be regarded as in itself law, whether it be the doom of an ancient monarch, the decision of a popular court, or the judgment of a modern judicial tribunal. Law being a general principle applying indifferently to all cases which in the future can arise under it, the decision of a court can be law only if the court has power in its decision to lay down binding rules for future con-

[1] [1893] 1 Q. B. 450.

duct; a power which is not inherent in judicial action as such. Law operates by extending its power over acts done throughout the territory within its jurisdiction and creating out of those acts new rights and obligations. In order thus to act there must be a general rule existing previously to the acts and ready to create the resultant rights. Unless the rules of law are thus general they can have no reference to future action.

§ 130. **The Universality of Law.** — It is unthinkable in a civilized country that any act should fall outside of the domain of law. If law be regarded as a command, then every act done must either be permitted or forbidden. If law be regarded as a right-producing principle, then every act must in accordance with the law change or not change existing rights.

"No plain or valley, no nook or corner, to which the dominion of man has extended itself, is without some law of the land. Indeed, law is the breath of dominion." So said Judge Grosscup, in Swift *v.* Philadelphia & Reading Railroad.[1] A hiatus or vacuum in the law would mean anarchy.

It follows also that not only must the law extend over the whole territory subject to it and apply to every act done there, but only one law can so apply. If two laws were present at the same time and in the same place upon the same subject we should also have a condition of anarchy. By its very nature law must apply to everything and must exclusively apply to everything within the boundary of its jurisdiction.

§ 131. **The Continuity of Law.** — Another necessary characteristic of law is continuity. "From the day of its promulgation to the day of its repeal the law must always be heard and obeyed."[2]

There can be no break or interregnum in law. From the time law comes into existence with the first felt corporateness of a primitive people, it must last until the final disappearance of human society. Once created, it persists until a change takes place, and when changed it continues in such changed condition until the next change, and so on forever.

[1] 64 Fed. 59.
[2] Pillet in Clunet, xxi, 417.

Conquest or colonization is impotent to bring law to an end; in spite of change of constitution, the law continues unchanged until the new sovereign by a legislative act creates a change. The law of today must remain the law of tomorrow, except for such changes as may be made in the law by legislative action before tomorrow.

The social need of continuity in law is most clearly felt because society needs to know the law in advance of judicial action upon it. In order that law may help rather than hinder the carrying on of the work of society it must be possible for every person, of his own knowledge or by the help of others' knowledge, to discover the application of the law to any contemplated act. He must be in some way secured against unexpected legal consequences of his actions. Business could not go on, industry could not be maintained unless it were possible for the producer or the merchant to learn how he could conform his activities to the law. For this purpose it must be possible for one learned in the law to speak with authority on the application of law to the proposed acts and to predict with reasonable degree of certainty the decision of courts in case the legality of the acts should be called in question. If there were any discontinuity in the law, — if, for instance, a judicial tribunal had the power to change the law as it liked, or the discretion as to the application of law to the facts, — the client would seek advice in vain, for counsel however learned could only vaguely guess what the law would be at the time of possible future litigation. Predicability of judicial decision is necessary if the law is to serve its true social purpose; and this predicability is possible only if the law is continuous.

§ 132. **The Purpose and Method of Law.** — Law has been defined from the point of view of its own nature, but law, to be fully understood, must be considered also with reference to the place it fills in the life of the world.

Thus considered, law will be seen to have two principal objects: first, the satisfaction of the desire for right and justice in the minds of individuals; and second, the protection of the interests of individuals and of society.

So far as satisfaction of the desire for justice is concerned, this plays its part in the development of law only in affording a continual standard by which the law is tried and improvements in it suggested and carried out; and since the ideal of right and justice held by the average man constantly tends to rise with the progress of thought and civilization, the law is in this way continually made better by the progressive working out of the purpose to secure justice.

The effect of the purpose to protect interests, however, is far more important in the immediate condition of law. The whole body of law will arrange itself into a system, more or less well conceived and clearly recognized, which is based upon the protection of such interests as are deemed worthy of protection. These interests may be divided into two classes, social and individual; and according as the spirit of the time tends to prefer organized society to the individual or *vice versa,* social or individual interests will be most favored by the law. Individual interests, on the other hand, may be divided into personal interests and interests of property; and according as one or the other is more in the mind of the law-giving sovereign, the law will give most thought to the protection of one or the other.

§ 133. **Social Interests.** — The general social organization becomes, as has been seen, upon its coexistence with law, what is called a state or, to put it in other terms, the state is society politically organized. The state, then, is the representative of the social interest. In theory the state must always be supreme before the law, and while in certain periods of civilization society has deemed it better to magnify the rights of individuals against the community, this individualistic condition is always unstable and tends to fall into the more natural condition of social supremacy.

The interests of the state are, in general, the personal interests of existence, constitution, peace, and so forth; and the property interests, that is, public rights over the persons and property within the state's jurisdiction. One interesting example of the protection of state interest is the doctrine of public policy; a doctrine by which every private right may be modified in the interest of the state.

It has been common to make a complete and fundamental distinction between the law which protects social interests and that which protects individual interests. It is believed, however, that no such fundamental distinction exists, but that the law deals with social interests in the same way that it deals with the interests of individuals.

There is, to be sure, one class of public interests which does not have an exact counterpart in the private law. It has been seen that a sovereign has full power of choice, first in creating protecting rights, second in furnishing remedies, and third, in issuing execution on judgment. In determining action on these matters of choice the law is unquestionably influenced by the nature of the social interests involved in action or non-action, and to that extent social interests play a different part in the development of law from private interests.

§ 134. **Private Interests of Person.** — Private or individual interests comprise roughly interests of person and interests of property. Interests of person may include every personal desire which is purely personal and does not involve the use of any property in a thing. Existence itself, so far as law is concerned, is an interest. It is quite possible for law to ignore the very existence of a man; human existence, therefore, must be regarded as an interest desiring recognition and protection. Life, liberty and the pursuit of happiness, the human interests named in so many of our declarations of right, are among the principal personal interests, to protect which must be an object of law.

Beside these interests which are common to all mankind, there are certain kinds of personal interest which are peculiar. Such, for instance, are nationality, honor, office and condition, and in general all permanent personal conditions. There is also a class of important interests in the relations between persons, such, for instance, as marriage and legitimacy. Every civilized law must protect many out of all possible personal interests, and no law has as yet undertaken to protect all of them. The quality of any particular law, therefore, is determined in this respect by the number of personal interests which it protects or leaves unprotected.

§ 135. **Interests of Property.** — Interests of property comprise every thing which a man may desire to possess. Not every such thing is protected as a private interest; such generally diffused objects of desire as air and water are usually not protected as private interests, but as social interests of the state. Under certain circumstances, however, even such things as air or water may be treated as individual private interests.

Interests of property are not necessarily confined to tangible things. Much valuable property, the private interest in which is protected, is entirely intangible; such, for instance, are good-will and patent rights, franchises, and interests in corporations. In addition to these intangible interests there is another class which may in some aspects be regarded as property: that is, power over the property or the services of another; a power created by contractual and other obligations. Interests based upon such obligations, it will be noticed, are interests only in the relative sense. It is the interest of the creditor to have the right protected, but the wealth of the debtor is diminished by the exact amount that the wealth of the creditor is increased by the obligation. The protection of such relative interests is, however, acknowledged to be a function of the state.

§ 136. **Interests of Will and Act.** — It is not only in his person that an individual needs protection. For his full development in society he needs protection for his freedom of will and of action. In some aspects this is a mere personal interest, in other aspects it is closely allied to property interests; but the exercises of the free will through the permitted act is a special interest of so great importance as to justify separate consideration. Protection of the human desire to will and act is a duty of the law, always important and in some conditions of life essential. The protection or the restraint of the will as it operates through the act is apt to constitute the most plastic and the most characteristic portion of the law. It is in thought and action that new ideals first express themselves; and the law which protects interests of will and action, in order to subserve its purpose, must be capable of rapid growth to meet the quick development of contemporary thought. On the other hand, the interdiction and restraint of anti-social thought and act is a necessary feature of any law that is well adapted to the protection of all interests.

The interests under consideration are even more constantly than other interests the cause of conflicting claims. One may hold property or enjoy personal rights without in any way infringing the rights of others; but the full enjoyment of freedom in thought and action is quite incompatible with a similar enjoyment by others, since few acts can be done which do not in some way limit the power of action on the part of others. The task of the law, therefore, in protecting the interests under consideration, is the most difficult which it has to meet.

§ **137. Vested Rights.**—It will be seen that legal protection of interests of property and person results in the creation of legal rights in persons or personal relations and in things. If my interest in my own existence is protected by law, it becomes a vested right to exist. If my interest in my house is protected by law it becomes my vested property. It is the nature of such a right to continue in existence until the law puts an end to it or until the interest itself ceases to exist, as by my death or by the destruction of my house. A process exists, then, by which a right to a person or thing once created continues unchanged by ordinary circumstances or by lapse of time until finally destroyed by nature or by the law that created it. Such an interest as this may be called a vested interest and the right created by the law is a vested right. It will be noticed that every right which is in its nature continuous and capable of continuing without change may be a vested right. This of course includes rights in intangible things, which have already been discussed. A contract once made may be given this quality of remaining in existence until it is performed or discharged by law, and the right in the contract then becomes a vested one. The same thing may be said of any obligation, whether created by act of the party or by mere operation of law: if a continuous obligation is created by a law it then may be regarded as a vested right.

On the other hand, it will be noticed that the obligations of thought and act recently considered are not of this nature. Thought and action are necessarily discontinuous. There can, in the nature of things, be no vested right to think a certain thought or to do a certain act; unless, indeed, it takes the form of an obligation to think or to act. There being no obligation in question, any protection of one's interest in freedom of thought or action can mean no more than legal permission to think a particular thought or to do a particular act; or, perhaps more accurately, to think and act as often as one pleases, but still necessarily disjunctively. The general freedom of thought and action for the future can therefore never become a vested right, since it is incapable of continuous expression.

The power to think or act may indeed be coupled with an obligation to permit the power to be exercised at any time in the future or during a certain fixed period in the future. To take a specific instance: when one is given power to deal with certain property for value paid by him, the transaction involves a binding obligation on the part of the creator of the power not to interfere with the action. This obligation constitutes a vested right, and in a certain sense the power to act would therefore be a vested power. The vested right, however, is one merely of obligation, and can concern the law as a vested interest only through the operation of the obligation.

§ 138. **The Legal Protection of Interests.** — It is often conceived to be the duty of law to take care that interests protected by the law be not violated by wrong-doers. This, however, is not strictly true. Only exceptionally does the law make provision for the prevention of wrong-doing. There are, it is true, certain police measures taken for the prevention of serious crimes, and in a few cases legal power is given to individuals to protect their own interests. These, however, are rare exceptions. The law does not generally attempt to carry out preventive measures against the violation of rights.

What the law does is to create right after right, in a long series, in the effort to repair injuries to protected interests. An interest which receives the protection of the law, that is, which becomes vested, is protected by a class of rights created by the law to safeguard the vested interests; for instance, a vested interest of personality is protected by a provision against assault; and a vested interest in land by a provision against trespass on it. If a wrong-doer violates one of these protective rights, the law then creates a new right which is regarded as equivalent to the one destroyed by the wrong-doing, and this new right takes the place of the violated right. This is a right to damages or other reparation. If the wrong-doer fails to satisfy this right by making due reparation, the law, upon the case being proved in court, creates by means of a judgment of the court still another right, which in turn it gives the wrong-doer a chance to satisfy by performance. If the wrong-doer still continues to violate his obligation, the law, in its effort to redress the wrong, gives one more right still, by providing for some method of executing the judgment. It is by the execution of the judgment that in the usual course of events the law for the first time provides for the actual carrying out of a right and the prevention of a violation of it through action of the state.

Around social interests the law spreads the same enveloping series of protecting rights that it does about private interests. These protecting rights may be violated just as is the case with the rights protecting private interests, and the wrongful act which violates them, called a crime, results, like a private wrong, in the creation of an equivalent remedial right. This right, in turn, if a remedy is offered, results in a judgment, and the judgment is an execution; and so the cycle of the law is completed in criminal as in civil cases.

The law, then, in protecting an interest first creates a vested right; second, it creates a series of protecting rights to protect the interest from moment to moment; third, in the case of violation of the protecting right it creates a right of action; fourth, in case of failure to satisfy this right and as a result of a law suit it creates another right by a judgment; and finally, upon failure of the defendant to satisfy the judgment, it creates a right of execution; and this right for the first time is regularly specifically enforced by the state.

CHAPTER V

RIGHTS

§ 139. The nature of rights.
140. The analysis of rights.

Topic I. PRIMARY RIGHTS

Sub-topic A. Static Rights

141. The nature of static rights.
142. Distinction between a static right and the rights that protect it.

PART 1. PERSONAL STATUS

143. The nature of personal status.
144. Personality.
145. Artificial personality.
146. Other examples of personal status.
147. Relative status.
148. What law governs status.

PART 2. RIGHTS OF PROPERTY

149. The nature of property.
150. The sort of interest protected.
151. The sort of things which may be subject of interests.
152. Transfer and extinguishment of rights of property.
153. What law governs rights of property.

Sub-topic B. Dynamic Rights

154. The nature of dynamic rights.

PART 1. ABSOLUTE RIGHTS

155. Interest-protecting rights.
156. Interest-enjoying rights.
157. What law governs absolute rights.

PART 2. RELATIVE RIGHTS

158. Contracts and debts.
159. Quasi-contracts.
160. What law governs relative rights.

Topic II. SECONDARY RIGHTS

161. The nature of secondary rights.
162. Rights of redress or restoration.

Topic III. REMEDIAL RIGHTS

163. The nature of remedial rights.
164. Right to sue and to be satisfied.

§ 139. **The Nature of Rights.**—The primary purpose of law being the creation of rights, and the chief task of the Conflict of Laws to determine the place where a right arose and the law that created it, a more careful study of the nature of rights is of course desirable before the examination of actual cases of conflict is begun.

As has already been pointed out, many European languages make no discrimination between the system of law and a legal right; *ius, Recht, droit, diritto, derecho* are words meaning, equally, law in general and a particular individual right. The application of a foreign law and the enforcement of a foreign right might be expressed by a European lawyer in the same phrase; and to deny the application of a foreign law would seem to be the denial of enforcement of a foreign right.

Since we are fortunate enough to have different words for these ideas, it is all the more necessary that we should fully understand each of them.

A right may be defined as a legally recognized interest in, to, or against a person or a thing.

Professor Roscoe Pound, in an article in the *International Journal of Ethics* for October, 1915, entitled "Legal Rights," has so exhaustively considered the meaning and nature of rights that little more is desirable than to summarize his conclusions; expressing here the indebtedness that every scholar must feel to him for his remarkable studies in Jurisprudence.

He distinguishes five senses in which the word "right" is used in law books.

(1) It is often used in the sense of interest; as in Gareis's definition of an interest (in his *Enzyklopädie und Methodologie der Rechtswissenschaft*, 3d ed., §5): "a subjectively perceived relation derived from necessity, between the person feeling the necessity and an object; that is, the object for which the necessity exists and is felt, and through which, by use or consumption, actually or probably, it will or may be satisfied in whole or in part." So far as such a right is a legal one, it means an interest as recognized and delimited for the purpose of securing it through the legal order.

(2) It is used to designate the chief means which the law adopts in order to secure interests, namely, a recognition in persons, or a conferring upon persons, of certain capacities of influencing the action of others. As Merkel puts it (in *Juristische Enzyklopädie,*

2d ed., §159 note), the idea in the second use of "right" differs from that in the first use as the fortification from the protected land.

(3) A third sense of the word is the capacity of creating, divesting, or altering "rights" in the second sense; that is, a legal power.

(4) Another use of the term signifies a condition of legal immunity from liability for what otherwise would be a breach of duty; that is, a legal privilege.

(5) Right is also loosely used to indicate that which is just; so that, even in legal speech, we not infrequently say one has "a right" to this or that because, without any definite legal claim, we feel that on a balance of equities we should like to see him have it.

For other discussions of legal rights, Professor Pound refers to numerous authorities. [1]

In the analysis of rights which follows, rights in the first sense discussed by Professor Pound have been called static rights; rights in the second sense, dynamic rights. Powers and privileges are of importance in our law chiefly in their effect as limiting dynamic rights. Rights in the last sense are not, properly speaking, legal rights at all, and will not be considered.

§ **140. The Analysis of Rights.** — Many methods might be devised of analyzing and classifying rights; and one would be bold indeed who should claim his own method to be the best. Nor is it possible to find in the authorities to which we turn for our knowledge of law any classification of rights to which we may assent. Such essays in this direction as have been made by courts and by the authoritative writers on law have been little considered by the authors themselves and little regarded by their successors. In fact, the law is on its face an amorphous body of principles, and it can be analyzed only by going below the surface; nor is there any received method of proceeding. The classification indicated by its division into currently received topics — Con-

[1] Hohfeld, Some Fundamental Conceptions as applied in Judicial Reasoning, 23 Yale Law Jour. 16, 28; Salmond, Jurisprudence, §§ 70–74, 78–85; Gray, Nature and Sources of the Law, §§ 22–62; Wigmore, Summary of the Principles of Torts, in his Cases on Torts, vol. ii, App. A, §§ 4–8· Korkunov, General Theory of Law, transl. by Hastings, §§ 27–29; Gareis, Science of Law, transl. by Kocourek, §§ 31–35; Brown, The Austinian Theory of Law 172 *et seq.;* Schuppe, Begriff des subjektiven Rechts, chap. 2; Bierling, Kritik der juristischen Grundbegriffe, ii, 49–73; Dernburg, Pandekten, 8th ed., i, § 38; Windscheid, Pandekten, i, § 37; Kohler, Lehrbuch des bürgerlichen Rechts, i, §§ 44–46; Cosack, Lehrbuch des deutschen bürgerlichen Rechts, i, §§ 16–20.

tracts, Torts, Property, Procedure, Equity, and the like — is purely unscientific and unhelpful; it is useful only as furnishing labeled compartments into which the multitude of decisions may for convenience of study be sorted.

For our purpose, however, some kind of analysis and classification of rights is absolutely necessary; unless indeed all rights should in the conflict of laws be treated alike, which, as we shall see, is not the case. The classification here adopted is based upon a difference made by our law in treating rights of the different classes with respect to the law creating and having power over them.

All rights may first be divided into three main divisions: 1, primary rights; 2, secondary rights; 3, remedial rights. The first division, primary rights, includes all the rights created by law and existent in the ordinary proper course of events, unaffected by illegal interference. The second division, secondary rights, includes rights which arise upon the violation of primary rights, by the wrong of some responsible human actor; they are created by law in order that reparation may be made for the wrongful destruction of each primary right. The third division, remedial rights, consists of rights to sue and to enforce judgment; all rights, in short, which are created to secure the actual enforcement of secondary rights.

In the following sections, each division of rights will in turn be examined with a view to determine the exact nature of the various rights included in it, and to fix the law which creates these rights.

TOPIC I. PRIMARY RIGHTS

Sub-topic A. Static Rights

§ **141. — The Nature of Static Rights.** — Primary rights may be divided into two classes; static rights and dynamic rights. A static right, or as it is commonly called a vested interest, is a legally protected interest in a person or thing. Such an interest is one which continues indefinitely, and protection of it therefore requires a right which, like the interest it protects, has the character of permanence. Accordingly a static right remains in existence until either the subject of the interest ceases to exist or the law itself by a special act puts an end to the right. Take, as instances of static rights, marriage and land. A marriage once created continues in existence until the death of a spouse or until a divorce. A title to land continues to exist until the land itself disappears, or until the law, by an act of taking by eminent domain or by the operation of a statute of limitations, destroys the title.

When we say the right persists we do not mean that it may not be transferred from one to another. Most static rights in persons are to be sure incapable of transfer; but most property rights are freely transferable. The transfer, nevertheless, is the transfer of a right which continues in existence, not the creation of a new right.

In addition to this characteristic quality of permanence, static rights have another important peculiarity. Static rights are objective; they concern not merely the party or parties to them, but every member of society as well. Marriage, for instance, is not merely a private relation between two spouses; it is a relation which everyone must notice and respect. Property is not only a private right of the owner to the thing owned; the owner's right affects and abridges the rights of everyone else, and it enters as well into their relations with the thing as into those of the owner. Static rights, then, concern all the world.

The state itself is interested in the continued existence of all static rights which it does not choose to terminate; and parties cannot usually by their own will put an end to such rights. Thus personal status cannot be terminated, in general, by consent of the parties; a collusive divorce, even, is wrong, though granted in the legal method by the proper tribunal. In England, special counsel is employed to test the *bona fides* of suits for divorce. Rights of property, also, are of interest to the state; and although it ordinarily permits the abandonment of property, yet it may and sometimes does forbid it.

The characteristics of a static right are, then, these: the quality of permanence, the relation of third parties to it, and the interest of the state in its existence.

§ 142. **Distinction between a Static Right and the Rights which Protect it.**—A static right, as has been seen, is the interest of a person in a thing or in a person; the right is created by law, and once created it is permanent, that is, it persists until the proper law puts an end to it. The law that creates it, as will be seen, also provides for its preservation, by creating a hedge of protecting rights about it; rights of the owner or possessor to have it free from interference or destruction. One cannot conceive of a state creating a static right without providing for its protection; and so important is the existence of protecting rights that it is often said that the static right is really nothing more than the sum of its protecting rights, and if these are removed, the right must die.

This opinion quite loses sight of the real nature of the static right. It is to be regarded as a legal entity, quite apart from the particular protection with which it may be endued by law. A man travelling through the world may now be passing through a country which protects him from fright and horror, or again through one which guards him only against physical injury.

"If a Turkish or Hindoo husband were travelling in this country with his wife, or temporarily resident here, we should, without hesitation, acknowledge the relation of husband and wife between them; but the legal pre-eminence of the husband as to acts done here would be admitted only to the extent that the marital rights are recognized by our laws, and not as they are recognized by the law of his domicil. If a Roman father, or a father from any country which had adopted the Roman law of paternal power, were travelling in this country with a minor child, we should acknowledge the relation of parent and child, but we should admit, I presume, as a general rule, the exercise of the paternal power no further than as it is authorized by our own law."[1]

The fact is, that the static right itself remains unchanged, though the protecting rights change; and it would remain equally unchanged though they ceased altogether. In other words, a static right may be deprived of all present power to operate by the subject of it being carried into a country which does not recognize or give any effect to the right; but

[1] Ware, Dist. J., in Polydore *v.* Prince, Ware, 402; 3 Beale, 2, 5.

the right continues to exist so long as any vestige remains of the entity once created by the law. If, for instance, a husband and wife travel through a country in which there is no law recognizing marriage, they do not for one moment cease to be husband and wife, although the relation has no legal incidents in the country through which they are travelling. If a man carry his horse or his slave into a country which recognizes no private property in chattels or in human beings, the same thing is true; the static right does not come to an end merely by the present loss of its incidents. When the subject-matter is brought again into a country which recognizes the right, the property is found again to be in existence. The spouses returning from the country which recognized no marriage would not need again to go through the ceremony of marriage, nor could one of them regard the sojourn in the marriageless country as tantamount to a divorce; nor would the horse, returned into a country that recognized property, be regarded as *bonum vacans*. Though shorn of its incidents, the entity, the static right, remains in existence until its object perishes or some law having power over it puts an end to it.

Another sort of subsidiary right is often confounded with the principal static right. Thus it is often said that a static right, — for instance, a right in land or a marriage, — is made up simply of the bundle of rights which are necessary for its enjoyment. In the case of land, it is said that title to land, which is, as we shall see, the static right, is made up of a bundle of smaller rights; the right of possession, the right to use, the right to destroy, the right to transfer, the right to devise, the right to prevent interference or annoyance from third persons. In a similar way, marriage is said to consist of the right of each spouse to the society of the other, and the right to prevent strangers from breaking up this society. If this method of thought amounted merely to saying that a static right is of present use only in so far as some such elements are recognized and enforced by the law, it is doubtless true. If, however, it is taken to mean that a static right is a mere composite which may be resolved into these elements, it is an unsound manner of thought. Marriage, or title to land, is a thing of itself, a separate entity, out of which certain smaller rights may be carved, but without altering the nature or the existence of the entity. For instance, one who has the complete title to land may grant a right of way, a right to use, a right to possession, a power of transferring, a right of inheritance; he may strip himself of all power to object to anything that may happen to the land; and yet he may not part with his legal title. The title, though stripped of its value, may still remain in his own hands. So, a machine made up of wheels and cogs, of screws and bolts, may be stripped of one after another of its members without losing its character as a machine. It may be deprived of all present power to function, and laid on the shelf until the missing parts are supplied; but when they have been supplied the machine is not another machine. It was, is, and will be the same machine until it is destroyed, in spite of the destruction and replacement of its parts. In the same way a static right once created continues the same thing until finally destroyed, though during its existence it may be subjected to the laws of various countries, which may supply very different rights of enjoyment and protection, or even no rights at all.

Part 1. Personal Status

§ 143. The Nature of Personal Status. — Personal status is a vested personal condition or relation; a condition or relation created and destroyed by an act of law, not by the mere consent of the parties, and of legal importance to all the world. The quality of permanence distinguishes status from consensual relations, such as those of master and servant, or of principal and agent, where the relation depends upon the mere will of the parties; and the close analogy between status and property is shown by the fact that these two kinds of static rights possess in common the above-stated characteristics of static rights.

Personal status may be divided into two general classes: absolute status and relative status. Absolute status comprises cases of static personal condition, such as personality, natural or artificial, legitimacy, nationality, servile condition, office or rank. Relative status comprises cases of static relation between persons, such as marriage, guardianship, legitimate descent.

§ **144. Personality.** — Of all interests, that of a man in his own personality is the first and most necessary; and it might be supposed that any civilized law would tacitly recognize this interest without the need of special legal sanction. This however is not always the case. In the early stages of our own law, for instance, the outlaw was a man who by regular judicial process had been deprived of legal personality; as the phrase ran, he had become *caput vulpis,* no longer recognized as a human being. An affirmative act of the law, inlawry, was necessary to give him again a vested right in his own personality. A similar instance of loss of legal personality is the so-called civil death, either by becoming a monk or by being convicted of felony. A slave lacked legal personality in the slave states of the United States, while slavery existed there, though in some of the free states he still possessed legal personality.[1]

By the first provisions of the French Civil Code, foreigners do not ordinarily enjoy civil rights in France; that is, they have not full recognition of their personality.

§ **145. Artificial Personality.** — Personality is not confined to individual human existence. There is also in the human mind a tendency to personify an institution, an association, a thing, or even an ideal: thus a country, a college, a club, a ship may be thought of as a person; even such abstractions as patriotism, fame, or rumor may be imagined, and represented in literature, painting or sculpture, as a person. Such personality is not fictitious, though it exists only in the minds of men. The concurring affections of the people make a nation a real thing, a thing apart from the mere individuals who owe it allegiance; the devotion of her sons creates a real living university, differing from its teachers and students, and more than their sum. In the same way, a growing sense of individuality may affect the nature of a business association. A partnership may be but a name to partners, clerks, and customers. On the other hand, by reason of age, success, striking peculiarities of action, or other-

[1] Dred Scott *v.* Sandford, 19 How. 393; and see Polydore *v.* Prince, Ware, 402, 3 Beale, 2.

wise, it may be regarded as an institution quite apart from its associated partners; as important department stores or printing plants are regarded as entities, with individual qualities, and their names no longer connote the names of partners, but the names by which the institutions are distinguished.

Such personality may or may not receive legal sanction; but in every law some such artificial personalities are made the subject of static rights. Thus in maritime law ships are personified; in India idols may become persons in the law; in the middle ages animals were sometimes endued with personal qualities. But the principal artificial persons are business associations. Any business association may be, and in every civilized country many such associations are, endued with personality, or in the language of our law, incorporated.

It is often said that the subject of incorporation is the individual persons who are thus associated together for a business purpose. It is far more accurate, however, to say that these individuals by their agreement together form a new thing, an association, which has in fact in some greater or less degree the quality of an institution, an artificial personality; and that by incorporation the state merely gives the legal status of personality to this institution.

§ **146. Other Examples of Personal Status.** — All matters of personal rank or caste are examples of personal status. Such, for instance, are nobility or serfdom. Since status of this sort is neither created nor recognized by the American law, it is not essential to consider the question at greater length.

Slavery is another example of personal status closely analogous to those just considered. This, also, is a status from which our own law is, fortunately, free, and it will be necessary only to mention it here.

Full age or minority are in many laws treated as kinds of personal status; and as such they will be considered later. The same thing is true of interdiction, that is of loss of civil powers, by reason of insanity or other mental incapacity. It will be necessary to consider these examples of status in the course of our discussion, although they do not exist in our own law as static conditions.

Public office is a status that is of great practical importance in this country. The holder of a public office is vested with the office, and his position has all other qualities of static right. Its terms are fixed by law, and every person must take notice of the existence of the office and its rights and duties.

The similarity of a public officer to one who owns and maintains a public utility has often been noticed. A common carrier, innkeeper, or person employed in any similar public service, owes duties and exercises rights which are in all respects analogous to those of public officers; and the two may be considered together. Our law sets apart certain business activities as endowed with a public interest. These are now often called public utilities; or, in a similar phrase, public service. Office and public service, as will be seen, have certain peculiarities which distinguish them from ordinary kinds of status; but, generally speaking, the analogies are so close that they may be properly included within this category.

§ 147. **Relative Status.** — Of all varieties of relative status, often called in our law domestic relations, the most important is marriage. In all Christian nations marriage is a relation which is of interest to the State; its creation and destruction are regarded as matters which are to be determined by the State alone, and not in any degree by the mere will of the parties themselves. In other words, the mutual relations of the spouses are static, to be taken notice of by all the world and to continue in existence until either the subject-matter itself is destroyed by the death of one of the parties or until it is put an end to by an act of the law, that is, divorce.

The relationship between a father and child is, obviously, a purely natural one, and as such, the law can neither create nor end it. This natural personal interest, however, before being of any importance in the law, needs to be raised by the law to the character of a legal right. When thus recognized and given effect by the law, the natural relation becomes what is called a legitimate relation. A natural child, recognized as such by the law, is called a legitimate child; but if the relationship is not recognized by the law, the child is illegitimate, and the blood relationship is treated as if it did not exist.

Such legitimate relationship exists in the ordinary case from the birth of the child. In cases, however, where at the time of the child's birth it is illegitimate, the possibility always exists of its being later recognized as a child by some subsequent act of the law. This act of the law, after the child's birth, is known as legitimation.

A relation similar to that of fatherhood and sonship may be established between persons not naturally related in the blood. Although this has many qualities analogous to that of blood relationship, it is nevertheless not the same thing. The process by which such a relation is established is called adoption; the child is called the adopted child, and the parent the adoptive father.

A relation of care and obedience exist by nature between a minor child or other person not capable of caring for himself, and the person who actually cares for him. This relation has many qualities analogous to that of father and child, although there are very characteristic differences. The relation is often recognized by the law, which creates out of it the status of guardian and ward. Guardianship may be created by the law in any case where it deems the ward incapable of caring for himself.

Guardianship of this kind must be carefully distinguished from that office, called in our law by the same name, where the so-called guardian is merely a custodian of property. Custodianship of property obviously involves no personal relationship whatever, and is not an example of status, but of power over property.

§ 148. **What Law Governs Status.** — It is obvious that such interests as have been considered do not fall within the territorial jurisdiction of any sovereign. They have no situation in space, and are in their nature not only intangible, but capable of indefinite transfer from place to place in so far as the movement of the person in question may be regarded as a transfer of the right. Under these circumstances some conventional mode must be found to determine the law which shall control the interest or right. It would be possible to have such rights under the control of any sovereign in whose territory for the time being the person or persons interested happened to be. This, however, would be an interference with the nature of the right; which, as has been seen, is not a temporary or easily changed right, but one that has permanence as a most important characteristic. In order to preserve the permanent character of status by putting it under the exclusive control of one sovereign, a tacit convention has been adopted by all states, giving to one single sovereign the sole control for the time being over personal status. Unfortunately there is a difference between different systems of law as to the sovereign who has control. In the middle ages, the sovereign who by convention had control of personal status was the sovereign of the domicil of the person concerned. This has continued to be the rule in common-law jurisdictions and in several civil-law states. In most of the civil-law states, however, the sovereign of the allegiance of the person concerned has been selected; and nationality, rather than domicil, therefore controls personal status in most of the large states of Europe today.

Such a difference of opinion as to the law governing personal status is quite unfortunate; but the difficulty of removing the conflict has already been considered.[1] Meanwhile, since our courts deal with the problems in accordance with the principles of the common law they must continue to apply the law of the domicil to questions of personal status.

Part 2. Rights of Property

§ 149. The Nature of Property. — Property being a protected interest in a thing, any sort of interest may be protected, and any sort of thing may be the subject of an interest. It remains for later investigation to determine the nature of the things and interests in question.

This use of the word property, which may claim to be the accurate legal use, is to be distinguished from a very common application of the word to the thing itself which is the object of the interest. Thus where the object of the interest is a horse, the property in the true sense is the legalized interest of the owner in the horse; but the horse itself is very commonly spoken of as property, the property of the owner. So

[1] Ante, § 42.

common is this latter use, that one can hardly hope not to fall into it at one time or another; but the effort should be made to confine the word to its proper use.

In its proper use, the word *property* should be applied to any legalized interest in the thing, whether greater or less. As now commonly used in our law, it is restricted to the complete interest, the ownership or title; and when one now speaks of *property* in a piece of land he means ownership of the land in fee. Formerly it was common to apply the word to other special interests; thus, one having the legal right of possession was said to have property, or a special property, in the thing. This use is practically obsolete.

Where, however, property is spoken of in the broader sense, it is still understood as defined above; and it will thus be used in this discussion.

§ **150. The Sort of Interest Protected.** — Interests of any kind may be protected by the law; though the kinds of interest protected by a particular law, as for instance by our own, are limited. Within such limits the interests may be very numerous; but it is possible to divide them into well-recognized classes.

Thus, interests may take effect in succession; there may be present and future interests in a single thing. Each successive owner of the interest has, while he enjoys it, a complete or nearly complete enjoyment of the thing.

Interests may be greater or less; thus there may be ownership in fee, power to appoint, easement, right of possession. Each of these interests is, in the sense in which we are using the term, property. The power of appointment by will, the right of way over the neighbor's land, the right of possession of another's horse, are all alike property. Such interests differ from those considered in the preceding paragraph in that the smaller and the larger interests are enjoyed simultaneously.

Interests may be recognized or enforced in different courts; thus there may be legal or equitable interests, free tenancy and copyhold, equities of redemption, and similar interests recognized in a single court only, and not in other courts.

It has often been denied that the interest of *cestui que trust* is an interest in the land; but, on the other hand, it is said to be a mere personal claim against the trustee. And this is doubtless the theory on which the common law proceeded. For our purposes, however, as we study the nature of the right with a view to determining its real qualities and its relation to other rights brought into conflict with it, we cannot rest satisfied with the theory of a particular law, or even of that common law which is the basis of all our particular laws; for the theory may be, as legal theories often are, a fictitious form into which the substance of progress is forced. It is necessary for us therefore to examine the case more fully. The court of equity, when it first restrained a trustee from depriving *cestui que trust* of his so-called beneficial interest in land, created or recognized a new right; was it a right in the land, not recognized by courts of law, or a new kind of contract, not recognized by courts of law? While it is true that equity can act only *in personam*, did the chancellor, so acting, give relief to *cestui que trust* as owner of an interest in the land, or as the mere beneficiary of a contract which a court of law would not allow him to enforce? Equity, the chancellor said, followed the law; which law did he follow, the law of property or the law of contracts? When law and equity are fused is *cestui que trust* recognized as the owner of an interest in land, or as the beneficiary of a contract?

The real fact is, that courts of law and of equity differed as to the existence of an interest in the land; and the power of courts of law was broader, so that their view appeared for a time to represent the accepted doctrine as to ownership. But as time went on the chancellor's view came more and more to be recognized as the true view of the case, and the court of law really to be the court whose power to do justice was limited by its own blindness. Instead of administering an exceptional and limited justice, the chancellor came to be recognized as having the last and controlling word. So it has proved. Law and equity have been fused by lawyers even more fully than by legislators; the doctrines of equity are now fully accepted as a constituent part of the law, and the interests recognized in equity are legal interests.

§ 151. The Sort of Things which may be Subject of Interests. — It is clear that any tangible thing may be subject of interests. Land, animals, and movable things are usually so subject. The most generally disseminated things, like air and water, may be, but usually are not, the subject of legalized private interests; not that the interests do not in fact exist, but because the public interest is so much greater that it is not desirable to recognize the private interests.

How far interests in animals are to be recognized depends entirely on policy; where the general or public right is greater, as in the case of ordinary wild animals, private interest is not recognized. On the other hand, private interests of man in man, regarded as a mere animal, may be recognized; as in that sort of slavery where the slave is regarded as a thing.

But in addition to tangible things, there are many intangible things in which a man may have an interest, and the interest be recognized by the law. Thus a man may have an interest in an idea: an invention, a poem, a musical composition. Such an interest might be recognized by the law of patents and copyrights. So a merchant may have an interest in the good-will of a business. The things which are the subject of these interests are none the less real because they are not corporeal. Intangible as well as tangible things may be the objects of interests.

But there are other intangible things which have no actual existence, but are mere creatures of the law; debts, contracts, franchises and monopolies are of this sort. That these may nevertheless be regarded as things, the subjects of recognized rights, is very clear; and in the modern law most legal creations of this sort are the subject of legal rights. Thus, a contract between A and B, though in its nature not at all a static right, but merely a relative dynamic right, is nevertheless treated by the law as the subject of a property right. Accordingly, third parties are legally bound to respect it; the parties themselves do a legal wrong by repudiating the obligation before the time for performance; and equity provides an action for repossession of the right by judicial proceedings. So far has this tendency to create a vested property right out of a mere dynamic relation gone, that the contract is frequently regarded as sufficiently fixed in place as to be the subject of taxation and of seizure on execution. The true nature of such rights as these will frequently arise for consideration in later chapters. Although an ordinary contract may be treated by the law as a thing only to a limited extent, certain obligations evidenced by or inherent in written documents may and frequently are dealt with as things. Thus any kind of commercial paper — bills, notes, cheques, bills of lading — are in many respects dealt with as ordinary things; so to a less extent are certificates of stock and insurance policies. Bonds are in our law in all respects dealt with as things.

Not only may a thing be the subject of rights; collections or aggregates of things, treated as forming a single unit or entity, may be the subject of an interest. Thus the stock in trade of a merchant may be regarded as a single thing; it is so regarded for purposes of taxation. Perhaps the commonest and most important example of this unification of a number of things is the treatment of an aggregate of property owned by a man as a single estate, as for instance for the purpose of transfer at marriage or death. In the common law this is confined to an aggregation of personal property; land is never so treated.

§ 152. **Transfer and Extinguishment of Rights of Property.**— It is a characteristic quality of rights of property that they continue in existence until extinguished by act of law or by destruction of the thing. Such a right must be capable of transfer, at least upon death, since the right is of a nature to outlast human life; and in fact in all civilized communities rights of property are also transferable *inter vivos*.

A right is transferred when the transferee is put into exactly the same relation toward the thing that the transferor previously occupied. A transfer of title places the same title in the transferee; a transfer of possession puts the transferee in and the transferor out of possession.

Rights in tangible things may of course easily be transferred, by consent of the parties; and the same is true of real intangible things. In the case of commercial paper, a transferee takes the exact place of the transferor by the very terms of the instrument.

Choses in action, including contract rights and debts, are by their very nature incapable of transfer; for they are two-party relations, and the personalities of the parties are fundamental qualities of the relation. A new party could be inserted only by such a complete change in the nature of the obligation as would be a destruction of it and the creation of a new one; and this can be done only by mutual consent of both parties. Such a right, then, is incapable of transfer; it can only be assigned. An assignment is merely a contract that the assignee shall enjoy all the benefits of it, including that of suing. It does not put the assignee into the position of the assignor, or affect his right except collaterally.

§ 153. **What Law Governs Rights of Property.** — A right of property being a right in a thing, the sovereign who has control over the thing is obviously the sovereign who must, generally speaking, have jurisdiction over the right. So far as tangible property is concerned, whether land or a movable thing, this is quite clear: questions of the creation of rights in the thing, transfer of rights, and extinction of rights, are determined by the law of the place where the thing is at the time the right in question is created or dealt with. In the case of intangible property, other considerations control. Certain intangible things have, as has been seen, a real existence, and such a thing is sometimes so closely connected with a tangible thing that a situs may be predicated for it at the place where the tangible thing is. Thus, for instance, the good will of a business, or a franchise to run a ferry or a mill, is situated where the business, the ferry or the mill is situated.

Other intangible property consists of the interest of an individual in some intangible thing, like an idea or invention. Where the law turns such an interest into property, the property has this quality, at least, of a mere creature of the law, that it can exist only so far as the law that creates it extends; thus, a patent for an invention, the copyright in a book or picture, a legal monopoly, exist only within the territory of the sovereign creating them. Such a right, being a mere creature of a single law, must always remain within the jurisdiction of that law and can be dealt with only in accordance with it.

Where the law is dealing not with a single thing, but with an aggregate, like an estate, different considerations must prevail. The very purpose of the law is to pass a whole estate as a unit, and the estate may be scattered through the territories of several sovereigns. In order to accomplish the purpose some express or distinct agreement between the sovereigns is therefore necessary, in order that those portions of the estate within the different territories may all pass together, and the entire estate thus remain unbroken. Only by some such agreement can this result be reached, as of course the portion of the estate which lies within the territory of a sovereign must, in fact, pass in accordance with his legislative will without regard to the will of other sovereigns. In order, therefore, that the purpose may be accomplished, it is necessary to find either some principle of international law, some express treaty, or, at any rate, some identical provision in the municipal laws of the countries concerned. Such a provision is in fact found in the common law, and forms, therefore, a portion of the law of each common law state which has not changed the original principles of the system. In only one or two of all the common-law jurisdictions has such a change been made; and it is therefore possible to say generally that in common-law states an entire estate may be expected to pass as a unit, in cases where that is found desirable. The principal cases of this sort are death and marriage; in each of which cases, by the common law, the property of the deceased, or of the woman, passes as a single estate.

One of two laws might obviously be adopted as the law which should govern the passing of such an estate: the law of the domicil or the law of the allegiance. As in cases of status, countries governed by the common law and countries governed by the civil law differ in this respect. In most civil-law countries during the last century the law of the allegiance of the person in question, whether the deceased or the husband, is allowed to govern the passing of the entire estate; in common-law countries the law chosen is always that of the domicil.

Sub-Topic B. Dynamic Rights

§ 154. The Nature of Dynamic Rights. — It has been seen that a static right is of indefinite continuance; that it concerns third parties as well as the owner; and that it is of interest to the state, which guards its creation, its transfer, and its extinction. Dynamic rights are in all these respects the opposite of static rights. Instead of being permanent, they are evanescent; they come to maturity, and at that moment come to an end, either by satisfaction or by destruction. Instead of being objective they are merely subjective; they concern the parties alone, and no one else has right or interest in them. Instead of being matters of state concern, they are of no public interest. The parties may deal with them as they please; they are incapable by their temporary and personal nature of transfer, but they may be released or extinguished by the mere will of the parties, without act or consent of the state. Static rights, in a word, have to do with vested conditions; dynamic rights have to do with the permission or forbidding of acts.

Dynamic rights are of two classes: absolute rights and relative rights.

Part 1. Absolute Rights

§ **155. Interest-Protecting Rights.** — Absolute rights are created by the law; and are rights, not against a definite party, but against all the world; that is, against each person who comes within the sphere of their activity. Such rights may properly be called interest-protecting rights.

The law hedges about every interest which it recognizes as a right with a number of interest-protecting rights. Thus, the ownership of land is protected by the right to have others refrain from any act injuring such ownership; for instance, from trespass to the land, from destruction of any part of it, or from a nuisance that injures it. The interest of personality is protected by forbidding others to violate personal security or sense of security, to harm reputation, and in other ways injuriously to affect the personal interests of the person. A marriage is protected by forbidding all persons to interfere with the marital relation, whether by causing loss of service or by injuring the marital tie itself.

It will be noticed that each of these rights forms a continuous series lasting as long as the interest exists; every moment new and every moment coming to an end. A particular right existing for the moment only is at that moment either satisfied or destroyed; but whether satisfied or destroyed, it is succeeded, if the interest continues to exist, by another right in the same series. The destruction of it results in a new right, a right of action.

The interest protected may be that of a private individual, in which case the destruction of the interest-protecting right constitutes what is called a tort; on the other hand, the interest involved may be that of the public at large, organized society, or, in other words, of that specialized legal personality, the state. In that case, the destruction of the interest-protecting right becomes a crime.

It will be noticed that an interest-protecting right had to do with the legal permissibility of acts; and that it is purely negative, forbidding the doing of acts by others in violation of the right.

§ 156. **Interest-Enjoying Rights.** — Similar to interest-protecting rights are the rights which enable the owner of a static right to do acts in the enjoyment of his interest. Thus, the interest of marriage requires for its full enjoyment the right of cohabitation; but it is within the power of law to withhold this right from the spouses. So the law may annex to the interest of a person the right to "stand in justice" in the courts; to the interest of a father in his child a certain right of correction; to the interest of an owner in land the right to use it in a certain way; to the interest of an owner of a patent for an invention the right to dispose of the invention in return for a royalty.

These rights are not so obvious as the interest-protecting rights; indeed, to one dealing only with the law of a single jurisdiction it is the denial rather than the existence of such rights that is noticed. For a state that legalizes an interest will naturally confer all such rights of enjoying the interest as are compatible with the interests of other individuals and of the state; and it will seem that the limitation of an owner's acts by reason of competing interests is a limitation upon a general and essential right to "do as he pleases with his own." "Shall I not take mine ease in mine inn?" is the natural quære of a man who assumes that the ownership of property involves every right of enjoyment which he could conceive.

When, however, one studies a number of different laws with a view to determine their mutual spheres of action, one is struck with the fact that the right to do acts in the enjoyment of interests varies from state to state, and that no right of enjoyment can be predicated as absolutely essential; and with the further fact that the right of enjoyment created by the state which creates the static right receives no recognition as such in another state. Each state creates and has a right to create its own armory of enjoyment-rights, as it creates its own fortress of defensive rights. Each right of enjoyment is as entirely a creature of the law as each right of protection; and each, as has been seen, is quite distinct from the static right itself.

§ 157. **What Law Governs Absolute Rights.** — The law which applies to an absolute right must be the law of the place in which it is to be exercised. Since such a right cannot be transferred, the law is concerned only with its creation, and the question whether it is discharged, satisfied or destroyed. Since an absolute right, as has been seen, is a mere creature of the law, and has to do with permitting or forbidding acts, it must be created by the law within whose jurisdiction the acts are to be done. What acts are forbidden, so that their commission constitutes a tort, and what use of property is permitted, are questions which concern only the sovereign within whose dominion the acts are proposed. What is a tort, what use of property is a nuisance, what acts of discipline a father may commit, what civil rights a person may exercise, are all determined by the law of the place where the alleged rights are to be exercised.

PART 2. RELATIVE RIGHTS

§ 158. **Contracts and Debts.** — Relative rights are obligations between two persons created by their will or act; consensual obligations of all kinds, like debts, covenants and simple contracts; they do not consist, like absolute rights, of a continuous series of momentary rights, but are single obligations, due at a certain fixed time. It has already been seen that a contract tends to become a piece of property and as soon as it comes to partake of the nature of property, it becomes a permanent right, outlasting a breach and capable of being enforced after the date for performance, and the subject of interest-protecting and interest-enjoying rights. Regarded, however, merely as a relative right, it is a single obligation, either satisfied or destroyed at the moment fixed for performance. After that, the mere relative obligation exists no longer, its place being taken, as will be seen, by a claim for damages.

It has already been seen that a contract right is not capable of transfer or modification by the act of either party; even, indeed, by consent of both parties the obligation cannot be altered and persist in the altered form. A relative obligation, being created by the parties, who in creating it settled its terms, it can never exist as the same obligation with altered terms. The parties may, to be sure, modify their obligations by mutual consent, but only by extinguishing the old obligation and creating a new one; and the creditor may assign it, but only by a contract that the assignee shall enjoy the profit of it.

At the maturity of the obligation it, like a single absolute obligation, must either be performed or destroyed; and if it is destroyed, the law is no more concerned with it as a relative obligation, although, as will be seen, it creates a right of action for its breach.

§ 159. **Quasi-Contracts.** — The relative right which for want of a better name may be called a right of quasi-contract arises when one man is by law obliged to pay money to another, though no agreement has been made to do so, because of circumstances which make such payment proper. Among instances of this sort are obligations to pay salvage or average; to return an unjust enrichment; to pay for services properly rendered in an emergency. The primary obligation in such a case is not performable at any fixed time; but at least upon demand (and this may be made by the act of bringing suit) the obligation matures and unless fulfilled is violated.

§ 160. **What Law Governs Relative Rights.** — Relative rights, being ordinarily created as a result of some act or event, are properly governed by the law of the place where the act or event occurs; since that law alone can determine the legal significance of the event. Thus a contract should be created by the law of the place where the agreement took place; a bond or other specialty, by the law of the place of delivery; a quasi-contract, which usually arises upon the happening of an event, by the law of the place where the event happened. In case of obligations in admiralty a difficulty as to the application of law arises which will be considered at length later.

So far as transfer of the rights is concerned, the simple relative right, as has been seen, cannot be transferred; it can only be assigned, and that by the making of a contract. This contract is of course governed by the same law that applies to the making of any other contract. A bond or a mercantile specialty is capable of transfer as a chattel, and the law of the place where it is at the time would therefore govern the transfer; but such an obligation is rather a static than a relative right.

All matters that have to do with the satisfaction of the relative right, or its destruction — in other words, with performance, discharge, or breach — should on general principles come within the dominion of the law which governs the performance, that is, the law of the place of performance.

Topic II. SECONDARY RIGHTS

§ 161. The Nature of Secondary Rights. — Secondary rights arise upon the interference with or destruction of primary rights. The law does not generally undertake by preventive measures to guard against the destruction of primary rights of individuals; but it safeguards those rights by providing, in case of destruction, a substitute for them. A wrongdoer, according to the theory of the law, can gain nothing by his wrong, nor can the injured party really lose; and the law assumes that this will be enough to prevent all preventable wrongdoing. A certain amount of wrongdoing can be prevented neither by preventive nor by retributive measures, as the history of the criminal law shows; and the machinery of the law for preventing wrongdoing by the comparatively inexpensive method adopted seems on the whole to have proved successful.

§ 162. Rights of Redress or Restoration. — Wrongs to static rights may be of two sorts; by dispossession or by destruction; wrongs to dynamic rights can only be by destruction. Wrongs of dispossession call for a remedy which shall give restoration of possession; wrongs of destruction, however, are incapable of being repaired in kind, and must be redressed in some other way. Each of these methods of remedying wrong will be considered in the succeeding sections. But before there can be a remedy there must be a right; and it is the business of the law, upon a wrong being committed, to furnish a right to take the place of that infringed. This right is assumed to be such an equivalent of the injury that by reason of it the injured party will be kept whole. In case of dispossession, the law creates a right of repossession; in case of destruction, it creates a right to compensation. When the right destroyed is that of an individual the compensation takes the form of damages, which are so measured as to be the nearest possible pecuniary equivalent of the right destroyed.

This right to damages needs a word of further explanation. It is, as has been seen, a secondary, not a remedial right; and the size of it is a matter concerning the nature of this secondary right, and has nothing to do with the remedy offered for enforcing it. The effort of the law is not merely to create a right to damages, but to create a right which shall be the equivalent of the right destroyed.

The right to restoration of possession must of course concern merely the sovereign who had control of the property at the time it was dispossessed; that is, the right is created by the law of the situs at the time of dispossession. The right to damages, however, since it is based on the destruction of a right, which must have been the result of an act, concerns the sovereign within whose dominion the act was done; that is, the law of the place of the wrong, whether tort or breach of contract, creates the right to redress. But since all secondary rights are mere creatures of the law, they are naturally subject to be affected at any time by the law that created them.

Topic III. REMEDIAL RIGHTS

§ 163. The Nature of Remedial Rights. — The law, as has been seen, deals with a wrong by creating, as a result of it, a secondary right; and it enforces the secondary right, first by a right to sue for satisfaction of it, and next by giving a judgment as a result of the suit. Thus the destruction of a primary right results in a secondary right; the failure to fulfil a secondary right in a right to sue; the right to sue, when exercised, in a judgment. In this way the law creates right succeeding right, in an effort to keep the peace and enforce the requirements of justice without the resort to force. If this effort fails, and the wrongdoer finally fails to satisfy the judgment right, the law for the first time regularly interferes forcibly, by requiring the executive to force the wrongdoer to fulfil his judgment obligation.

This succession of right upon right is not always recognized. It is often said, for instance, that a court of law sits to redress wrong; and that it will or should act whenever a wrong has been proved. "Every wrong has its remedy" has even become a maxim, and represents the common view of those who have not especially considered the question. And yet it must be clear, from every consideration of justice and from every detail of practice, that a court can give a man only what the law has already given him a right to receive. That the right to damages must precede the suit for and recovery of damages is well settled. Thus, as Blackstone says, "The primary right to a satisfaction for injuries is given by the law of nature, and the suit is only the means of ascertaining and recovering that satisfaction. . . . The injured party has unquestionably a vague and indeterminate right to some damages or other, the instant he receives the injury." [1]

The English Court of Appeal, by overlooking this fact, reached an apparently erroneous result in the case of Machado *v.* Fontes, (1897) 2 Q. B. 231. That was an action for damages for a libel upon the plaintiff, contained in a pamphlet published by the defendant in Brazil. The defendant offered a plea alleging that a libel "cannot be the ground of legal proceedings against the defendant in Brazil in which damages can be recovered"; which was explained to mean that a libel in Brazil creates no right to damages, but is only a crime. The court, however, refused to allow the plea; on the ground that since the act was a wrong in Brazil the proper

[1] 2 Bl. Com. 438; quoted in 1 Sedg. Dam. 9th ed., § 5.

remedy for it in England was by an action of tort. The Lord Justice Rigby said: "The act in question is *prima facie* actionable here, and the only thing we have to do is to see whether there is any peremptory bar to our jurisdiction arising from the fact that the act we are dealing with is authorized, or innocent or excusable, in the country where it was committed."

This case, and the doctrine laid down in it, will be fully discussed in a later chapter.

§ **164. Right to Sue and to be Satisfied.** — When a static right has been taken away from its owner by a wrongful act, and a right of repossession is created by the law to take its place, he needs a remedy which will give him restoration of it. Not all such wrongs have been provided by our law with this sort of remedy; in many cases of dispossession of chattels, for instance, no remedy is provided by the common law. But usually such a remedy exists: in the case of outlawry (in the old law) by the process of inlawry; in the case of denial of or interference with marriage, by a suit for restitution of conjugal rights; in case of intrusion upon a public office, by writ of *quo warranto;* in case of land, by a real action; in case of bailment of property, by an action of detinue; in case of taking of property, by an action of replevin or by a bill in equity for restitution; in case of denial of performance of a contract, by a bill for specific performance. In each of these cases, the remedy is given as a separate right; and as has been seen it may be withheld. For instance, upon dispossession of a chattel by a wrongful act a right of repossession is always created, though at common law, as has been seen, a remedial right is not always granted. Under proper circumstances, however, the right of repossession may confer on the owner the legal privilege of retaking it from the dispossessor.

Where a dynamic right (or an entire series of dynamic rights, as in case of the destruction of a thing) has been destroyed, and a right of redress has been created to take its place, a law will probably give effect to this right by a right of action to recover the damages; but this right of action, again, is quite independent of the right to damages.

The affording of a remedial right, being independent of the secondary right, is a matter solely to be determined by the sovereign from whom the remedy is demanded; in other words, the allowance of a remedy, the methods of carrying on the suit, the judgment, and the execution, are matters entirely for the law of the forum sought by the complaining party.

Bei Fragen zur Produktsicherheit wenden Sie sich bitte an:
If you have any questions regarding product safety,
please contact:

Walter de Gruyter GmbH
Genthiner Straße 13
10785 Berlin
productsafety@degruyterbrill.com